SEVEN YEARS
in
CHINA
in the 1930s

LETTERS HOME FROM
TWO YOUNG MISSIONARIES

by
Jean Wemyss-Gorman

Grosvenor House
Publishing Limited

This book is published by
Grosvenor House Publishing Ltd
Link House
140 The Broadway, Tolworth, Surrey, KT6 7HT.
www.grosvenorhousepublishing.co.uk

A CIP record for this book
is available from the British Library

ISBN 978-1-83975-589-7

Dedicated to my parents,
John and Ruth Carpenter,
on the 90th Anniversary of their sailing to
China in 1931

John and Ruth 1929

ACKNOWLEDGEMENTS

It has been such a help to share this journal every step of the way with my husband Peter and brother-in-law Rodney Bessent, husband of my late sister who was born in China. I am so grateful for their opinions, interest and support. Thank you too to my family and friends for spurring me on with their enthusiasm and encouragement, and to Jo Monroe for her professional advice in putting me on the road to self-publishing and helping this project come to fruition.

JWG
July 2021

PROLOGUE

This journal consists of extracts from nearly 550 letters written by my parents while they were in China, the majority by my mother to her parents. It is thanks to them for keeping the letters that we now have this amazing first-hand account of missionary life in China in the 1930s. My parents' experience was, of course, simply a microcosm of all that was going on in the world around them, but it gives a fascinating glimpse into life as seen through their eyes.

I have always known that these letters existed but had no idea how many there were. It has been a massive but thoroughly rewarding task ploughing through a veritable mountain of thin Chinese paper covered with close writing on both sides, and discovering the unique treasure that lay within.

My mother particularly used to love talking about China and I wish I had taken more notice as I really only gained a vague impression of life out there. I certainly had no idea what my parents had been through and it was not until I transcribed the journal that the picture became clearer and everything fell into place. I have been completely caught up in the world they inhabited and travelled with them along a truly emotional journey, sharing their pleasures, fears, tears, fun and laughter, perplexities, uncertainties and joys. It has been a real eye-opener and a profoundly moving experience and I consider it a great privilege to be acting as their mouthpiece now and sharing their story. I feel immensely proud of them, though I know they would want to have the last word and say that it was not they who should receive praise but the One in whose name they went.

JWG
July 2021

JOHN AND RUTH CARPENTER

INTRODUCTION

This journal is taken from letters written by John and Ruth Carpenter to their respective families, friends and supporters during their time as missionaries with the China Inland Mission (CIM) in the 1930s. John's letters home were addressed to his parents and sister in Chislehurst, Kent, where his father was vicar. Ruth's letters were addressed to her parents and, until they left home, her sister and twin brothers in Hatherleigh, Devon, where her father was vicar.

History of the China Inland Mission (CIM)

The China Inland Mission (CIM) was an interdenominational and international mission founded in 1865 by James Hudson Taylor whose vision was to evangelize the inland provinces of China. It was a "faith mission" whose policy was never to appeal for funds. Workers had no guaranteed salary but everyone was given a remittance according to donations received. They were also expected to adopt Chinese dress and the lifestyle of those they were trying to reach. The first party of missionaries went out in 1866 followed 20 years later by the "Cambridge Seven" and by 1915 there were over 1,000 missionaries working in the field.

In 1927 nearly all the missionaries had to evacuate at the beginning of the Civil War between the Chinese Nationalist Party and the Communist Party of China and it looked as though the door was closing. In 1929 the Mission had a strong conviction that God was calling them to advance in two ways, firstly that the Church in China should become increasingly self-supporting and self-governing, and secondly that there should be a well-planned effort to take the Gospel to the un-evangelized millions. This was known as the Forward Movement and an appeal for 200 new workers was made of whom John and Ruth were among the last.

China in the 1930s

The 1930s were a time of great turbulence in China, not least in Szechwan Province, South West China, where John and Ruth worked throughout their time. There were still five warlords in the province controlling their own divisions and, as well as the many short-lived skirmishes between them, bandit activity was rife and fierce fighting persisted between the Chinese Nationalist Party and the Communist Party of China. In Szechwan, this was virtually continuous from the time they arrived until October 1934 when the CPC Red Army set out on a year-long retreat from South East to North West China. This later became known as The Long March during which Mao Zedong became the firmly established leader of the party. One of the routes passed through the north of Szechwan which, like the previous battles, affected the more northerly mission stations and had repercussions throughout the province. In another province two CIM missionaries were forced to join the

March and remained captives until well after it had ended.

Throughout this decade, President Jiang Kai-shek was the political and military leader of the Chinese Nationalist Party. Within this role, and influenced by his wife, he professed his faith as a Christian in 1930 and was baptised. He had a high regard for missionaries and was very supportive towards them. In 1935 he introduced the New Life Movement, a strict programme of cultural reform intended to stamp out corruption and immorality.

Simultaneously the situation between China and Japan was deteriorating and finally broke out into full-scale war in July 1937 which particularly affected John and Ruth on their homeward journey. There was a temporary uneasy lull in hostilities between the Nationalist Party and Communists as they combined forces to oppose Japan but later this reverted to civil war, finally ending in victory for the Chinese Communist Party in 1949. At this point, missionaries were no longer welcome in China and they either left or were expelled. The China Inland Mission then switched its focus of activity to East Asia and in 1964 changed its name to the Overseas Missionary Fellowship (OMF).

Background

Both John and Ruth came from clergy families and their parents were friends, in fact distant relatives. John was born in China where his parents were missionaries and Ruth was born in Dorset. They met in 1925, became engaged in 1929, sailed to China in September 1931 and married two years later.

John was 26 and Ruth 21 when they left their sheltered backgrounds and set out on their journey into the unknown, at the peak of their energy and full of missionary zeal. John was ordained into the Church of England and both shared a deep faith and a strong conviction that they had been called to China, confident that the Lord would guide, protect and provide for them.

That assurance would be put to the test in the years to come as they had to adapt to a different culture and difficult climate, often living in primitive conditions and having to face danger, illness, disease, discouragement, homesickness, loneliness and disappointment. When they set out, everything was new and exciting, but gradually as they faced the realities and challenges of life they began to see the world in a different light. However their strong unwavering faith and sense of mission remained with them throughout the rest of their lives.

Missionary Life in China

In East Szechwan there were 24 mission stations. The larger towns/cities had mission compounds and the smaller ones just had a mission house, and there were numerous outstations in the country. Between two and five "foreign" missionaries worked at each station and a varying number of Chinese staff:- pastors, evangelists, colporteurs (distributors of Christian literature and tracts), Biblewomen (women evangelists), teachers etc. Szechwan province, through which the Yangtze River flows, was worked by several different missionary societies and there was a large Church of England diocese led by a Bishop.

Despite the long distances separating the stations, the missionaries got to know each other well and some remained life-long friends, and a surprising number married! They were all in a similar situation and the camaraderie they shared and the support they gave each other was of vital importance. They would stay with each other and use their homes as staging posts on journeys and refuges when evacuating, sometimes turning up unexpectedly and sometimes not turning up at all and there was no knowing what had happened to them. Always there would be a warm welcome and usually a small contingent to meet them some way out of town.

Apart from the cities there were no proper roads or motor vehicles and the "roads" were little more than lanes. The missionaries had to walk everywhere or be carried by coolies in *sedan chairs or *hua-gans and other coolies would be hired to carry their loads so they were never completely alone on a journey. Many stations were situated by the river so that boats were a common form of transport. Every station had "servants", typically a cook, house-woman, gate-keeper, cowman etc, so that the missionaries were relieved of some of the more arduous tasks to free them for their work.

---

*sedan chair Enclosed "box" with windows on two horizontal poles carried by one coolie at either end and bearing one passenger

*hua-gan/hua-kan/hua-kanri Light chair, sometimes called a coolie litter. Bamboo frame suspended from two bamboo poles and a bar suspended by string as a foot rest. With a pillow for the head it was a most comfortable mode of travel but heavy to carry so the missionaries tried not to use them more than necessary.

Letters from home took anything from three weeks to four months, depending on which route they came and other eventualities. They were an absolute lifeline and bitter was the disappointment when they didn't arrive. Weekly letters and many "snaps" were exchanged and Ruth, in particular, hung on every word from home and replied in detail. Inland mail was generally quick and reliable, given that everything had to be carried on foot in the country, and urgent letters were delivered at record speed by specially hired coolies. On the other hand, there could be delays of up to six months for certain stores and medicines which could only be ordered from Shanghai.

There was little snow in Szechwan, but huge swings of temperature and a high rainfall which often made travelling difficult or impossible. At the height of summer the heat in the cities was so intense and humid that it was impossible to work. Recognizing this, the CIM provided retreats in the cool of the hills to which their workers could escape. John and Ruth's was a hill bungalow at Chiu p'an shi where they spent many refreshing weeks, revelling in the stunning scenery, going for long walks and enjoying much fun and fellowship with eight or nine like-minded colleagues.

The monetary system was complicated. Dollars and cents were intermingled with the old Chinese currency and the calculations which had to be made to convert "cents" to "coppers" were intricate and differed from day to day. Moreover, the currency in one place was not the same as in another.

Conversions

Distances
1 li = ⅓rd English mile
30 li = 10 miles

Weights
catty = 1⅓rd lb.
shen = 5 lbs
burden = no more than 80 catties
2 loads = 1 burden

Currency
$1 = 1/3d old money (0.06p today)
cash or copper coins – infinitesimal value

Temperature
100°F = 38°C
20°F = minus 6°C

Distances between places in approximate day's travel – walking and/or by boat

Chowkow to Nanpu 2 days
Chowkow to Shunking   8 hours or 3 days upstream
Chowkow to Yingshan ½ day
Chuhsien to Chowkow 2 days
Chuhsien to Kwangan 2 days
Chuhsien to Pachow 5 days
Chuhsien to Tahsien 3 days
Chuhsien to T'uch'i 1 day
Chuhsien to Yingshan 1½ days
Chungking to Chuhsien 7 days
Chungking to Shunking 8 days
Shunking to Hochow 2½ days
Tahsien to Kiachang 1½ days
Tahsien to Paoning 5 days
Wanhsien to Liangshan 2 days

This map gives a very rough idea of the places in relation to each other. It is impossible to be more accurate with the locations as many of the names have changed and become unidentifiable.

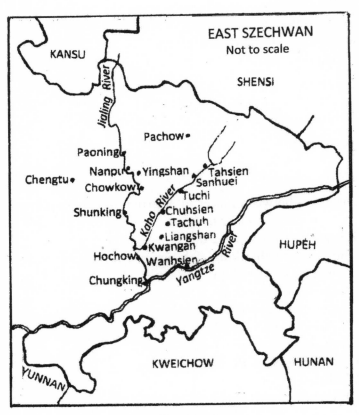

Map of East Szechwan

1931

Ruth's Mother

The Vicarage   April 1930
Hatherleigh, Devon

Darling Ruth

Thank you and John for the letters received this morning. You know that Dad and I are willing for you to serve the Lord wherever you feel He is calling you, and it is with our full consent that you take the step of offering yourself for work as soon as the Society sees fit to send you after you are twenty-one.

I need hardly tell you what it will cost us both - I cannot think of it – but we are willing and ready for we believe it is God's plan for you.

Your loving
Mother

John

Christ Church Vicarage   August 1931
Chislehurst, Kent

Dear Friends and Supporters

On September 24th I shall be sailing to China with a party of 19 new workers (men) to take up missionary work with the CIM (China Inland Mission). The Lord has been leading me to this point for many years, but

1

I am very conscious it is not going to be easy. The partings will be hard, China is unsettled at present and the language is very difficult; it may take months, even years, to be fluent enough to preach the Gospel.

We will spend six months at the men's language school at Anking before being designated to our stations to continue language study and begin elementary missionary work. My fiancée, Miss Ruth Rossiter, will be sailing with the ladies' party two days earlier and going to a women's language school. We look forward to being married some time during our second year. Our first term of service will probably be about seven years.

I feel very inadequate for the task but go in God's strength knowing He will be with me and supply every need, whatever the future may hold.

Yours sincerely
John Carpenter

•••

Ruth set sail from England on September 18th followed two days later by John

•••

Ruth

CIM Headquarters   October 27th
Shanghai

Dear Mother, Dad, Mary, Jack and Jock

Here we are in China and it is almost too wonderful to be true. My arrival was made sweeter by a big budget of letters from home waiting to greet me, and to add to my joy John arrived this morning and we will have a few precious days together before I leave next week.

<u>November 4th</u>

The parting of the ways has come and John came to see me off at the station. It was hard saying good-bye, knowing we won't see each other again for at least six months.

With love
Ruth

Ruth

Women's Language School   November 8th
Yangchow

Dear Everyone

After a long train journey we arrived at *Chinkiang* where we spent the night in the CIM station. We were met at the station and set off walking along cobbled streets, where there were jaunty rickshaws, men wheeling squeaky wheel-barrows laden with bulky goods and others carrying loads on long poles. Crowds of people were beating little gongs in special rhythms to denote the type of wares they were selling. As you can imagine, eleven foreign women walking along the street together aroused quite a lot of curiosity.

The next morning we boarded our launch at 6 a.m., squeezing into a small room with eight Chinese people and all our luggage. While we were waiting, pedlars came on board selling fruit, sweets, watch chains, penknives etc. and boat attendants poured us tea into little handleless teacups.

We crossed the Yangtze to join the Grand Canal where there were many boats with square, patched sails and some painted with dragons' heads. We saw a fine-looking Yangtze steamer and a smaller boat which can go further up the river. On either side were little low thatched huts made of bamboo and mud plaster. Many people were about and women were sitting in doorways sewing, probably patching their menfolk's clothes – you never saw such patched garments!

At last we arrived at *Yangchow* where we were met by a staff member who led the way to the language school in her *rickshaw. We turned off the moderately broad street on to what appeared to be a back alley but was, in fact, an ordinary street just a few yards wide with high walls on either side. Soon we met a rickshaw coming in the opposite direction and the two coolies had quite a heated exchange before one would give way to the other!

We were, of course, intensely interested in everything, shops with rolls of funny-looking dough, dumplings and brown square things, meal shops, chopstick shops, material and embroidery silk shops, sweet shops selling round sweets of weird colours on sticks and brightly coloured ones shaped like little tea-pots, flowers and fruits. There were eating houses with little charcoal

---

*rickshaw Small wooden two-wheeled vehicle carrying one passenger and drawn by one coolie

stoves being vigorously poked, boys with bamboos over their shoulders peddling interesting wares, men with two wooden buckets in which fish lay gaping in a little water, others carrying buckets of pale grey shrimps and someone selling giant radishes. Picture the narrow streets with all these shops, babies, people jabbering away in this strange tongue, pigs grunting, mangy mongrels wandering around, squeaky barrows, men with loads crying "oh! oh!" to get people to make way and the odd soldier in grey-blue uniform. Making their way through it all was a party of foreigners heading towards their new home, feeling very new and strange.

The language school is in a quieter street and has two big iron doors beyond which is a long house with two storeys and lovely balconies. We were given a very warm welcome by Mrs Macfarlane, the head, and the other staff members. Meg (Scorer) and I were so pleased to find that we were sharing a room again (we shared a cabin on the voyage) and I think will be very happy. We more or less live in our bedrooms and do all our study there. We soon unpacked and had the room looking jolly with our lovely things from home. There is a large garden with about 20 trees and quite a few birds, including some very big ones with beaks like eagles' which fly over and slap their wings against the leaves of the trees.

There are 47 in our party, a marvellous mixture of women from at least nine countries, predominantly American. Our day begins at 5.45 a.m. and as well as six hours language study there are times of prayer, domestic duties, relaxation and exercise in the garden. On Saturdays we can go for walks, six at a time with one of the women servants. Yesterday we went down to the canal, crossed over by ferry and walked through the cemetery, such a dismal place where the coffins are placed on the ground with earth packed around them in mounds, with no grass, flowers or tombstones.

The money system is truly amusing and complicated, and you can end up with a good heavy purse to carry round. Also it does not have the same value everywhere in China, and even coming here we had to get all our Shanghai money changed. We have been given $80 for our outfit expenses and $160 for our first quarter's remittance. Our board here costs precisely $1 a day (1/3d!)

I must tell you about our Chinese lessons. When we enter the room, we have to bow to our teacher from the waist. We then sit down, but not until he says so – he is our superior. We must sit very demurely, our neckline must be very high, and we must never cross our knees or let our toe or foot touch his by mistake. We must never look him straight in the eye – only his mouth may we watch. We may never laugh – that would be immodest in the extreme. We sit and he takes a pen and points to some words and we say them after him. We do tonal exercises and read from the primer. Once or twice I have felt an almost irrepressible urge to laugh which, with great difficulty, I have managed to control! At the end of the lesson we bow to him and he bows to us and we back out of the room, gradually facing round. Chinese etiquette is very quaint!

We will soon be having our Chinese gowns made and I will try to send you a little bit of the silk. They have patterns woven into them with beautiful silks and are enormously thick and beautifully warm. We also have cotton coats to wear over them to keep them clean whilst working. Yesterday it was very cold and I was so glad of the mittens you knitted me, Mother. It will get very cold soon and the things we brought will be none too thick.

I was the only one without letters waiting for me when we arrived which made me feel very lonely, but I'm sure they will come soon. As I write it's 2.30 on Sunday afternoon so about 6.30 a.m. at home, and I am visualizing the scene at Hatherleigh Vicarage as the day is about to get going. Mary will soon be up, lighting the stove and making tea for Dad before he goes off to early Communion. Doris will arrive and open the shutters, light the fires and lay the table for breakfast, and down you will all come just as we are having high-tea.

Monday

Today I have had three classes, firstly the group grammar class with Miss Griffiths then group reading with Mr Boh. Say "bock" to rhyme with "sock" only don't pronounce the "k" and say it very staccato with an explosive sound, and you have the correct pronunciation. He wrote characters on the board and we had to read them after him. He is awfully nice and wears a long pale blue gown. Thirdly I had my individual lesson with Mr Kuang, reading a lot of characters after him to practise the tones. I am not finding them too difficult but it's too tantalizing for words to hear people talking all around you and not being able to understand what they are saying, especially for a quizzy body like me! I'm simply longing to be able to speak this delightful language and be able to communicate the Good News to others.

(The light has just been turned off at the mains, but now we've lit Meg's oil lamp.) I've been given a new name – Miss "Deh", or Miss "Virtue"- something to

live up to! Meg's new name is Miss "Suh" but she doesn't know it means!

This city is full of soldiers. It is blessed with a Christian General who is a great disciplinarian and his soldiers are said to be the most orderly in China, whereas soldiers can be as bad as brigands. We are very sheltered in this compound as we are enclosed by a high wall and can't see much of the city even from our windows. It is washing day today and the back-yard has been full of white linen bleaching in the bright sunlight. We can send 33 pieces to be washed for $1 and it is done beautifully.

Well my dears, how are *you*? You seem so far away and I'm longing to know all about Home, sweet Home and am continuingly picturing you all.

With love
Ruth

John
Men's Training Home   November 1931
Anking.

Dear Friends and Supporters

After a most interesting voyage, we arrived at *Shanghai* on October 29th.

We spent a week in the beautiful new CIM headquarters, an especially happy time as the ladies had arrived only two days before and I was able to see Miss Rossiter before we went our separate ways to our language schools. We spent a good deal of time sorting out everything we would need for the next six months and packing them into two Chinese pigskin boxes and a

Chinese basket. The rest went back into our own boxes ready to be despatched when we reach our first stations next spring. During the week we each had the opportunity of telling briefly how we had been led to China, and some of us spoke through interpretation to over 250 Chinese children who had been rescued by the "Door of Hope" Mission.

From *Shanghai* we travelled by river steamer to *Anking*, a 2½ day journey up the Yangtze. On the Sunday we held two services attended by several of the ship's officers and also the "guard" of eight English soldiers who were on board in case of bandits higher up the river. There were no landing stages but at each port-of-call a sort of junk-barge came out from the bank, heavily laden with standing Chinese people, and moved alongside the steamer as close as it dared. Before they actually touched a number of men got on and off by jumping. Then a rope was thrown and made fast and when the "bump" came everyone got a good shake-up but no-one fell over because there wasn't room. With both boats now moving side by side there was a mad scramble as luggage, men, women and babies passed from one boat to the other. The steamer then speeded up again and continued on its way.

When we reached *Anking*, we all scrambled aboard the waiting ferry and were rowed to the bank where we extricated ourselves from our luggage and each other. Our passports were stamped and we set off walking to the training home near the North Gate. It was thrilling to be back in the narrow streets among familiar sights, sounds and smells for the first time for 18 years, and wonderful to realize that I had been called to take the Good News to these people. Our luggage was carried on poles by a long string of coolies, and we understood the wisdom of having brought all our goods in Chinese boxes etc. for ease of carrying and arousing less curiosity. *Anking* is not too keen on foreigners, but as long as they make themselves inconspicuous nobody minds, which is why only six of us are allowed out of the grounds each day.

So we have begun our language studies, and what a language it is! Each day we have a class with one of the staff, another taken by the head Chinese teacher who teaches us in Chinese, and then a period of private tuition with our own individual Chinese teacher. Can you picture me sitting at a table opposite my teacher with his pot of tea and a little cup, handy for mixing the ink to write the characters! The lesson consists mainly of me trying to imitate his sounds. He can't speak a word of English and we have to understand each other by pointing to characters and gesticulating and it is surprising how well we can communicate like this.

Yours sincerely
John Carpenter

Ruth
Yangchow   November 11th

Dear Everyone
Since I last wrote, I've had a lovely budget of seven letters by post, including one from John.

I'm very much enjoying the language study and look forward to each day's work. Today one student was struggling to read some characters and ended up with completely the wrong meaning. Mr Boh fairly exploded with mirth so we joined in. As you know, we aren't supposed to laugh in front of a Chinese man although it doesn't seem to matter if he laughs first. Mr Boh is such a dear and a splendid teacher. He is also very nice in his ways and actually possesses and uses a handkerchief. Most Chinese people think the "foreign" habit of blowing one's nose and putting the contaminated cloth in one's pocket is simply disgusting, whereas we "foreigners" regard their method of nose blowing, which I won't describe, as positively foul – it's all a matter of culture, I guess. Today Mr Boh and another teacher were drinking tea in a splendidly noisy manner which would be most impolite in our society but here it is rude *not* to make a noise and the noisier you are, the more it shows your appreciation.

Saturday

Thank you for the little card of kirby-grips which came just at the right time because Meg and I have had to alter our hair-style. The Chinese think that we have some sort of disease on our ears which we want to disguise with our "earphones" so we now have just one bun at the back and the kirby-grips help to hold it. It is *not* a beautiful sight, on me at any rate.

Once a week we can buy fruit - pears, tangerines, bananas etc. Yesterday it was my turn to collect the money and I finished up with $4.52¢, equivalent to about 5/8d. It had to be in coppers which are a little larger than a halfpenny and I finished up with 1,131 which all had to be bound up in 100 copper rolls! I have never carried such a heavy load of money before!

Having a bath is quite a ritual. The man from the street comes into the house carrying a pole over his shoulder with a bucket of hot water at either end. He goes upstairs and at the top he gives a hoarse cry to signify his arrival. The baths are oblong fairly large wooden frames lined with zinc. A nice hot bath is most refreshing and only costs sixteen coppers each (1d.)

Sunday

This morning I went to a service at the Chinese Church on the CIM station and felt very bucked to find I could understand some of the words. The country folk couldn't get in because of the weather. It was a filthy, muddy day and the streets were full of puddles and I had to keep my eyes glued to the ground. There appears to be absolutely no drainage system and the streets are full of the poor people going about barefoot or with just straw sandals. We saw two men carrying a sick man on a "stretcher", i.e. a door taken off its hinges, and an old blind beggar slushing along barefoot, feeling his way before him with a bamboo stick and holding his little bowl.

The rickshaw men had capes made of fine grass and big straw "umbrella" hats. All the women have such small feet and were wearing tiny galoshes. I saw one woman in a shoe shop trying some on with bare feet! There were numerous people with baskets of fish and we came across one whose basket had spilt and he was picking up all the fish from the muddy ground. It was fascinating to see what is sold in the shops - spectacles, wigs, safety pins, spoons, forks, materials, trilby hats which are very popular amongst Chinese gentlemen, lovely selections of brass and silver things, Singer sewing machines and all manner of odds and ends. There were also florists, fruit shops, butchers and numerous dough shops with all sorts of different dough strips.

I am very happy here, but sometimes the longing for you all and dear Hatherleigh with its freedom, lovely rambles with the dog, wind and wellingtons, makes me feel a little homesick and then I think of my calling.

Mrs. MacFarlane, our head, says that the word "sacrifice" is wiped right out her dictionary as she always spells it "J-O-Y". I want to do that.

With love
Ruth

Ruth

Yangchow   November 22nd

Dear Everyone

Yesterday we went for a most interesting walk across the ferry and about a mile down the other side of the canal along a rough narrow path. The canal was full of boats including some small houseboats with roofs made of a sort of coconut matting being propelled along by a man or woman with an oar. There were some slightly bigger boats with huge square sails and bamboo yards which were being pulled by ropes and gliding along gracefully.

Some of the houses had advertisements with characters attached to the walls, and I was thrilled to see an English one advertising Wills Cigarettes. (Imagine being excited by a cigarette poster!) Of course, we had to walk very demurely as it is not done to hurry in China and we were the object of many curious gazes.

Meg and I have ordered some foot-warmers. These are small rounded brass caskets with handles and lids full of holes. You put the charcoal inside and then rest your feet on them. They only cost $1.50 and about two coppers a day for the charcoal, so it is a simple method of keeping warm.

With love
Ruth

Ruth

Yangchow   November 24th

Dear Everyone

Your welcome letters arrived today and I loved all the news about home. It is such a joy knowing John is here and I'm longing for the day when you begin to address my letters differently! Won't it be lovely to meet again and the seven years will fly. When "we" come home, my Ma, your hair will be a sweeter colour than ever. One thing I ask of you – please stick to blue and don't go wearing black. And please have yours and Dad's photos taken frequently.

November 29th

This is my Christmas letter to you and I do hope you have a very happy time. I'm longing to know about everything, whether you had any visitors, what presents you had and gave each other etc. We won't have much holiday here as we wouldn't know what to do with ourselves, our chief occupation being language study.

I have got my Chinese gown now and it is very warm. Today is the coldest day so far and I'm so grateful for all the woollies you knitted me, my Ma, the mittens, bed socks and under slip. Also the cosy dressing gown and lovely rug are most useful for me to wrap up in to study. We have been moved to a different room which faces north and although it is possible to sit out on the south facing veranda with no extra clothing when the sun is shining, when we come indoors it is freezing. We can have oil stoves if we want, but have ordered the foot warmer instead which will be healthier and cheaper because we will share the cost.

It was my turn to collect the fruit money this week and I gathered 1,616 coppers including 324 from one person. I had to go and change a dollar which meant a delay and it took me three hours but I quite enjoy it because it gives me a chance to meet the others. Next time there will be a notice on the board reminding people to have the correct money ready.

Meg and I have had quite a number of visitors to admire our new room and yesterday we had a little tea-party with biscuits spread with a wonderful concoction of condensed milk and cocoa mixed with bananas. One of the girls showed me a photo of her sister and fiancé who are also in China and are getting married soon. The fiancé had completely shaved his head so that although he is quite young he looked like an old man. I hope John won't feel the need to shave *his* head!

We are getting quite used to seeing people wearing thick-padded garments, women in long trousers, men in long skirts and black skull caps over their close shaven heads, girls with long shiny plaits, children with bright brown eyes and dirty padded clothes, some with dreadfully scabbed heads, babies with a smear of black or a spot of vermillion on the tip of their noses or in the middle of their little foreheads, coolies walking along with their loads accompanied by quaint "musical" groans and chickens strutting about in the shops.

With love
Ruth

Ruth
Yangchow   December 5th

Dear Everyone
We are still having gloriously hot sunshine and bitterly cold weather at the same time. Saturday dawned

with a marvellous sunrise and the quaint roofs of the two temples over the other side of the canal and the graceful bare branches of the trees amongst the houses silhouetted against the orange-pink sky made the most beautiful, breath-taking picture. Later we went for a lovely walk away from the main street and through the narrow little roads between brick walls with abrupt right angle turnings, as they all are. We reached the edge of the town and created quite a lot of interest to a group of children, who shouted after us "yang kuei tsi" (foreign devils) until we were out of earshot. We then met a procession of little grey donkeys each carrying three sacks of flour. The sacks were arranged across their backs, one in the middle and one either side so that they balanced each other and didn't need to be tied on. They go over the canal on the ferry. We also passed an incense factory with hundreds of tin trays of incense sticks lying out in the sun to dry.

We've been practising some Christmas carols, but people don't seem to know my favourites. I shall miss the carol-singers coming round on Christmas Eve.

I have bought myself a wedding present, some Yangchow-ware made of black polished wood and inlaid with mother of pearl figures and pictures. I also bought three little trinket boxes of different shapes and sizes, a little photo frame, a small pin-tray and a larger round tray about 12" long. They are all topping and only cost $4 – about 5/-. I would love to send you some but they would only get smashed, but I hope to bring you some lovely presents when I come home.

Last week, the President of China, General Kiang Kai-Shek, invited Christian leaders to a conference to see what Christianity could do for the country at this time and one of our senior CIM missionaries was invited to lead the prayers. Last year the President was baptized into the Christian church which is a great thing for China.

With love
Ruth

Ruth
Yangchow   December 11th

Dear Everyone

A fortnight today is Christmas Day! So "bring forth the holly, the box and the bay"! It will be over by the time this reaches you but I hope you'll have had a very happy time. Meg and I have been comparing notes about each other's family Christmas traditions! I am anxiously waiting for the postman because I haven't had a whisper from home for over two weeks.

At present, six of us are sitting round the stove trying to warm our feet. Today is the coldest day we've had and my flannel was frozen! For the first time I am wearing my long-sleeved vests and thick woollen stockings and they aren't a bit too warm. Much to the amusement of our Chinese servants, we have been playing quite a bit of netball and other energetic games in the garden, which make us delightfully warm.

The prayer meeting this morning was taken by a local CIM missionary, who has just returned from a month's famine relief work among the people who have suffered so dreadfully during the floods. He told us that in a similar situation ten years ago the CIM entrusted much of the food distribution to the officials, but only one-tenth of it ever reached the people for whom it was intended. So this time, the CIM took responsibility, but even so, some of the bags were cut open and flour taken.

<u>December 16th</u>

Your lovely letters of November 16th have just come with all their topping enclosures and have made me want to jump for joy! I had 13 letters from various friends, relations and Sunday school children and they have been like a breath of heaven. Thank you ever so much, Dad, for sending a sprig of holly. It hasn't arrived yet but it's so exciting to think of seeing a real bit of Hatherleigh holly.

With Love

Ruth

Ruth

Yangchow   December 18th

Dear Everyone

I've had a busy evening writing letters and in the intervals dealing with the bath man who has paid us four visits with nine buckets of water, the last brought by his two little boys.

I must tell you about last week's happenings. The CIM girls' school adjoins the premises of the language school, divided by the garden. The headmistress is Miss Todman, a CIM missionary, who told us a fortnight ago that the Students' Federation in *Yangchow* had sent a delegation with a letter asking if the girls would join them in a demonstration against Japan. This led to a feeling of unrest amongst the girls who said they must be patriotic at all costs and they must join in with the students to save their country from Japan. However, Miss Todman pointed out that the best thing to do for their country was to pray and she couldn't allow her school, a Christian school, to join in a movement which stood for war and must be backed by Russians, and so the tension eased.

However, last Thursday, Miss Todman received another letter demanding to know immediately whether or not she would allow her school to join the demonstration. Once again she refused, but on re-reading the letter she found it very threatening and when one of the parents advised her to send all the girls home she immediately closed the school. Fortunately all the boarders had relations or friends in the town they could go to. Word went around that a procession of some thousand students would begin the next day and we were advised not to play games in the garden. In the morning some students came and interviewed Miss Todman, and Mrs Macfarlane stood at the gate waiting to prevent them from coming to our house. Then the noise started and white banners appeared over the top of the wall though we couldn't see anyone. Lots of little flags with characters on them were hurled over and the students made a terrific din and a dozen or so came into the garden where Mrs. MacFarlane was.

We went down to dinner feeling rather awed but at peace, though twice the gatekeeper burst in unceremoniously shouting something we didn't understand. We had prayer round the table then went up to our rooms to study with the multitude outside still raging and Mrs MacFarlane still standing by the gate. Somebody carried out a chair for her and the table boys took out her dinner. By 3.30 p.m. the noise had abated and the students had dispersed and classes continued as usual, though I don't know when I have found it harder to concentrate. Before they went, the students nailed up all the class room doors in the school and demanded that as a condition of the school being re-opened it must join the student league, so we are waiting to see what will happen.

We hear that the students have been up to *Nanking* and pulled the Foreign Office to pieces. The soldiers were told to shoot and some people were wounded. Also General Kiang Kai-Shek, the President, has resigned, and altogether things look pretty grim. The students, prompted by the Reds, want war with Japan, and can't see that China isn't in any way prepared for that. They say that if it happened, China would become "Red" which looks very likely. Apparently the students want a general strike and the Postal Union is in favour, so that means no letters may get through.

We hope you have not been alarmed by any reports you may have read and I can reassure you that we have been kept safe and apart from this, the doings here have been as usual. The time is flying and the studying progressing and I now know how to write about 100 characters.

I loved hearing about the coatee you made, Mary. Please get a snap taken of you wearing it, and you in your new suit, Dad, you in your new frock, Mother, and you in your plus-fours, Jock and Jack.

Later

Today several of us went for another interesting walk by the canal taking a different route through this maze of streets. We passed a bridal party with the bride and groom each seated in a gaudy "box" trimmed with very bright red, green and white coloured streamers, being carried on the shoulders of two men. All eyes were turned on us as children shouted "foreign devils" and the like, and mothers nudged their babies to look at us curiosities. We then saw a young man throwing himself about, shouting in a shrill voice, gesticulating wildly, chucking his clothes about and attacking a man, a truly ghastly sight. Further on we heard strange sounds and saw two figures dressed in black with white things round their heads and two long tails hanging down behind. They were bowing and wailing and shrieking in front of a wayside shrine where there were some little idols, and were burning little bits of paper which were floating about in the air while others laughed at them. I felt an overwhelming sense of hopelessness at it all.

The bath man has been coming up and down the stairs with the hot water and every time he comes I have to stop writing and conduct him to the bath rooms, turn on the lights, put in the stoppers, wait until he has emptied the pails and gone, then fly round to the bedrooms of the next on the list for baths.

It's actually Christmas week and I feel quite excited though it is so strange to be away from home. I can't really believe it but know we're going to have a happy time and already there are great plans afoot to involve everyone in decorating the home with paper-chains, pretty Chinese lanterns, evergreens and even holly. Won't it be delightful!

With love
Ruth

Ruth
Yangchow   Saturday December 26th

Dear Everyone

To my great joy the Christmas posts brought a wonderful pile of letters from all of you and other friends and relatives and a big fat one from John. Your parcel is still on its way, teeming with mystery, but I haven't minded that so long as I have your letters. I had so many lovely presents, including a flashlight from John, a rice bowl and pair of chopsticks from the staff and two sweet little Chinese pots for salt etc. from the girls; we all clubbed together so that each student had one present from all the rest.

I have been thinking of you all so much and hoping you had a joyous time. Meg and I have had a wonderfully happy Christmas, and trying to make each other happy helped us not to feel *too* homesick. We both had the idea of filling stockings for each other and smuggling them in when we thought the other was asleep, and had such fun opening them on Christmas morning.

After breakfast about ten of us hurried off to the American Episcopalian Church where they were holding a special Communion service in English. It was a gloriously sunny day with a white frost as we walked through the streets. Everyone was going about their ordinary business and the old Buddhist bell tolled out its doleful tones, while for us it was such a special day. The house had been beautifully decorated and we had party games, carol singing, Christmas dinner with chicken and plum pudding. The day concluded with a jolly entertainment after which I rushed upstairs to read all your letters which I had been looking forward to all evening.

I was so interested to hear all the news of home. I do so hope you won't move before John and I return because I long to come home to dear Hatherleigh, but seven years is a long way ahead, isn't it. Meanwhile, the wedding day is getting nearer and the weeks are flashing past. I shall soon be taking my first language exam which I'm doing in "character". I have to know at least 400, and write every one of them.

I do hope you have a very happy New Year. When we are having breakfast on New Year's Eve you will be having your watchnight service so I shall be able to picture you in the dear old church with the bells pealing out. Perhaps if I listen very hard I shall hear the Hatherleigh chimes, though as a matter of fact, I expect the only bell I shall hear will be the mournful, eerie tolling of the Buddhist Temple bell.

With love
Ruth

Ruth
Yangchow   January 3rd

Dear Everyone
   Today 14 of us were invited to a Chinese dinner with
some friends of Miss Todman. There was a round table
and at each place a pair of chopsticks and a big bowl of
"mien" on a small plate. In the middle were five smaller
bowls containing little bits of fish chopped up with
edible fungus in a sauce, chicken similarly treated, slices
of egg pickled in lime which were black and the whites a
green-black jelly and radishes with salt beef and a kind
of seaweed. Our hostess placed some of each on our
plates to have with the mien.
   This was our first attempt at using chopsticks and it
was fun trying to grapple with long strings of mien and
doing the polite thing of having one end in your mouth
and sucking up the rest. To be *truly* polite one must
make a *really* good noise as the slippery strings are
drawn up into your mouth. I was glad I'd kept my
cotton gown over my silk one and that there was no
cloth on the table because everything got pretty
spattered. There is a lot to be learned about Chinese
table manners because it would be easy to do something
highly offensive.

Recently Mrs MacFarlane was invited to a feast where the lady next to her removed her false teeth and put them on the table between them. Another guest remarked politely that she thought there was not really room for them there, and would she mind putting them elsewhere! The feast was given by two brothers who are not Christians but they are very kind to the missionaries. They run the motor bus and steam launch company and will always help when someone needs transport to *Shanghai*.

With love
Ruth

Ruth

Yangchow   January 16th

Dear Everyone

After a burst of spring weather it has turned bitterly cold again. At long last, your lovely Christmas parcel has arrived. Thank you for all the wonderful presents, including the surprise Christmas pudding made by you, my dear Ma, and Dad's sprig of holly. Meg and I invited two friends for "Christmas Dinner". We heated the pudding in a saucepan on the oil stove, and the holly, though faded, looked grand stuck into it and everyone thought it was too good to be true to have a real "made in England" pudding.

China is in a very sad state with practically no government as so many have resigned. Kiang Kai-Shek, the Christian ex-President who resigned, is being implored to return to sort things out, but he is in no hurry to do so. At one mission station, occupied by two ladies, a regiment took over the chapel and some of the rooms. They moved on leaving the place in an appalling mess and were followed by another group who commandeered more of the house. While the ladies took shelter with a Chinese Christian the soldiers ordered the servants at bayonet point to tell them where the missionaries were, but they refused. The missionaries returned to find the house in complete disarray and many things missing.

January 25th

Thank you all so much for your letters and presents. I had a very happy 22nd birthday and John sent me a lovely table-cloth embroidered with lanterns and six little napkins to match. Meg and I invited the six English girls to a party, the chief item being *real* English jelly which I had got on the Shanghai order. It *was* a treat, but never again! It was priced at 25¢ but cost more like $1½. The cook also bought us some cakes and biscuits and everyone put on nice dresses, chatted and knitted happily and altogether we had a jolly time.

January 30th

The other day, 500 officials formed a welcome party on the road at *Nanking* in anticipation of the return of Kiang Kai-Shek, but, much to their chagrin, he flew right over them and went to his summer residence. We hear that there are no trains or ships going to *Shanghai* and part of the railway has been destroyed. Evidently all foreigners have been summoned to the foreign settlement and refugees are going to be refused entry. We don't know how all this might affect this and other missions.

On our Saturday walk yesterday we saw a man by the little pond behind the "graveyard" stooping over a sort of drag-net picking out lots of dirty little fish which our chaperone told us he would sell on the street. Then we met a very large man riding a very small donkey and were followed a long way by some ragged children asking for money, and we were amused to hear our residence called "The Foreign Devil Hall"!

With love

Ruth

Ruth

Yangchow   February 5th

Dear Everyone

Meg and I were invited to tea with such a nice couple who have been missionaries in China for years and suffered much. They lost three children as babies, and a fourth was killed when they were fleeing from the Boxers at the turn of the century. They had to wrap him in a sack and bury him by the roadside. They have a lovely home and garden, and we had dainty afternoon tea in their pretty drawing room, solemnly waited on by their table-boy who also removed a 2" poisonous lizard with a pair of pincers!

A big world map has been put up so I was able to point out to my teacher where the various countries were and told him that all the red was British and he seemed quite impressed. He brought some Chinese money for me to see and gave me two very old coins with holes in the middle.

It came to light that some of the servants had been stealing, mainly the cook who has been here about 30 years. He was quite unrepentant and made all the boys go on strike, which they did for one meal, i.e. our breakfast. They put their pots on the stove for their *own* breakfast, but Miss Wilson removed them and said "If any man will not work, neither shall he eat". So they all started work again and the cook was dismissed.

I wonder how you all are. How is the garden, Dad? Here it is beginning to look quite spring-like and one little tree in the garden is covered with pale pink blossom and looks so pretty. I think the summer is going to be *very* hot and already it is roasting in the sun.

February 13th

We now have a third person sharing this room. Meg and I had a hectic time rearranging the furniture to make room for her. She came up from *Shanghai* by steamer and motor-bus and at one point saw shells skittering along the water. She told us that in *Shanghai* the noise of bombs and shooting was continuous and crowds of refugees were fleeing to the Concession for refuge. A truce had been called to give the women and children time to get out of the Chinese district where they are expecting a big attack from the Japanese and an anti-foreign uprising is also feared.

This week is the New Year lantern festival and there is a marvellous display in the town. The narrow streets are packed with people pushing and jostling, selling lanterns, rickshaw men pulling their loads, mangy dogs lying asleep or slinking along, women buying little flowers for their hair. Everywhere there are bright lanterns made in every shape and size - animals, men with horse heads, huge grotesque dogs, big fish with open mouths, ships, motor buses or even aeroplanes - the cleverest things you ever saw!

The other day the bath-man's little girl came to see us. She walked upstairs with her father looking like a little queen in her pink silk frock, white stockings and black galoshes, wearing a pretty little flower in her beautiful sleek black bobbed hair.

Goodbye my dears. I think about you so much and feel so cut off, but I hope all is well at home.

With love
Ruth

Ruth
Yangchow   February 15th

Dear Everyone

A lot of Japanese troops have landed in *Shanghai* and are preparing for a big attack on the Chinese district. Many people have evacuated the Yangtze valley in the *Chingkiang* and *Nanking* area, and it is possible we may have to do the same. Meanwhile the break-up of our happy party has begun and the first one has left us.

Thursday

This morning we received a visit from General Chang tsi Kiang with his Aide-de-Camp and about 20 soldiers. He is a highly regarded commander and a fearless Christian and has spent vast amounts of his own money on Bibles and circulating them among his men. We all assembled in the drawing room and bowed when he came in. After a few preliminary remarks we had a hymn, sung by half the company in English and the other half in Chinese! Then the General addressed us graciously by interpretation and followed this with a most inspiring message.

We also had a visit from four gentlemen from the British Consul and two gunboat officers who came from

Chingkiang to assess our situation and the best way to evacuate if we had to. There are about 90 foreigners in *Yangchow* at present, of whom 64 are in this compound. It was great to see some Englishmen and their beautifully groomed dog.

<u>February 27th</u>

Thank you so much for the sweet pressed snowdrop which I showed my teacher. He was charmed and interested to hear about our bluebells too. He told me that in spring there are many beautiful flowers here, and I think they are going to be a real joy to me. Thank you, Mary, for telling me all the old familiar sounds you heard when you were writing. I can't tell you just how my heart aches for you all and home sometimes.

Today's news from *Shanghai* is terrible with great loss of life not only through the fighting but also smallpox. John tells me there is a possibility of evacuation in *Angking* and certainly things look worse, but life goes on calmly here and we get on steadily with our work.

<u>March 13th</u>

Our General Director is coming soon to designate us and as our escorts are waiting at *Shanghai* it should not be long before we leave for *Szechwan*.

With love
Ruth

John to Ruth's Parents
Angking   March 5th

Dear Cousin Margaret and Cousin John

Thank you for your most welcome letters. I have been very busy revising for my first language exam which includes the geography of China and legal duties of missionaries. I wish Ruth could get on a bit faster. Here at the men's training home there are six graded classes into which students are placed according to their abilities with no distinction made between missionaries' sons and the rest. However, at the women's school they are all kept together except the daughters of missionaries, which is frustrating for Ruth but means she will get a thorough grasp of the subject. As you know, one of the conditions of marriage is that we must have passed grade two, so Ruth and I intend to get on as quickly as possible!

By the time you receive this, we will have entered our fourth year of engagement. It seems such a long time but we are both at peace with it.

With love
John

Ruth

Yangchow   March 20th

Dear Everyone

I loved hearing all about the garden and snowdrops around the lawn, and by the time you get this the orchard will be a perfect picture of blossom, primroses, aconites and daffodils. Your description of the river with those lovely big primroses growing by the water's edge brings back special memories because it is one of the first walks John and I had together. I often think of the beautiful quiet wanderings by the river in Hatherleigh.

Yes, Dad, I have seen a lot of women with bound feet. They walk awkwardly but fairly quickly. None of the younger generation have their feet bound but they are naturally very small. I've not been into a temple yet but have peeped inside two or three and we see plenty of Buddhist priests in their black and grey voluminous clothes.

There is no fighting at present, but I think it is by no means over. The timing of the sale of the old CIM premises in *Shanghai* when the market was at its best was wonderful. It is now in the heart of the Japanese territory and filled with soldiers, whereas the lovely new premises are further out and away from the troubles.

<u>March 27th</u>

Out of the window I can see five or six little children playing about, such bonny kiddies with glossy hair, rosy cheeks and black sparkly eyes. Some of the bigger girls are walking round in twos arm in arm, in bright colours and lovely plaits. Certainly the girls in China today have advantages their parents never had.

Mrs MacFarlane told us about two Chinese women she'd known. One was the wife of a prominent official who made a great show of his devotion to her in public but behind the scenes made her life hell and had four other wives living in the same house. Many husbands keep as many wives as they can afford, which is illegal but of course still happens.

The other was a local teacher, a devout follower of Confucius, who had a beautiful daughter still unmarried at the "great age" of 20. A family offered a good price for her to marry their son and arrangements were made. She was paraded through the streets in a lavishly decorated sedan chair and taken to her husband's home only to find he was a complete simpleton. The poor girl was devastated and cursed her parents for allowing themselves to be deceived just to make money. She threatened to kill herself but they implored her not to because if she did, they would have to refund the father-in-law with all the money he had spent on the wedding.

We have seen many pathetic old women with shrunken, shrivelled faces, blank expressions and bleary, half shut eyes, reflecting a life of abuse and sense of hopelessness. But there are many beautiful women with good husbands and such appealing children, happy despite their poverty.

The time in this happy home is nearly over and it is wonderful to think that we will be branching out soon. It is three years ago this week that John and I got engaged and I long for the time when we are married.

With love
Ruth

Ruth
Yangchow   March 29th

Dear Everyone

Today I showed Mr Boh some pictures including one of a GWR train that has the record speed of nearly 80 mph. He was most impressed and wanted to know how far my home was from London and how much the train fare was!

Saturday was very hot but by Sunday it had dropped by 28°! As always, there was plenty to see on our canal walk. By a house there was a mother shaving the head of her tiny son with a very fierce looking razor! Another boy picked up his young brother and "offered" him to us, much to his violent protests. We walked through the graves, huge mounds where the people are buried kneeling or standing, each grave with a clod of earth on the top shaped like a rice bowl. We came across some big odious-smelling round brick-lined pits, about 6' deep, into which the drainage from the city is dumped. Every day it is carried away in wooden pails for use on the fields and very often the loads accompany us on the ferry.

The country seemed delightfully quiet after the town and the willow trees looked fresh and dainty, the crops were green and men were ploughing with oxen. We passed a woman "washing" a garment in the muddy water and banging it against the landing stage and a man washing his hands in the canal and giving his mouth a good rinse out.

<u>April 2nd</u>

This morning we had the most glorious sunrise with the sun coming up in a perfect orange ball in a crimson sky. It's been a beautiful day with the birds singing and nearly all the women are wearing their pretty foreign frocks, so refreshing after going around in our unflattering "eiderdowns" for so long. Some of our party are about to leave for their designations and gradually our party is beginning to break up.

With love
Ruth

John
Angking   April 7th

Dear Friends and Supporters

We are progressing with our study of this difficult language and have passed our first exam. There are still five to go, each with another six months' study.

Mr Hoste, the General Director has just been to tell us our first designations, and I will be going to *Chowkow* with Mr Fred Purchas. We will join the Rev and Mrs G Denham who are very experienced missionaries and although we will begin at *Chowkow* and have that as our base, it is likely we will soon be delegated to open up a work at *Pengan* across the river, as part of the "Forward Movement" scheme (see Introduction).

Yours sincerely
John Carpenter

Ruth

Yangchow   April 10th

Dear Everyone

Mr Hoste has arrived to tell us our designations and it is thrilling to be near this next step of the journey.

This month is the "lucky month" for attending to graves and on our canal walk we saw a lot of people in the "cemetery". On our ferry was a coffin accompanied by two men with white cloths on their heads, white shoes and a piece of white cloth from shoulder to waist. One was carrying a stick decorated with white paper. They seemed to be having a great argument about the place of burial, or the price. One group of people looked very prosperous, but so dissatisfied. A man carried a basket full of red paper packages in which we could see little paper money which would be burnt before the graves. The most pathetic sight was a woman sitting cross-legged by a grave, rocking to and fro and wailing in utter misery.

<u>Monday</u>

Well, my dears, I have been designated to *Wentangching* to be with an older lady whose colleague is on furlough. I shall be a long way from John though hope we will still be able to meet as much. Meg is going to *Chuhsien* which is not far from *Chowkow*. I will miss her *so* much.

<u>April 17th</u>

Meg's and my destinations have been swapped because the missionary at *Wentangching* wanted someone more permanent. Also the powers-that-be realized John and I would be too far apart. I must say I'm very glad.

Our party is now scattered over the provinces and there are just a few of us left waiting to go to *Szechwan*. There have been great thrills over the designations and not a few tears. Two of our number had been longing to get into the field, but have been designated to HQ and *Chefoo School to do secretarial work.

Thank you so much for the wild daffodil and primroses – a real little bit of home.

<u>April 24th</u>

Tomorrow we leave for *Shanghai* where we will stay about a week before proceeding to our designations. Both Meg and I need some dentistry which would be very difficult once we are in *Szechwan*, being so remote from dental and medical help. I expect by now John will be on his way to *Chowkow* and I shall be chasing him up the Yangtze.

With love
Ruth

Chefoo School, situated in northern China, was the CIM boarding school for missionaries' children from all over the country.

Ruth

In the Launch   April 26th

Dear Everyone

We left by launch yesterday morning and spent the night at the CIM station in *Chingkiang*, and hope to catch a steamer to *Shanghai* tonight. As we sailed up the Yangtze I reflected how last time I was here I couldn't speak a word of Chinese but now, six months later, I can understand so much more.

Chingkiang is a pretty place with rugged cliffs and fresh green trees and here and there quaint little buildings with curved roofs. We walked to a beautiful park from the top of which there was a marvellous view of the Yangtze. At the bottom we passed through the cemetery and were shocked to learn that the newest grave belonged to a lady missionary who had become obsessed with the idea that she had committed some deadly sin and took her own life.

<u>April 27th</u>

Last night a whole cavalcade of rickshaws arrived in the pouring rain to take us to the wharf. We set off in a long procession through endless bumpy streets, down a slippery, muddy slope, over a 2' wide plank and on to a small boat. We were rowed across to another landing-stage where we climbed up some steep steps into a crowded shelter, all this in the dark with the aid of torches. Eventually a big steamer arrived and we elbowed our way through the jostling crowds until finally we reached the first-class deck. (Foreigners are not allowed to travel on the Chinese decks.) Very soon the boys had put up camp-beds for us in the dining saloon and in the morning we rose early so they could put it straight again for breakfast. As we neared *Shanghai* we saw ruined houses and the havoc caused by the war and passed many gunships, American, Japanese and English, such horrid things.

With love
Ruth

Ruth
CIM Shanghai   May 4th

Dear Everyone

We are enjoying our week in *Shanghai* and it feels strange to be in a city again after six months when the widest street is no wider than our gravel path at home. It's interesting to see crowds of beautifully-dressed Chinese women, with marvellous silks and satins, waved hair, pencilled eyebrows, lipstick, powdered and rouged faces.

There are several missionaries here who are going home on their first furlough and it makes me think of when John and I will be going. Sometimes I have a big ache inside and simply long to see you, but we've got a lot of work to do before then! This happy, relaxed time in *Shanghai* has been like an oasis and set us up for the next chapter of the journey as we step out into the unknown.

<u>May 6th</u>   Ta-kiang River

At last we're off to *Szechwan*, travelling up the Ta-kiang in a large luxurious river steamer, almost too luxurious for missionaries but we're making the most of it while it lasts as the hard part is to come! Meg and I have just been chatting to an official of the shipping company and his wife (Mr and Mrs Lamb) and she has invited us to go into the kitchen tomorrow and make some cakes. Fancy passengers doing some of the ship's cooking!

May 7th

At 3 a.m. we made a stop where we picked up the other three members of our party, making seven in all. Much to my delight there was an airmail letter from John waiting. He was on a Chinese houseboat with another fortnight to go to their final destination.

I've been studying hard all day apart from every now and then when I jump up to view the scenery, and believe me, we have seen some amazing sights. All along the bank are big nets suspended from large bamboo poles which are lowered and raised, a very primitive but most effective way of catching fish. We passed through rocks which rose sheer out of the water and saw picturesque towns and villages, small brown houses snuggling in amongst the trees, little houses carved out of the cliff, a town protected by a long wall stretching over the mountain tops, pagodas, pretty boats with huge sails, many labourers returning to their thatched mud huts, buffalos and oxen grazing and the black silhouette of a soldier on duty. We passed one of the great lakes of China, the second largest naval base where we saw several warships.

May 8th

We were anchored all last night due to rain and mist. The river is very dangerous in some places as there are continually shifting sandbanks and we have to go very carefully. We passed a place where one of this company's steamers was wrecked. We are due at *Hankow* in two hours' time.

<u>May 12th</u>

We have just arrived at *Ichang* having had a very pleasant overnight stay at the *Hankow* mission station. The scenery today was nothing special but I was busy swotting and then taking my three exams (on board!) so didn't miss anything. I have spent many hours on this voyage studying, and it is nice to have this behind me so I can enjoy the rest of the trip. The last two ports of call are *Kweitu* and *Wanhsien* where we will leave the ship and spend a few days before starting the five day road journey by sedan chair, evidently through the most magnificent scenery.

With love
Ruth

Ruth
Yangtze River   May 15th

Dear Everyone

We have now entered *Szechwan* province and are making good progress. We are just going through a rapid and the boat is reeling like a mad thing - thrilling! It is being such a marvellous trip and I wish you were all here to share in it.

We spent 2½ days in *Ichang* and on our last afternoon twelve of us set out in a motor-boat for a picnic. We headed towards the mountains and stopped at a place where a pretty little stream joined the river. With the usual commotion we disembarked, and much to our surprise, about 50 Chinese people emerged from the back of the boat where they had been sitting quietly - friends of the captain taking the opportunity of a free trip!

It was a beautiful day and the scenery was amazing. Great cliffs towered up on either side and in the valley nestled little houses shaded by the trees. People were going about their work, babies were playing half-naked and the water was green and clear, so different from the muddy yellow water of the Yangtze - it made me long for a swim! We had the picnic tea which the table-boy and pantry-boy had brought, then several of us climbed many steps till we came to a very old temple which was a huge cave with a few rooms where two or three priests live. There were at least 50 fierce-looking idols leering out at us from dim corners at the top of a flight of rock steps. An old, very talkative priest very politely offered us tea and oranges and happily accepted $1 at the end. We climbed down the other side of the cliff and reached the jetty and had a lovely breezy spin back, laden with all kinds of beautiful wild flowers and grasses.

While I was at *Ichang* I re-packed my luggage and found to my delight that, over and above the CIM allowance, I will only need one man to carry it which means I won't have to leave anything behind. I also met a colleague who was going on furlough and she kindly gave me her sedan chair.

Yesterday we were up at 5 a.m. to see the gorges. I simply can't tell you how spectacular they were, towering sheer out of the water with little houses nestling here and there on rocky slopes, and ledge above ledge of cultivated strips of land bearing crops. No piece of land is too small to be cultivated and the Chinese are models of economy. The "trackers'" path was sometimes a mere ledge, with or without a railing, and sometimes dropping down to a lower level by means of rough steps hewn out of the rock. Trackers are the men who pull the boats along through the gorges, about eight to a boat. Originally this was the only way to get up the rapids and steamers like ours are relatively new. We passed several boats being pulled by trackers and in one place the current was so strong that they were all bent double, motionless, making no progress at all and when the wash of our boat caught theirs they were all dragged three steps backwards. It was pitiful. They only get $4 for a trip which can take a matter of weeks.

Last night we anchored at *Kweitu* where once again we were warmly welcomed by the resident missionaries. It was interesting to see their nice big church, complete with the familiar ecclesiastical furniture. A local carpenter had been commissioned to make a lectern in the spread-eagle design, and being proud of the little English he knew, had sent in a bill for "one piece holy chicken"!

May 19th

On Monday we reached *Wanhsien*, the final destination of our 12 day voyage. Yesterday we said good-bye to Meg as she headed off to her station, and on Thursday the remaining four of us will leave. All our loads had to be most carefully weighed for the coolies to carry, and we are allowed to take a few things inside the sedan chair for the journey. I have nine coolies, three to carry my sedan chair (two in the front and one at the back) and four to carry my two burdens of luggage. Each one comprises two loads strapped to the middle of two long tiao (poles) borne on the shoulders of two coolies, one at either end. A burden must weigh no more than 80 catties (1 catty = 1⅓ lbs). Those carrying the sedan chair frequently change shoulders and sometimes ask you to ride in a rickshaw at their expense. My fellow travellers have 26 coolies between them plus two head coolies to keep the others in order, 37 altogether! I hope we shall be able to do quite a good bit of walking.

So good-bye my dear ones until my next letter which will probably not be posted until we reach *Chuhsien* in six days' time.

With love
Ruth

Ruth

En route to Chuhsien   May 22nd

Dear Everyone
We are at the end of the first stage of our overland journey and I feel that my experience as a missionary has really begun!

We spent the first night at a Chinese inn. There was one main room with a smaller one off it occupied by a cow. We were given two large rooms containing a mouldy table and wooden beds with a layer of straw and coconut matting (hosting visitors we won't name). The floor was damp mud, well dirtied by generations of feet. The walls were of unfinished plaster perforated with cracks, no doubt the home of unseen enemies and providing a good view for the residents next door. There were oil sheets right over the bed on which we laid our own thin mattress and bedding. The head coolie was most attentive, wiping down the table, laying it, washing the dishes, packing up the basket, and with two others rigging up our mosquito netting and getting hot water.

The only place we could relieve ourselves was the pigsty which was built over a huge writhing cess-pool with boards to separate us from the pigs. Here one and all were free to "squat" (at the risk of being nuzzled in the back by a pig.) This was something I had not anticipated and was a great misery to me.

After supper, most of which we had brought with us, there was a good deal of haggling over the price of board and lodging for which we eventually paid $1.50 for the four of us and the 36 coolies! Despite our apprehensions about insects and rats we actually spent a most peaceful night once the loud voices outside had died down.

After staying the night at the *Liangshan* mission we are now on the road again. The coolies are going along at a good pace and there are oft repeated shouts of "pang ko" (change shoulders) and "y'ai tso" to passers-by telling them to keep to one side. My chair is made of wicker and is very comfortable. There is a good space under the seat for things I need for the journey with a lantern and aluminium holder for food slung on the back and my fan stuck in the roof.

<u>May 23rd</u>

Last night we stayed at another inn which was not quite as bad as the first! I am writing this while the coolies have a much needed rest. A small crowd has gathered around my sedan chair and is watching me make these strange hieroglyphics. The crowd increases and I have just counted 11 pairs of feet. A woman is surreptitiously removing the mackintosh cover to have a look at my feet, and now an old woman is examining my dress and lifting it up and they're having a friendly, wheezy laugh at my expense! I told them my family lived in England and they asked if I had any children, then they, most politely, talked about my stockings, clothes, watch, brooch, skin, hair etc.

On our travels we have been at the centre of a large audience at every meal and the children come as near as they can without actually touching. They must be amazed to see us laying the table with all sorts of paraphernalia when they just run home, fetch a bowl of rice and a pair of chopsticks and eat their dinner on the street.

While the coolies were having their breakfast this morning, one of our party preached to two of the women and I took the opportunity to sketch them...

Sketch of women

<u>May 25th</u>

After a lovely night at another mission station we have arrived at *Tachu (Big Bamboo),* and this time tomorrow we will be at *Chuhsien!* The coolies have only just arrived with my baggage (10.40 p.m.) and I'm just going to bed having got up at 4 a.m. this morning!

With love
Ruth

Ruth
Chuhsien   Saturday May 28th

Dear Everyone

Here we are at *Chuhsien,* our final destination, and what a delight it was to find a lovely budget of letters waiting when we arrived on Thursday evening.

It was a long day's travel, made longer by our coolies' frequent stops for opium smokes. Several people from the mission station had walked miles to meet us. At the end we had to cross the river, climb a long flight of stone steps on to a wide paved area and there we were in this city. It seems so clean, has lots of wide streets and nearly all the houses have two storeys.

The General of this city has decreed that men wearing long garments should have them cut off, and women must have their hair bobbed. Spitting on the streets is punished by fines and subsequent offences by imprisonment. Soldiers with electric torches inspect the houses for sanitary condition and reach under the beds and the darkest places!

Although the General has done some good things, he is not a nice man and has had many wives, his latest a girl of 17 years. He has numerous children whom he supports by heavy taxes which means that, although the people work so hard, they don't have enough to buy adequate food.

Outside my bedroom window is an old single-storeyed house over which there is a lovely view. In the distance against the light grey sky, runs the long dark mountain range which we came over, and below are the green and brown foothills dotted with trees. In front is the silver-brown streak of the river, and then the town. The old house is being pulled down and a new one built for the General's brother, possibly two-storeyed, which would ruin the view and make this room extraordinarily dark!

There are two senior missionaries here, Miss Allibone and Miss Tucker ("the Ladies") who are both lovely people, and the junior worker, Lilian Harte-Wilden, is also very nice and most fluent in the language. Miss Tucker tends the little garden which is a perfect picture and the house is full of flowers.

The house was once an ancestral hall. I have a dear little room and have used every inch for all my clothes, books etc. and am surrounded with many precious photos and trinkets which make it very homely. There are three dogs and some cats and cows are coming. The gate woman sleeps just outside my room and if the dogs bark in the night, she yells "na-di-ko?" (who?) and wanders around investigating.

With love
Ruth

John
Chowkow   June 2nd

Dear Friends

On April 18th a party of 12 of us left the training home bound for *Szechwan* Province. We began our month's journey on a comfortable river steamer, carrying about 30 foreigners and several hundred Chinese passengers. We started by getting stuck on mud-banks and further on had to sail through Communist-infested territory. We saw men with rifles on the banks, but with an armed guard of six marines behind armour plates on deck we were well protected.

At *Hankow* we said goodbye to Western civilization and entered the famous Yangtze Gorges and Rapids. The swirling, torrents seemed to come rushing to meet us, while on either side towered the mountains and crags, hundreds of feet high. The great thrill was the Rapids. In one particularly strong rapid our vessel was tossed backwards and sideways alarmingly and we later learned that the captain was expecting it at any moment to crash on the submerged rocks which he said we must have missed by inches!

At *Wanhsien* some of our party continued their journey overland and the rest of us went on to *Chungking*, a big city with a major CIM station which is a hub for comings and goings of workers in their travels as well as the normal missionary team. The last four of us stayed here a week then took a Chinese houseboat for an eight days' journey to *Shunking* on the *Kialing* River which meets the Yangtze at *Chungking*. It is known as the "Little River" although it is about as broad as the Thames at London Bridge, and yet 1,500 miles from the sea.

Including the captain and his wife, there were 18 of us on a boat about 45 ft. long with no divisions or partitions. The middle section was covered with a semi-circular roof of bamboo matting. At night the crew rigged up a similar cover over the front section, and two of us slept on camp-beds and two on the floor.

There were seven tow-men, a good, willing team, who walked at the end of a plaited bamboo rope while a young man stood at the bow with a pole to keep us in deep water and yet as close as possible to the bank. An old man steered with the rudder and when he and "bow" disagreed they simply shouted at each other over or through the cover while the captain slept and his wife cooked the rice on a charcoal fire. Our slow progress became somewhat tedious after a week of being towed at walking pace and sometimes we walked and even helped for a change.

At *Shunking* a group of colleagues gathered to welcome us to *Szechwan*. Two of our fellow-travellers remained here while Mr Purchas and I set off overland for the last lap to *Chowkow,* leaving the luggage to take its time along the winding river. This was the first time I have walked 40 miles in one day, apart from the help of a *wha-gwi for the last few miles.

Mr Denham came to meet us some way out, and as night fell we arrived at *Chowko*w where we were warmly welcomed by Mrs Denham – and a big thunderstorm! After placing buckets where the rain

---

***wha-gwi** Sort of bamboo deck-chair seat slung between two bamboo poles, carried by a man at each end. They are much lighter and faster than sedan-chairs and you can hire them at villages or even on the road when you are getting tired. In fact they correspond to the "taxi" in England and cost about 1d. per mile.

was coming in through the roof, we finally retired about midnight, tired but happy. This was May 17th.

Our mission house is situated on a main street leading down to the river. It is a converted Chinese inn which Mr and Mrs Denham have turned into a comfortable, though hardly luxurious, little home. It has two storeys and stretches right back with a little "garden" on one side next to a flight of steps on the street.

The front room opens on to the street and is boarded up at night. This is our "preaching hall" which is opened every market day, i.e three times every ten days, when the streets are crowded with people mostly from the surrounding villages. Benches are put out to seat about 30, but as soon as we start singing, two or three times that number congregate, standing inside and outside and sometimes up the street steps. Someone will preach illustrated with brightly coloured pictures, and the crowd will listen eagerly to the gospel, many for the first time.

John's study, Chowkow

Our "guest hall" is just through the preaching hall and is where visitors are entertained. Our new pastor, Mr Liu, sits there most of the day, and will talk to anyone who comes in. The third room is our dining room which has an earth floor and is also our "church". We push the furniture back and replace it with benches and stools to seat about 50 people, men on one side and women on the other, Chinese fashion. Our Sunday services have been very encouraging but we do need new premises before we can extend the work or start any regular children's work and are encouraging the church members to accept their collective responsibility in finding a place of their own.

On the other side of the river is *Pengan* which is regarded as the residential and business city while *Chowkow* is the market town, but the two are one. We are based here and so far have only made the occasional visit to *Pengan* to do a little preaching and bookselling on the streets, but we are looking for some small premises where we might spend a few days and follow up the open-air work by inviting enquirers to come and see us.

Yours sincerely
John Carpenter

Ruth

Chuhsien   June 4th

Dear Everyone

It's not easy concentrating while a house is being built under one's nose, with hammering, chopping and sawing, and underneath hymns being sung! The house is progressing but I'm awfully afraid they are going to keep a pig or something obnoxious under my window.

My room is full of rats running around and nibbling my soap. They are flea-ridden and sometimes carry lice which can cause typhus so they are especially loathsome and so far we have had no success with rat-traps. There are also legions of mosquitos but I have a net and have had some white gaiters made to protect my legs. Before wearing them I had to wash them because the tailor has a rather objectionable method of making the material soft and workable by filling his mouth with water and squirting it over the cloth, repeating the process several times. He has made me a foreign frock and treated the cloth in the same way, but the stitching is beautiful.

June 5th

There were about 80 children at Sunday school today, all with very lusty voices and singing any note but the right one. They are adorable and I was able to talk with them a bit and am longing to have my own class when I'm a little more fluent.

Lilian and I have started going on some lovely walks without a Chinese escort and we have been over the hills on tiny steep paths generally between paddy fields. This is such a nice station to be starting at although in the autumn Lilian and I will be moving on to *T'uch'i* (*"earth creek"*) an outstation about a day's journey away. It is our first assignment under the "Forward Movement" to which we are pledged.

With love
Ruth

Ruth
Chuhsien   June 13th

Dear Everyone

We hear that Mr. Ferguson of the CIM has been captured by brigands and that the government official who was trying to negotiate his release was shot though fortunately not fatally.

It is almost unbearably hot and trying to study and sleep is really difficult, though it is great to have the *punka going during meals. We enjoy our walks in the cool of the evening and last night we were accompanied by the teacher's grandson. He and his brother are such handsome, serious little boys, always dressed in white suits and bare-footed. The elder brother has his head shaved and the younger one has the back shaved and the front long, which is the fashion. We stopped to talk to a crowd of "soldiers", mere 12-15 year olds, who were playing outside some barracks and they asked all sorts of questions and mimicked our attempts at "broken Chinese". Evidently all the soldiers are very well disciplined so not a threat to the general public.

Yesterday we had two classes at Sunday school and I helped to keep the under eight year olds in order. Already I'm feeling less foolish as regards the language and getting used to the change of tones. The singing is simply deafening and it is the girls who have the hefty voices whereas the boys' voices are quite pleasant. We had a good congregation at the later service including some young students who kept coming and going. As is customary, the men sit on the right side of the aisle and women on the left.

---

*punka   Large cloth fan on frame suspended from ceiling

Today is washing day and all the clothes are hung on long bamboo poles in the front courtyard. Our cook has turned up in a new suit, bare-footed and shaven-headed; it is cooler to have no hair in this heat. His wife brought their baby daughter to see me and was very interested in my photos and everything in my room. The Chinese are celebrating the "Fifth Moon Feast" and we have received heaps of peaches, eggs, sugar, corn on the cob, fans etc, all from church members wanting to show their appreciation of the Ladies.

In a few weeks' time we will be going up to the CIM bungalow in the hills to escape the intense heat of August (see Introduction). The Ladies have invited John to join us and I *do* hope he can.

Later

It is dusk but the men are still working hard on the roof next door. When they get going they sing in weird monotonous tones and are always shouting. Sometimes I catch them surreptitiously peeping up at me and grinning. One of them was given a beating the other day and stood for ten minutes with his arms straight down by his sides crying at the top of his voice! They have just dropped a load of tiles off the roof which they are finding hilarious. They rarely use a ladder and climb about like cats.

It is almost dark now, but if I shut my eyes I can see Mother, Dad and Mary sitting round the dining-room table with Brandy at the window pleading to be let in, the boys at Oxford just finishing hall and John at *Chowkow* writing letters, possibly one to me, and both of us thinking how lovely it will be when we meet on the hill for the summer and talk about our plans for next year!

With love

Ruth

Ruth
Chuhsien   June 19th

Dear Everyone

This week Miss Allibone took me to see the Confucian Temple behind our house. We entered the courtyard under a huge stone structure with the most beautiful carving, then approached another courtyard by a broad flight of steps, the top ones of which were covered with carving to prevent people going up directly in front of the Tablet of Confucius. There were no idols, only tablets. Twice a year sacrifices are offered and a lot of money is spent. There is a beautifully tended little flower garden and behind it another small temple with the tablets of Confucius' mother and father. There are three temples close to our house, one to the Goddess of Mercy, one to the God of Literature and the other known as the City Temple; two others have been pulled down to make way for a new school.

It is swelteringly hot, 85° in the shade, and I simply don't know what to do with myself; I don't know how I got through my five hours study today! Lilian is away at present and I am going for my evening walks with such a nice young Chinese woman. Today we were accompanied by about 12 girls and one boy and had frequent rests in the shade. The children picked maize from the fields and ate it with great relish and a woman at a house gave them a big wooden dipper of cold water.

I can imagine the green lawns and beautiful rambler roses at home and the countryside in all its June glory. Our garden isn't quite as luxuriant as it was but I can still pick armfuls of flowers for the house and the vine is heavy with unripe grapes.

June 27th

After I wrote last, the temperature dropped by more than 20° and it poured with rain so we went back to our warm clothes, but it is now getting steadily hotter again.

Yesterday, two chickens walked into Sunday school but the children took no notice as they are so used to having chickens in their homes. Lilian and I went for a walk with about 30 children, a long single file trail along the muddy "roads", i.e. paths, between the rice fields, with plenty of laughter and chatter. The procession dwindled steadily as one by one they took their road home. We met a huge procession of priests dressed in voluminous mustard coloured robes, beating cymbals and gongs. There were four idols made of bright red, green and yellow paper sitting on chairs, each carried by two men. One idol had six arms and three faces and another had three eyes.

July 2nd

John preached his first sermon last Sunday and tomorrow I'm taking my first Sunday school with about 20 boys. I'm feeling a bit nervous but excited at the prospect of starting at last. I don't find it nearly as easy and interesting to study here as at *Yangchow* and miss the classes and the motivation. Five hours of looking up words or reading aloud does get somewhat monotonous, but I want to get on as quickly as I can.

There are now signs of unrest amongst the military factions, and yesterday we passed a huge crowd of soldiers lined up six abreast right down the road. They are called the "Rats of Szechwan" because they know the mountains so well and are difficult to catch. They are well disciplined but very poorly clothed and nourished, especially in the winter. In the evenings everybody sits in their front rooms (mainly shops) or on the pavements and it is not uncommon to see one woman sitting on the pavement catching things in another woman's hair, and the other day a baby was having a bath on the street corner! Chinese girls are called "visitors in the home" – isn't that sad?

You asked me, my Ma, what I'd like in a Christmas parcel and I'll tell you a few things, even though it's only July - an apple, good stiff toothbrush, shampoo, shiny writing paper and some *precipitated chalk. I'm anxious to take very good care of my teeth as the nearest dentist is 200 miles away and it would cost about $200 for a visit. Also, if possible, a *wee* pot of strawberry or raspberry jam, just for a taste; it would be such a treat. And you *will* put in some sweets, won't you?

With love
Ruth

Ruth

Chuhsien   July 3rd

Dear Everyone

This morning I played the organ in church, hard work because the pedals are pretty stiff. The congregation consisted mainly of men because it was pouring with rain and women don't possess mackintoshes and wellingtons and have little to change into if they get wet, whereas the men go barefoot and roll their trousers up over their knees and wear huge umbrella type hats so don't get so

---

*precipitated chalk Calcium carbonate used especially as ingredient of toothpaste powder for its whitening qualities

wet! My first Sunday school went well with about 25 boys, and I shall be having them regularly now.

July 8th

Yesterday a foreign man called. My teacher had seen him in the town earlier lying on a bed in a shop window, smoking opium. The story he gave Miss Allibone was that he was from Georgia and the nephew of a commissioner at *Wanhsien* . He was of truly remarkable appearance, head shaved bare but with a huge auburn bushy beard, wearing a white shirt and bright yellowy brown trousers. He claimed he was on his way to see our Chinese General about buying some aeroplanes and tanks. The real object for his visit was to "borrow" $10 to take him on his way to the General's house – a tall story and I doubt we'll ever see that again, but you never know, we may have been entertaining angels unawares! Later we heard he had also conned our fellow-missionary at *Tachu* out of $5!

July 11th

Last week, Miss Allibone took me to see the family of a Chinese official, now deceased. They have a shop which disguises the nice house behind it and we were taken through a small courtyard to a "guest hall" which contained all the ancestral tablets and chairs and tables for guests round the walls. Two little servant girls poured us some cups of very strong tea and soon came and took them away again. They were cups everyone had been drinking out of! We were then given some fresh hot tea in clean Chinese cups with no handles, a rim for a saucer and a lid. Miss Allibone and I sipped ours and thought we had escaped anything worse when a girl came in with steaming bowls containing two poached eggs in "gravy" i.e. sugar dissolved in hot

water. It was as much as I could do to get outside the
eggs let alone drink the syrup! Then the girl brought in
a little towel wrung out in very hot scented water to
wipe our hands and faces.

These people are very old friends of Miss Allibone
and stood by her when all other officials turned against
the foreigners, but sadly they have never turned from
idolatry to serve the living God. It was interesting to see
them pass the water pipe around from woman to
woman. They roll up a minute piece of tobacco, put it
into the pipe, have a puff, puff it out and start again – a
tedious business. After about ten puffs they hand it on
to the next person. I have seen quite young children
doing it and small boys smoking cigarettes.

One evening Lilian and I came across a tennis court
which was all marked up and looking most inviting.
The next day we took some girls from the CIM school
who often come for walks with us and one of them
bought a ball. She could only get a soft rubber one
which had to be hit very hard. Three or four boys
appeared and were delighted to be ball-boys and we had
an imaginary net. Next to the court was a drill ground
where soldiers were exercising and as soon as they were
dismissed they all crowded round and silently watched.
When another squad was dismissed they and their
officers immediately joined the spectators. We felt a bit
embarrassed, but *did* enjoy the game.

We are going to the hill bungalow on Thursday.
Miss Allibone and I will go first, followed by Lilian in a
few days while Miss Tucker will remain down here
seeing to things and preparing the food which has to be
sent up. We have just made a huge Chinese stone pot of

plum jam to take. I am still waiting to hear if John can come.

With love
Ruth

Ruth
Chiu p'an shi   Saturday July 16th

Dear Everyone

I'm writing from our hill bungalow where Miss Allibone and I arrived yesterday, a day later than planned due to various adventures!

Wednesday was simply sweltering, nearly 90° in the shade, and we got to bed late after an exhausting day getting ready to leave. Just before dawn a huge thunderstorm broke with torrential rain so we couldn't leave. In the afternoon the cow-man and cook set out with the cow and her big calf to do the 20 mile journey up to the hill in two days. About two hours later, back they all trooped. The calf had stubbornly refused to go on the boat to take them across the river and was getting increasingly fierce and in the end kicked the cowman's ear!

The next morning, the cook came and told us that nobody could go out of their house because the soldiers were doing an "inspection". This lasted half the day and many non-residents who were found in inns were taken off to be examined and probably heavily fined, not necessarily because they were breaking any law. The soldiers didn't search our house, but Lilian and I went to the gate to see what was happening and a soldier with fixed bayonet asked how many people were in the house.

All this prevented us from leaving that day, but yesterday, while negotiations were in progress for another cow, we set off, and as we climbed higher the scenery became more and more beautiful and it was delightfully cool after the unbearable heat. After about 14 li (5 miles) we stopped for our picnic, then carried on and saw the most beautiful flowering trees and huge white wild lilies growing everywhere, some with as many as seven or eight flowers on one stalk!

We arrived to a warm welcome from the caretaker's family. The bungalow was in the process of being spring-cleaned, walls and floors being brushed and washed and furniture washed and put out to dry. The new cow and calf arrived with the cowman and gospel hall gatekeeper who brought a letter from John and I quickly wrote one for him to be taken back. We can't post them up here so they have to go back with the man who brings things up.

Our loads arrived, somewhat wet as it had been raining, but our bedding soon dried in the sun and we were able to put up our camp beds. Then we unpacked the crocks and stores. Fortunately there is a hanging store cupboard with gauze sides, an absolute necessity because you can't leave anything out for fear of rats.

Originally this was a very nice bungalow, but a few years ago some "soldiers" (brigands) set fire to it and destroyed virtually everything. Nearly all that remains are the blackened/yellowed walls on which every conceivable space is written or drawn on, crude pictures of pistols, boats, faces or birds, and you can imagine how disfigured the place looks. Walls have been pulled down, but there is one mud wall with wide gaps at the top and sides and round the window. There is nothing to separate our bedroom from the one next door but a few pillars and a cross beam over which we have hung clothes, etc. We have one shelf each of a cupboard and I have a shelf made of two boards by my bed. Our "ceiling" is composed of a lot of loose boards laid on the beams where the floor of the attic used to be. Sparrows fly about under the tiles and one night a bat beat up against my mosquito net. As you can tell, it's very makeshift but topping and clean, so it's not a bit of a hardship. A carpenter and another man are coming to do some repairs and improvements and are going to make a little room for John.

We have a Chinese stove for all our cooking and our housekeeper got some clay from the fields and repaired it so it is quite nice to use now. It has just a round hole, no flues or oven, but we can boil and fry on it - so what more does one need! All the baking is done in the city and sent up, bread, cakes etc. So far we have done the cooking between us and have not had to live entirely on eggs and tomatoes as we thought we'd have to. Today we feasted on venison from a deer which had been caught overnight. It cost 15 cents a lb (100 cents = about 1/3d at home). Today we had wild boar which was not nearly as tender but both were delicious. All night long the locals have to take it in turns to stay out and utter weird yells to keep the boars from taking the crops.

We are sitting on the veranda looking out at a dark blue starry sky after an amazing sunset with marvellous colours in a gap in the distant mountains with the black pines standing out against the sky, a true foretaste of heaven. I've been for two lovely walks along shady grass paths with marvellous ferns, wild flowers growing thickly, brilliant butterflies, beautiful birds both large and small, interesting insects – and a feeling of quiet and peace all around. The views, when you suddenly come out into a clearing, are breath-taking and it is so much cooler. I'm so hoping John can come as it will be wonderful to have these lovely walks together.

Tonight I tried milking the cow before a large audience of Chinese women. It was awfully difficult because she is so small and inaccessible and so far is giving very little milk because she's not used to being milked. Generally the Chinese don't milk their cows but use them only for working in the fields.

We have had quite a lot of people from the village to "do worship" today. I took the children, eight jolly little boys, and it was sweet to hear them singing a little hymn they had learned last year and hadn't forgotten.

<u>Monday</u>

We were having breakfast when a group of soldiers came along, each with his gun. They "marched" (slouched) past, came to a halt and we could hear them being harangued by their officer. They lined up on our "lawn" and were ordered to number off, and then the officer lectured them from our veranda. Now they have gone and Miss Allibone tells me they were being instructed that, whatever their job, they were to respect our property and not come around bothering us - very reassuring, but isn't it quaint to come and say it right under our noses!

With love
Ruth

Ruth
Chiu p'an shi   July 21st

Dear Everyone

Yesterday, Lilian and I set out on our usual evening walk with our young escort. We crossed over the "main road" continuing along forest paths. From the occasional clearing we had a marvellous view over the vast *Tachu* plain, with the city dimly discernible in a blue haze surrounded by a black-grey range of mountains with another range in the far distance and vivid green rice fields in the foreground.

We were going to climb to the top of the hill, but it was beginning to look very overcast and we could hear distant thunder. "Shall we go?" said Lilian; "It' going to rain" said our small guide; "Oh let's go" said I! So on we went, eventually reaching a house where some gipsies were sitting outside under the roof. They invited us to sit on some tiny benches, and suddenly the storm broke and we were enveloped in mist and torrents of rain with thunder clapping overhead. They pressed us to go into the house, and soon men and boys came running up the path and at least ten of us crammed into a tiny room which was pitch black until our eyes grew accustomed to it. There was a mud floor, two tiny benches, a table and a shelf with incense on it, the ancestral worship place. While I helped putting firewood into neat bundles for sale in *Tachu*, Lilian preached to them and we sang a hymn and invited them to come to our service. Finally it cleared up enough for us to leave and half-way back we were met by the caretaker's son who had been looking for us everywhere!

Life is lived very much in the public eye and ear here, because all the workmen sleep in the part of the bungalow they are repairing which is only divided from our room by a thin wooden wall! They have made masses of big strong bricks out of mud dug from behind the house which they dry outside and then cut to size. The cow is giving much more milk now but it has to be used quickly before it goes off.

With love
Ruth

Ruth

Chiu p'an shi.   Saturday July 23rd

Dear Everyone

John can come! I'm overjoyed!

I'm writing this in a beautiful glade about ¾ mile from the house, surrounded by green ferns and delicate pines, the hum of bees and insects and the twittering of birds. Alone in the forest! But I must go back as I didn't tell them I was coming and they may get anxious. I am longing for John to come and share all this beauty. Miss Allibone says we can have the bungalow for our honeymoon which would be perfectly delightful. I am going down to *Chuhsien* on Wednesday and he should be arriving on Friday.

Tuesday

I have wanted to try my hand at "t'iao"ing i.e. carrying two pails on a bamboo pole over one shoulder. The Chinese carry very big weights with such ease that it looks as though anyone could do it. So Lilian and I had a go with all the Chinese gathered around splitting their sides at our efforts. I managed to walk a little way, but oh my, the pole *was* hard on the shoulder and the buckets very heavy and difficult to balance, even empty. Eventually I began to get the knack and said I'd like to carry some water, so although it was dark and the well some distance away, quite a little procession set off, the cowman leading the way with a lantern. We stopped on a narrow path between two rice fields and filled the two pails which I managed to get astride my shoulders. Well, it is one thing to get them on but another to get them balanced. The next moment I felt myself swaying under the tremendous weight and the whole lot went crashing to the ground, one pail falling down a four foot drop, all this amidst screams of laughter. I won't be able to live that down for a long time!

Wednesday

Here I am again down in the city. By 5.45 a.m. everyone was outside the bungalow on the lawn to see me off, drinking tea and watching the first faint signs of dawn, with the moon and a beautiful big star high in the sky. I set off with Lilian accompanying me a long way before she turned back. I was carried for a while then finished the journey by foot through paddy fields and glorious mountains, chuckling to myself what a strange way it was to be meeting one's fiancé! There were other sights too - people in grubby quilts lying asleep on beds, boards, or mats on the dirty road, soldiers doing their morning ablutions, fires smoking in every house, women cooking breakfast, sweeping mud floors and combing their long hair, naked children with fat little tummies wandering about, dirty babies whimpering, little boys driving goats, men and women working in fields and water buffaloes or cows along the high road.

Friday

He's arrived! He's walked *miles* and is looking tired but very fit. I'm in a whirl!

With love

Ruth

John

Chiu p'an shi   August 1st

Dear Cousin John and Cousin Margaret (*Ruth's parents*)

It's just lovely to be together again after nearly nine months' separation and we are so happy in this beautiful place.

I set out from *Chowkow* on Wednesday, and the first day's journey was 120 li (about 36 English miles). I had to walk all the way because I was unable to hire a hua-kan. I stayed at an inn where I shared a chamber with my two coolies. The next morning I was off by 5 a.m. with the prospect of an even longer day's walk – 130 li, but the thought of seeing Ruth spurred me on and happily I was able to hire hua-kans for nearly half the way, walking the rest of the day in the heat of a very hot day. The next day another 60 li finally brought us safely to the bungalow.

We have been talking about wedding plans and expect to be married in about a year's time, depending on advice from the mission and where we are to be designated, still a long time but we are at peace about it and await God's guidance.

Yours affectionately

John

Ruth
Chiu p'an shi   August 1st

Dear Everyone

It's so wonderful to have John here. Yesterday we went for a lovely long walk and came across a little house with two men sitting outside. They pressed us to join them and produced a water-pipe for us to smoke; it is the polite thing to offer visitors the "public pipe". John has been charming everyone with his string tricks, paper ships and boxes and handkerchief rats and now he is sewing some bamboo mats together to partition off his little room.

August 6th

Yesterday we were up before dawn to see off Miss Allibone who has gone to relieve Miss Tucker who will come up with our much needed stores. Recently many goods have been opened and searched by soldiers, ostensibly to see if any smuggling is going on. A new batch of 100 soldiers has arrived to take over from the last group and have been to see us today, several staying to the service and receiving tracts. Right now, there are five or six of them standing watching me and one commented that he doesn't understand this writing!

August 14th

We hear that a big Yangtze steamer went down with about 2,500 bags of mail on board, the latest of several wrecks on the upper Yangtze this year.

The time is going very quickly and I do wonder if John and I will meet again before we're married, perhaps at Christmas. It has been so lovely to talk over many things together, from wedding details to trying to imagine the scene of reunion when we come home for furlough - a very rosy picture!

Yesterday we went for a delightful walk around the side of the valley to the Pear Tree Abbey Temple. We managed to scale a steep slippery slope and continued down the "main road", a 2' wide path made of stone slabs winding between rice fields, beautiful woodland and grassy patches with the fir-clad mountains towering above us. Now and then we passed a solitary man or woman sitting by the road minding cows or water-buffalos. The temple was at the bottom of some steep steps and we were invited in by an old man who had very bad eyes and was dressed in a ragged grey cotton gown such as the Buddhist priests wear. We followed him through two nicely kept small courtyards into a larger one and gradually several men, mostly priests, appeared out of rooms encircling the courtyard. There was a huge wooden fish, its mouth wide open with a loose wooden ball inside which must have been carved inside the mouth when it was made. This was their dinner gong!

There were countless idols of all sizes, gaudily painted and set in alcoves and glass cases. We went from courtyard to courtyard seeing numerous rooms for worship until we reached the front door where there was a huge idol the size of an elephant, gilt and brilliantly coloured all over with a fierce-looking face, a third eye and eight waving arms some with dumbbells. Many come from far distances to worship them. The chief abbot, a youngish intelligent man, remarked that his worship and ours, though different externally, were the same in intention and inner meaning, which of course we could not agree with. We talked about the

Gospel which he had heard about, and longed to be more fluent to pass on the message more effectively.

<u>August 15th</u>

We had a very restless night with dogs barking, midges biting and unbearable heat. Then at some unearthly hour the boy came to collect the things for milking the cow and woke us all up for which he received a severe reprimand from Miss Tucker.

In the evening John and I had a picnic supper. We built a camp fire, boiled our kettle to make tea and used a handle-less tin to fry eggs and tomatoes and make pancakes, and then watched a beautiful sunset. It was dark by the time we started the long trudge back and we were glad of John's lantern as the path was very narrow and littered with big stones and it was most eerie passing through maize fields, rice fields and woods.

With love
Ruth

Ruth

Chiu p'an shi.   August 21st

Dear Everyone

The temperature has dropped from 90° to 55° within the space of four days and it has been raining solidly so we're now shivering in the few warm clothes we brought up with us. We can't go out because the roads are atrocious and we've been amusing ourselves by playing games and I've been studying which is much easier in this cooler weather. Our provisions are running out so we hope the messenger will be able to get up on Tuesday with replenishments. Meanwhile we feel a bit "cabined, cribbed and confined" on a little island in a sea of mist.

I had a long letter from Meg the other day. She had been very troubled with poisoned mosquito bites and I do hope her time on the hills will make her fitter. We are very much hoping to meet up at the staff conference in November, so we shall talk and talk and talk.

Before the rain Miss Tucker, our fellow-worker from *Tachu,* came up for the day, about 30 li (10 miles) away. She found it quite hard to speak English at first as she's been alone there for so long. While she was here there was news that a tiger had been seen on the hills just where we went for that picnic. In the end it turned out to be a leopard which is not nearly so dangerous. The two words sound very similar.

We have recently heard of five deaths in our mission through cholera. This is very prevalent in some parts of China but I don't think it has spread to *Szechwan.* Several people in *Chuhsien* have died of the heat in temperatures above one's own blood heat. Miss Allibone must be relieved it is cooler in the city now. Lilian is about to go down to relieve her so she can come back here.

With love
Ruth

Ruth
Chiu p'an shi   August 28th

Dear Everyone
It is harvest time and all the people are busy getting in their maize and taking the sheaths off the cobs and

hanging them up to store. Because the rice fields are still so wet they put the grain in a sort of boat with bamboo matting rigged up round three sides to contain it. They beat the ears on a frame so that the grain falls out and then leave the empty stalks standing in small stooks to dry. Rice looks very graceful when ripe and this year they have had a very good crop – but how I would love the smell of a hay field and the sound of a mower!

To answer your questions about *Chuhsien*, I've asked three people about the population and the answer varies between 10,000 and 70,000 including the outlying villages. The chief exports are tobacco, yellow-lilies which the Chinese eat, medicines and *hong-tang. They spin and weave both cotton and silk but not for export. There are countless small shrines each with three or four idols with holes in their backs to allow the spirits to get in, and people say they are not worshipping the *idol* but the spirit inside.

Our household comprises the Ladies, Lilian and me, the cook with his wife and baby, the cleaner, gatekeeper, cowman and the woman who tends the sick people. She also does some of our buying as we can't just go shopping ourselves but must have a competent Chinese person to do the transactions and everything then has to be brought to the house and weighed, generally in Miss Allibone's or Miss Tucker's sight. There are plenty of shops in *Chuhsien* selling rather poor quality clothing, china, watches, electric torches, tinned fruit etc. and a photographer of sorts.

---

*hong-tang   Coarse red ungranulated sugar

Yesterday I made a sponge cake using an old kerosene tin as an oven which I placed over an open wood fire and put red-hot charcoal on top. Much to my delight it was quite a success!

On Friday John and I went down to *Tachu* to see Miss Edwards. The first nine or ten li were all down steps by the side of a mountain. We stopped for our picnic breakfast by a dashing stream down in a rocky valley with cliffs going up high above us, and John had a lovely bathe with quite a little audience of coolies! We passed lots of people going to market and saw a posh red chair with glass windows and four bearers going to fetch a bride. Recently we saw a bridal procession with two men carrying half a pig on bamboo poles and another two carrying a heavy-looking box with a crumpled-looking cock tied to the front and a live duck strapped to the back - typical wedding gifts! We were given a lovely welcome by Miss Edwards whose house looked so civilized and pretty after six weeks of "camping out". She gave us a delicious meal and showed us all over the compound which seemed very big for one person. We started back at 3 p.m. and felt pretty weary by the time we had climbed all those steps at the end! It took 2¾ hours there and 3¾ back!

At supper time the other day, 90 soldiers marched up to the house, were dismissed on the lawn and given permission to watch us having our meal! They all crowded around the door, including the officers, politely making way for the women every time they went in and out to the kitchen and one asked what we were eating. They stayed until we had finished and then were lined up on the grass, numbered off and marched away!

Tomorrow we go down to the city and the next day John will leave and our holiday together will be over. I will miss him so much, but once I get back into the swing of a busy life there will be no time to be lonely. Then there will be the wedding to look forward to next September.

<u>August 30th</u>   Chuhsien

John's load was too heavy for one coolie to take back so he's having to have two and has just bought 200 walnuts to help make up the weight. He intends to do the journey in three days all on foot if possible.

With love,
Ruth

Ruth
Chuhsien   September 5th

Dear Everyone

Cholera has reached our city, worst amongst the soldiers, so we are not venturing outside our compound. *The* great cures are *bay nee-bar and *Condy's Fluid which fortunately are readily available. There is much disease and illness here because of the diet, climate and insects and there have been dire after-effects from the great heat when it was up to 102° in the city. Many children developed fearful sores and big lumps on their

---

*bay nee-bar (kaolin)   White mud which the Chinese used to whiten and starch their clothes

*Condy's fluid   Disinfectant solution of alkaline manganates and permanganates that could be taken internally or used externally. It had various uses including the treatment of some skin conditions.

faces and look so miserable and washed out, whereas by contrast the country children look very healthy, albeit dirtier.

September 8th

Tomorrow Lilian and I will be making an early start for our new station at *T'uch'i*. All the heavy things will go by boat and we plan to walk but can hire hua-gans if we need to. Today we had a visit from the foreign secretary of the famous General Jang-Seng, the warlord of this large district. He is not an altogether good man but he initiated various reforms including the enlargement of streets and is very keen on physical fitness and hygiene. His Secretary spoke very good English and had come by car from *Kwangan* for the birthday feast of our new next-door neighbour, General Jang's nephew, which is to be a huge affair. For the past three days his birthday theatre has been playing not far from us, consisting of incessant beating of brass things, intermittently with a dialogue in sepulchral tones and weird falsetto – an awful din going on all day!

The medicines we ordered from *Shanghai* have turned up at long last and are not in the depths of the Yangtze as we feared, and the stores are on their way.

Love from
Ruth

Ruth
T'uch'i   September 14th

Dear Everyone

Lilian and I set off early for our long walk on Friday accompanied by seven women and children and a dog as far as the river. We enjoyed the journey but were not sorry to get here. The first thing we did was to unlock our part of the house which was pretty dusty, and open up the shutters. No sooner had we started unpacking than the pastor and another man called to welcome us, and stayed for ages. Finally we got to bed utterly exhausted but happy and woke up ready for a hard day's work. We were just getting going when two women arrived, one of whom had a sick grandson she wanted us to see. We called in the afternoon and were led through the house, past the pigsty, water trough, kitchen and a bedroom, and out on to the street at the other side! We sat on benches drinking wee bowls of tea and quite a good crowd gathered. So did the mosquitos and Lilian and I were grateful to the daughter-in-law who stood fanning us vigorously. The sick boy was brought out on his brother's back and bandages were removed to reveal some curious hard swellings. We hope Dr Gray will be passing through soon and be able to see him.

We will be taking it in turns to do the house-keeping. Mrs Liu, our housekeeper, does the shopping and every night we pay her what we owe. We also have to buy our water which a man brings up from the river daily and we filter and boil it before we drink it. The *Chuhsien* cook is coming up to fix two kerosene oil tin ovens and meanwhile the cook here is improvising with a mud frame and wood. We have brought an eight gallon tin of kerosene which should last for ages. It will be interesting to see if we can live more cheaply here.

Mother dear, please could you send me a few recipes, e.g. Mrs Cardwell's pudding, your steamed plum pudding, ways to use up cooked rice etc. Also, how do you make floor polish and brass polish? We can get beeswax and Chinese vinegar locally and almost any colour for our distemper, either by using local dyes, yellow mud or our own washing bluebag! So you will see we will have fun making our mansion beautiful.

Our compound consists of the church, pastor's house, school, teachers' house and our house all built around a square courtyard. Our house has two storeys with wooden floors all needing a good scrub, and basic bamboo furniture. The upstairs is approached by a glorified ladder perched on a couple of big stone slabs and opening by a large trap door into Lilian's room which opens into mine. To augment the furniture we are using improvised baskets and boxes, and with curtains and various bits of old material for covers it is looking quite pretty and it has been fun getting it straight. You would laugh at our funny little house, but I think it is lovely.

House at Tuchi

The position is almost ideal, just outside the town and above it so that our drinking water comes from the clean river before it has been contaminated. Last night we slipped down to the river just as it was getting dark and stood there in the stillness watching the dark shadow of a junk moving along the river with the splash, splash of oars, dimly silhouetted against the pale water. It was magical. The country all around is so pretty with fertile plains, low hills and the mountains where we spent the summer just visible in the distance. We have traced a map of this district which the Military left behind when they occupied the premises. It is going to be very valuable because we can't buy maps like that.

On Sunday, Lilian took Sunday school and several children turned up. The church service was taken by the Chinese pastor who does Sunday duties in exchange for rice. The Chinese people are very friendly and there are no soldiers in this area and it is free from bandits.

We shall never complain of this place being "quiet"! The school children in the compound are either repeating their lessons, singing or playing football all day long, and when not otherwise engaged the two young teachers sing along to their little harmonium. Yesterday I was woken in the middle of the night by piercing wailing which went on for ages and I discovered it was one of the girls practising the *koo-jar.

Yesterday as I was breaking an egg it exploded! All I could do was to hold my nose, scramble out of my soaked, stinking dress and shout for Mrs Liu who plunged it into water. We had such a laugh but neither of us could face an egg for supper that night.

*koo-jar   Lament which girls sing when they get married.

Earlier Mrs Ch'u, our Bible-woman, came with me on my first "missionary journey". We could only walk very slowly because she has tiny bound feet. The streets were crowded as it was market day, and every eye turned on me and conversations stopped as people stared in silence. Many have probably never seen a foreigner before. We continued into the country and stopped under a big tree and I gave out tracts while Mrs Ch'u preached. Our audience was mostly men but there was one old woman who was asking questions while a younger one was catching things in her hair with her thumb-nails.

With love
Ruth

Ruth

T'uch'i   September 18th

Dear Everyone

Sunday services are over, and we are on the grassy cliff above the river enjoying the Sabbath calm. We are so fortunate to be able to walk 100 yards and come to the top of the cliff with such beauty all around us.

The other day, six mothers arrived with their babies wanting "santonin", so I made up some tiny packets of this very expensive drug and no sooner had they gone when a whole host of women arrived wanting to hear the singing on the "thing". The fame of the gramophone has spread abroad and we are glad that it brings people here and that they are willing to listen not only to it but also the gospel. So I opened the "toy" and it was just in the middle of the second tune when it started to make an ominous noise and the concert came to an abrupt end. The next day I took out the engine, oiled and greased it, put it on and it sprang to life again!

We were in the middle of dinner the other day when who should appear but Dr Gray. I had written to him about the little boy with the strange swellings and he had stopped on his way to *Paoning* to see him. Unfortunately the child had become so poorly that he had been sent away to an aunt in the country but Dr Gray did have time to see a sick neighbour. We saw him to his boat where his sedan chair and luggage were waiting and he was planning to stay the night at *Chuhsien* (unbeknown to the Ladies!) then leave early the next morning to continue his journey.

At church yesterday, the Chinese pastor preached for over an hour, something of a feat of endurance when one is perched on a 7" bench with no back! People were talking loudly and a man got tired of listening and started reading his Bible aloud. The pastor's chickens started cackling at the entrance so he signalled to his wife to go and still them. When she returned she gave a loud yawn and he said something to the effect that, even if you are getting sleepy please listen a little longer! We are trying to get out every day to do some evangelistic work, and it's lovely to feel I've started at last. For me it is just listening and trying to pick up the phrases, giving out tracts, smiling at all the mothers and children .... and fanning myself.

Some of the babies and children are so pitiful. At one house there was a small bundle of skin and bones in a wee bamboo chair, with a little wizened face with enormous brown eyes and flies clustering around on her face and nose. Her little sister picked her up and nursed her. Next door a large crowd gathered, one of whom was the very thin, undernourished mother of the baby who she proceeded to feed. There was another sweet-looking young woman with such a bonny baby of about a year old. The first mother gave her baby a big hug and a kiss, then handed it to the mother of the bonny baby for *her* to give it a feed. It was such a touching gesture.

Wherever we went, women young and old were spinning thread, making shoes etc. We went to two or three more houses where we were made to feel welcome and many people gathered to hear the gospel and receive tracts. While we were out about 30 guests had called, but Mrs Liu told them to come again tomorrow. Today I made yeast and three loaves of bread which I think are a success but it's very difficult baking in a kerosene tin, especially with wood as we have no charcoal except a little for our iron.

With love
Ruth

Ruth
T'uch'i   Saturday September 24th

Dear Everyone
On Wednesday Lilian is going to *Tahsien* to be a bridesmaid at a friend's wedding, so I will be missionary-in-charge for a few days! All being well, a man should be up from *Chuhsien* today with the silk for her dress, not what she ordered, but it will have to do because we'll only have two days to make it before she leaves.

Time is flashing past and we're getting many glorious opportunities for doing the *real* job, i.e. going out every day, visiting and preaching either in the homes or on the streets. Also we have engaged a teacher and read with him for an hour each day. It is great to be here in our own station, us two young ones, and we feel privileged to be responsible for the work in this district. I wonder where John and I will be this time next year.

Sunday

The cook from *Chuhsien* has just turned up in the middle of the service with Lilian's silk and letters from home. I have slipped out to have a quick glance to see if there's anything I need to comment on and am in an awful hurry as he has to go and I must get back into church again.

With love
Ruth

Ruth
Chuhsien   October 2nd

Dear Everyone

Lilian left at daybreak on Wednesday, and I had two busy fruitful days going out with the Bible-woman. On Friday I was going to bed quite late when I heard a lot of commotion, dogs, voices, people running and walking about just up the road, but it soon stopped and I went to sleep. The next morning Mrs Liu told me excitedly that there had been three robberies on the street and a man shot dead as he was trying to raise the alarm. The people are up in arms because they pay a lot of money to keep the militia, who then allow such violence on the street before most people are in bed.

Our two women were very frightened, though I felt absolutely calm. Mrs Ch'u and the old teacher were very serious and advised me to return to *Chuhsien* as soon as possible. So I hurriedly packed up, put things away, took down the curtains and barred the shutters, grabbed some lunch for the road and found a coolie who agreed to carry my load down for half a dollar. Finally at about 11 a.m. Mrs Liu and I set out for our 20 mile walk. I wore Chinese dress so as to be less conspicuous and Mrs Liu walked behind me. I was very sad to see *T'uch'i* fading into the distance. After a while we met one of the *Chuhsien* coolies coming along with a load on his back – for us! Inside were various groceries, a large parcel of tracts and a big packet of letters. I took out the milk, butter and letters and sent him on to *T'uch'i* with the rest. I then walked along reading the letters though at times this was impossible because the road is so uneven and narrow with sudden bits of rock jutting up so the letters lasted me about six miles and made the journey seem very short!

We stopped at a town for refreshments. Being market day the streets were packed and we had to elbow our way through. Inevitably, a large crowd came to watch me eat, whereupon Mrs Liu stood up and announced in a very loud and eloquent manner that I was a young foreign spinster who had come to preach doctrine and was on my way to *Chuhsien* and had stopped for a drink. It is considered most ill-mannered, particularly by the older generation, to stare at a young unmarried woman, so thankfully most of the crowd soon dispersed. The last mile we did by boat, by which time the *Chuhsien* coolie we met on his way to *T'uch'i* had caught us up.

What a surprise the Ladies had when we appeared at the house so unexpectedly! They gave us such a warm welcome and there was much to talk about. It was lovely to come to such a "palatial" house after our little "hut". Mrs Liu is going back tomorrow and taking some provisions for Lilian. What will she say when she comes back and finds the bird has flown? The women will see to her needs and advise her if she needs to come down. If it's merely a local affair involving the militia it will soon be dealt with. Also local people wouldn't dare do anything against the Gospel Hall, and if they did the matter would be taken up by the General and senior authorities. Please don't be afraid for me, my dear ones, because I can assure you we will be advised by those who are very experienced and will be most careful not to run risks.

Four big boxes arrived today, our stores from *Shanghai* for which we are most grateful. I foresee a useful cupboard being made from those boxes!

With love
Ruth

Ruth
Chuhsien   October 8th

Dear Everyone

I was advised it was safe to return to *T'uch'i* and planned to set off this morning but it poured all night and the roads would have been impossible.

We hear that that the two coolies who took Mrs Liu back to *T'uch'i* got half-way there when they, and some others, were seized by the Military to carry their officers. Our two managed to escape and one got back long after dark but the other hasn't turned up yet.

Last Tuesday Miss Allibone took me to see one of the locum pastors and his family who live in a big country house. On arrival we were requested to come and have some hot water and, with many apologies and protestations that they should not have troubled and that we were not worthy etc, we went into another room where a large square table was laid with nine saucer-like dishes arranged in a square in the middle, each containing some special Chinese cake or biscuit mostly made of nuts, rice puffed, sesame seeds etc. We were given foreign cups with handles, but the Chinese had their normal bowls. The hostess stood up and placed something from each dish next to each cup. What we didn't eat was wrapped up in a little parcel and given to Miss Allibone to take home, as is the custom.

<u>October 12th</u>

I got back to *T'uch'i* two days ago. After the jolly wedding house-party with all her friends, Lilian came back to find an empty house and had been quite lonely. This afternoon we went out preaching and found a place where there is a big tree and steps cut into the stone making ideal seats. An enormous crowd gathered, mainly boys and men, and listened intently. One of the men took a tract and sat down in the middle of the crowd and started reading it very eloquently, explaining it as he went, gesticulating and completely holding everyone's attention. I was absolutely fascinated though couldn't understand much of what he was saying. He was a very keen Buddhist but certainly showed interest in the Gospel and invited us to his house.

October 18th

I'm *so* thrilled to hear of Mary's engagement *(Ruth's sister)* and long to hear more. Every now and then a little prick of homesickness comes and the weather, your letters and Mary's news all make me long for home.

It has been raining constantly and I feel bottled up with lots of steam to let off! At least I've been able to get down to some hard study and will be so glad when I've completed all four exams, though that's a long way off yet. It has suddenly got much colder and I have started wearing my winter pyjamas, those old pre-war ones that Dad wouldn't wear – they're lovely and cosy!

October 20th

Last Saturday the two teachers from the girls' school came to "lunch". We gave them sandwiches, chocolate blancmange, fruit salad, oranges and nuts, but they didn't like any of it, and when Mrs Liu and Mrs Ch'u sampled the remains they quite genuinely thought the blancmange was pig's liver! The same day we had other visitors who asked if they might see upstairs and were most interested in all our photos, and examined our beds by poking their hands right in trying to find out between which of the many of the layers we slept!

Sunday was market day but we had quite good congregations and the two school teachers came to both Sunday school and church and seemed very interested. On Monday evening I did a bit of exploring and found a high path which brought me out on to a wild desolate place full of graves. I enjoyed my solitary walk, and in the evening Lilian and I had fun doing some acrobatics to gramophone records. On Thursday we visited the place with the tree and the stone steps where crowds of men listened and gladly received tracts and gospels which they are amazed they don't have to pay for.

There is fighting between the Military in the *Chungking* area and John said that *Chowkow* had been full of soldiers but most of them had moved on. There has been movement of the *Chuhsien* soldiers too but no definite news, and the *Tahsien* soldiers are said to be moving down towards *Chungking* today and will pass through here. There is also a rumour that Kiang Kai-Shek is sending troops to *Szechwan* to investigate. You can understand how difficult it is to get reliable information with such slow communication between places.

With love
Ruth

Ruth
T'uch'i   October 26th

Dear Everyone

It was simply marvellous to get the biggest budget of letters I've ever had from home, mostly delayed, and I didn't realize I'd missed quite so many.

Thousands of soldiers have been passing through and the local people are *eating bitterness because their rice, eggs and vegetables have been purloined by the hungry men. Not only that, but no youth or able-bodied man dare venture out of their home for fear of being taken by the "grab coolie" system. Plain clothes

---

*eating bitterness   Enduring something unpleasant in good humour

men are appointed by the Military to seize every man who may be out doing his ordinary work and he is compelled to go and carry heavy loads for the soldiers. Lilian saw a deaf and dumb man working in a field being collared, and a young man returning from market with his father who cried out in vain to resist them and implored Lilian to help him, but of course she couldn't.

The town is full to over-flowing and I've seen hundreds of small horses and countless men arriving looking so tired, each carrying his bedding, food bowl, gun, and umbrella, one to fight their brothers and the other to ward off the elements! We thank the Lord that so far they have made no attempt to enter our premises, probably because they respect the fact that the girls' school is here.

I'm very anxious to hear from *Chowkow* and Mrs Liu went to the Post Office to see if there were any letters. The mail bag was in, but they cannot or dare not open it because even the P.O. is full of soldiers. When I heard from John yesterday, he'd had a fever for ten days with temperatures of 102° and higher, so I'm simply chafing to hear the latest news. He could hardly eat and wasn't sleeping and last time he tried to write he was lying flat because he was sick when he sat up. The Denhams and Mr Purchas have sent for medical help but this all takes time. How I wish I could be there to help look after him.

October 27th

The post has brought a short letter from John and one from the Denhams. Dr Gray had just arrived and diagnosed a slight touch of typhoid fever. John was feeling very lonely and it must be horrid just lying there day and night feeling so unwell. How I wish I could pack up and go straight away but it just wouldn't be possible.

We hear the soldiers are moving on tomorrow. Men have been hiding in the sugar canes to avoid being caught, and the fields and hills, usually dotted with little groups working hard, are practically deserted.

Today Mrs Ch'u and I visited a house nearby where a poor woman was living with her two small children. Her husband had just died and she looked so miserable and the children were so ragged and dirty. Who knows what these people suffer. Whilst we were there we saw a fine young man being marched along by a soldier with two women behind pleading loudly for him. Later we saw two soldiers, no more than boys, trying to chase a young man who I was so pleased to see slipped behind a hill and got away. When the soldiers came back past me I gave them all a gospel which they accepted politely.

The only way this is affecting us personally is that our man who gets our water from the river hasn't dared go for two days, so today Mrs. Liu and Lilian went down with a pail and fetched some and hopefully things will return to normal tomorrow. We feel so blessed that all our needs have been provided for even when it has been difficult to buy things. Today we were able to buy some vegetables from someone we visited.

Now to answer your questions, Dad. Yes, mushrooms do grow in China. The cowman got some when we were on the hill and we had them for supper, but the next day we were all ill because they were not the real thing after all! Yes, there is a kind of blackberry but it is very scarce. No, there is no railway and the cinema has not reached *Chuhsien*, though they sometimes have a very noisy theatre. Yes, there are rich and poor and a sort of class distinction though nothing like ours at home. A family may have coolies, paupers, teachers, farmers, soldiers etc. all living in the same cluster of buildings. Even the officials spit in their houses and are the same in their habits as the poorest.

Next day

We had just finished breakfast when we heard a commotion in the courtyard, and saw three military "grey-jackets" pulling the pastor's servant out of the house by his collar. However the two teachers and their servant stormed at them and said he was the school water-carrier and suffered from ague, so they let him go. Then we heard another great noise at the back, and there were four or five soldiers with our old water-carrier on the ground. They had beaten him because he was elderly and ill and couldn't carry but I'm glad to say they let him go again. It is hard to blame them as they are put under such pressure by their superiors to catch men. It is such a relief that they have gone now.

With love
Ruth

Ruth

T'uch'i   November 1st

Dear Everyone

The news of John is that the German nurse from *Tahshien* arrived eight days ago and he is doing well. She said that his is the mildest case of typhoid she has ever nursed!

November 3rd

Good news! John's temperature is down to normal and he is making splendid progress. I am so relieved.

Today has been a happy day. With a coolie carrying our picnic basket, tracts and gospels, Mrs Ch'u, Lilian and I set off early to go to a market about 20 li away. It was such a pretty walk, fairly hilly which always means going up and down lots of steps. There were huge rocks and oil trees turning to most beautiful autumnal tints. Being market day the place was full of people. Lilian preached to a crowd of men resting under a tree. We then found another big tree and soon the people flocked around, tightly packed, to hear Mrs Ch'u who perched comfortably on a large root. They were rather noisy, and at one stage a quarrel broke out when a man tried to push and shove his way out. We distributed tracts and gospels and it was amazing to see how quickly they all disappeared! We hope they will really be read, and that our new supply will soon arrive.

We had our picnic at an inn watched by the usual crowd, some standing on benches to get a better view. They were most intrigued to watch us boiling our kettle on the little spirit stove, and there was a chorus of "boiling" (in Chinese) when it reached that point.

Our last pitch was at the edge of the town where we sat on a little mud bank beside a field. The crowd jostled to get nearer, and I invited one old lady who was being pushed about to come and sit by me. She listened well intermittently then started examining my hands and stroking them affectionately, and exclaimed "my, you're very fat". The people behind me were trying to lift up the rim of my hat to see if my hair was bobbed. An old man was talking to Lilian and he also remarked on my obesity! I'm glad our eyes didn't meet just then. We continued to the next place, where again the people were more interested in us than what we were saying. Some women commented on my eyes being a different colour from theirs and asked if I could see them clearly. Another old lady put her finger to her nose and said "see, our noses are flat and small, but hers is high and big", at which point she took my nose between her finger and thumb, gently pressing it! They are very endearing despite their strange ways. Quite a lot of them had heard of the Gospel and it is such a joy to me to be starting to preach a little and to be understood.

With love
Ruth

Ruth
T'uch'i   November 5th

My own dear Mother
Many happy returns of the day! I only wish I were with you to make it an extra happy day and how I would love a good long talk! I am so happy about Mary being engaged and longing to hear all about it.

Fancy, only ten months now until *the* day and I shall soon be sending my measurements. Please when you have time would you send away to Buttericks and Weldons for a fashion book with special patterns for brides, designed for 1933. Then I could choose what I liked and send it home so they could perhaps cut a pattern to the required measurements.

Today the messenger came up from *Chuhsien*. I had three letters all ready for him to take down but shortly after he left, I saw them still lying on the table. I tore out of the house and ran down to the little jetty, hoping to catch him. No-one had seen any sign of him, so I guessed he might be having his dinner in town and decided to wait. The inevitable crowd of 30 or 40 gathered around and someone kindly offered me a bench to sit on. They wanted to know what I was doing and to see the letters and count the stamps. I tried to tell them about the Gospel and invited them to the service. Eventually, to my joy, I saw the messenger coming down the steps and was able to give him the three precious letters. As I thought, he'd been having his dinner in the town.

Then Mrs Ch'u and I went on the street. Our method is to walk slowly until someone invites us to sit down and there is usually no difficulty in attracting a large crowd. Today I stood on a bench and held up some pictures which attracted quite a bit of attention and one woman asked how she could be saved. It is great when they ask such a direct question. We are delighted because one of our lapsed members has started coming to church again. He is a teacher who runs his own private school and yesterday he turned up with a train of small boys.

One day we were invited into the house of an old man who had evidently listened to the gospel under the big tree where we go on market day and it seemed had understood quite well. Then we went into two more houses where we were invited to "come in and be sociable for a bit" and Lilian preached to them. At one house we were entertained by a most engaging and enthusiastic young woman who gave us a huge bunch of new potatoes and asked us to go again. She says she is coming to see us because she wants to learn about Jesus.

John is a lot better but still very weak and he is going for a fortnight's recuperation to *Nanpu* where there is a trained missionary nurse. Poor John. He's not used to being quite so helpless and feels it's an awfully long time to be doing nothing, forgetting his book work and not even getting any spoken language.

I can imagine how beautiful everything is looking at home now with the autumn tints. The leaves are turning here too and it is very pretty. Turnips, carrots, red peppers, peanuts, hemp, sweet potatoes, broad beans are all being harvested and rice fields being ploughed. The ginger harvest is over and people are busy drying ingredients and chopping hot things for their pickles which make their food taste so nice.

With love
Ruth

Ruth
T'uch'i   November 11th

Dear Everyone

A very Happy Christmas to you all! It seems far too early to be thinking of Christmas but it's quite late enough for the post. I'm afraid I haven't sent any Christmas presents because there is nothing much to buy in these outlandish parts. How I would love to be with you all, but I know I can't, so what's the use of thinking about it! All being well, we will spend Christmas with the Ladies at *Chuhsien* and they have also invited John but I don't know if he'll be able to come.

Today we've spent 25,400 cash at the market, that's just over $1 = 1/3. For this we bought 22 eggs, 10 oranges, 4 huge pomeloes, 1lb lard, a cabbage, 12 turnips, 2 bunches of onions, a goat's liver and 4 pails of water. So you can see that, on the whole, the cost of living is very much lower than it is at home. The oven is still very difficult. I tried to roast a joint of mutton but it was not nearly done after ages and we couldn't eat it! Still, we're gradually getting used to a kerosene oil tin for baking bread and cakes.

The military movements continue to be unsettled but aren't troubling *T'uch'i*. We're getting on with the good work, preaching the Gospel every day and planning to visit the markets gradually.

November 17th

John is probably on his way to *Nanpu* now and I'm sure the change of scene will do him good and be a rest for the *Chowkow* folks who have done so much for him during his illness.

Yesterday we went to a town 30 li away via a road which was steep and hard-going but the scenery was marvellous. In one place two men passed us each leading a fair-sized monkey on a cord. When we reached the town we stopped at a wide open space where a huge crowd gathered, far too big, and it became a pushing swaying, shouting mass of people all trying to get a look at us! Some wanted to listen and shouted at the others, but eventually the crowd got smaller and more attentive. We then moved on to a better place with fewer people, but there was little interest. We had our picnic dinner at the home of a Christian family, and only after we finished did we discover they had bought 2½ lbs of mutton and had been about to prepare dinner for us! So we bought the meat from them and later enjoyed some Irish stew!

November 21st

At one house we visited recently there was a large table on which was a huge two-storeyed construction like a doll's house made of wood and paper and wallpaper on the walls. The chief interest was the provision for the inhabitants of the house, i.e. the souls of the departed. There was a retinue of about 12 little men, servants, each one standing on its own little plinth made of a rice bowl filled with plaster. There were cones of gilt and silver paper called the gold mountain and the silver mountain for use as money, and about ten dishes of plaster foods, marvellously modelled and realistic looking, e.g. a pig's head, a duck, a fish and a marrow. There were also grotesque "door gods". The whole "house" was covered with dust and cobwebs and there were signs of rats outside. The home was full of idolatry, but the people were willing to listen when we told them about our God.

At another house we saw a little girl about six years old who was having her feet bound up. She was sitting at the threshold resting one poor little baby foot with all the rags and bandages chucked on the filthy ground and covered by innumerable flies. I don't think she'd had her foot broken but just bound very tightly. Mrs Ch'u gave the women a good lecture which seemed to fall on deaf ears. A small group of men appeared from nowhere, and I was showing them a picture when suddenly a dog dashed up, nipped my leg and dashed away again, leaving three tiny marks which I treated later with iodine - rather a nasty experience but fortunately with no ill-effects.

The messenger has just arrived from *Chuhsien* and brought a lovely fat budget from home. Oh joy! Now I must stop because he is waiting to take this down.

With love
Ruth

John
Chowkow   November 23rd

Dear Friends and Supporters

I am writing from *Nanpu* where I am convalescing after a bout of typhoid.

At the kind invitation of Miss Allibone and Miss Tucker I was able to spend my summer holiday at their hill bungalow so Miss Rossiter and I had a delightful month together, the first time we had seen each other for nine months and worth every step of the 100 mile trek there and back in the heat of summer!

Like most provinces of China, *Szechwan* is overrun by "the Military", that is a number of generals each with his own army and ambitions. At times, when Japan is not occupying their attention, they fight amongst themselves, usually for a certain city or more land on which to grow opium and collect taxes, with fines from those who refuse to comply. Often the defeated army turns to banditry or defects to the victorious General.

About two months ago the Military had a scrap which has been more widespread than usual. Initially we were conscious of an unusual buzz of activity among the 1,000 or so soldiers in *Chowkow,* then literally thousands poured through the streets from elsewhere on their way to fight the *Shunking* troops. Fortunately the fighting did not come closer than 15 miles though quite a lot of wounded were brought back to *Chowkow*. Now that the trouble has blown over locally the main scene of action has shifted west.

Inevitably it is the poorer classes who are most affected by this. The soldiers go round seizing all the able-bodied men to carry their loads. I saw a group of 20 or 30 roped together, being driven down the street past our house and in the teashop opposite we saw at the attic windows a crowd who had been locked up.

Sometimes several troops would arrive at *Chowkow* and want to "stop a night or two" which meant they went into every house down the street and occupied whatever rooms they fancied, herding the owners into the back or elsewhere. We had several such visits, and one group marched right through our house during a Sunday service to investigate, and then returned to the dining-room walked up the "aisle" and announced to Mr Denham which rooms they wished to occupy! Fortunately he was able to turn them away by convincing them that our premises were far too small. On another occasion Mr Denham finally managed to get rid of a very insistent group by telling them it would be most dangerous to stay as someone in the house had typhoid fever!

That "someone" was me! On October 13th I got a headache and became increasingly unwell and when my temperature reached 103.9° Mr and Mrs Denham sent for a doctor from *Paoning* and a nurse from *Shunking*. They diagnosed it as typhoid and for a time I was flat on my back being fed every two hours with a teaspoon.

Thanks to having been inoculated before I left England it was a relatively mild attack, and after five weeks I was able to make a two day journey by sedan chair to *Nanpu* for a fortnight's convalescence, I am feeling much better. How good the Lord has been keeping me through my illness and I am much looking forward to returning next week and getting right back into the work again.

Mr Purchas and I had started making separate weekly visits to some of the surrounding market villages within about a ten mile radius accompanied by Mr Liu. We walked there and then preached for three or four hours and it was wonderful to see the eagerness with which the people left their marketing and crowded round to hear the Gospel and clamour for books. On our way back we stopped at one or two tiny villages, partly to rest and partly to talk to the villagers. We were just getting into our stride when the military troubles put a stop to it, but now the scare is more-or-less over Mr Purchas and Mr Liu have resumed the visits.

In *Chowkow* the streets are once again buzzing with activity after being deserted for weeks and the preaching hall is crowded. God is blessing the work and attracting such interest that there is now a full week of services and meetings, i.e. Bible school, enquirers' class, prayer meeting, men's meeting and women's meeting. After six months here in *Chowkow*, I am certain that the Lord has led me to this place with my fellow-worker, Mr Purchas, and I could not have wished for more kind, helpful and inspirational "seniors" than Mr and Mrs Denham.

Yours sincerely
John Carpenter

Ruth
T'uch'i   November 26th

Dear Everyone

Last week the Ladies sent up two cooked wild ducks complete with gravy and stuffing. Although Lilian and I did our best we couldn't finish them quickly enough and one went off so Mrs Liu took it and cooked it for their supper, reporting that it only had a slightly bad taste!

The other day we went to a Chinese feast with the two teachers on our compound. One of the guests was wearing bright mauve baggy sateen trousers, black flowery little shoes, a mauve woolly cap decorated with gay red and green ribbon and a pale blue top garment over all her padded ones. She did look jolly and you would have laughed to see her having a piggy-back on one of the other guest's shoulders all around the tennis court! I'm sure Chinese women weren't able to let their hair down like this a few years ago!

<u>November 28th</u>

It is midday and we have just come back from a wedding breakfast. We were out by the river having a "jump" to get our toes warm when a woman approached us, dressed in her best, to tell us that the feast was ready and we were invited to go along. The men were seated at tables on the pavement under the eaves of the house, about eight tables with six men at each. While they had their feast the women were led up some steps and through a trap door into a dark little room. Mrs Ch'u warned me to mind my head and I found it was nearly knocking against some pigs' entrails which were hanging from the ceiling!

We were led to the bride's room where she sat in a black silk robe with a very pale, tear-stained face, looking utterly miserable. I felt so sorry for her. The bridegroom was 17 years old and looked about 12, also wearing black silk and a trilby hat which nearly swallowed up his tiny, pale face. He was standing on his own with no-one taking much notice of him as the preparations were being made for their chairs. We smiled and said a few words, and his mother instructed him to give us a bow, which he solemnly did.

The bride had a nice, freshly whitewashed little room with skylights and a bannister overlooking the room beneath, which opened on to the street. The enormous bed had grass cloth curtains and a strip of silk across the front with a picture painted on it. There were new blankets and a gay satin square with brightly coloured stitching, two square pillows and two roll-shaped ones filled with rice which will gradually be emptied and substituted by chaff.

The twelve guests sat on the edge of the bed until the men had finished and then we were summoned to the feast where we were pressed into the seats of honour. Each place was laid with a pair of chopsticks, a china spoon and a wee wine cup. (The wine is like methylated spirits and we don't drink it!) Then the bowls of food were brought and placed in the middle of the table and when our neighbour said "ching ts'ai" we all dipped our chopsticks into them. There was pork, chicken, mutton, greens, turnips, fish etc. all in gravy and when one big bowl was emptied of its "solids", the gravy was tipped into another one; it is surprising how nice fish, mutton, chicken and pork gravy tastes all together!

Anything the guests hadn't eaten was wrapped up in paper and taken home.

The girl would be considered a well-endowed bride, but she had never seen the man until they were married yesterday! What a shock she must have had to see that such an infant (in looks) was her husband! She is a student and comes from a heathen family. The bridegroom has been a regular member of our Sunday school so we do hope she will be allowed to come along with him.

Such is a wedding feast in China, according to their customs. I do hope I shan't look quite as miserable as the poor little bride. There was none of that joyous feeling when everyone is brimming over with happiness, making speeches and congratulating each other.

With love
Ruth

Ruth
T'uch'i   December 1st

Dear Everyone

The other day we walked out to a house about 8 li away, then worked our way back, calling at a good many homes. It was a very pretty road and marvellous to see acres and acres of perfectly cultivated land on the hills and in the valleys, with circular paddy fields shining in the sun and the green sugar canes waving their last farewells before being cut down, stripped of their leaves and quickly carried off in bundles.

The sugar cane harvest is the chief preoccupation at present, and we passed a very friendly old man who we had met when we were preaching the other day. He was in charge of the harvesting and invited us to go and watch. The sugar cane is put between two huge stones which go round by means of cogs and the juice is thus crushed out, runs down a bamboo pipe and is caught in a bucket. It is then put into a huge pan and boiled to a certain temperature when it is passed on to another pan and boiled and so on, until it comes to the last pan where it is tipped out when ready. The finished product is known as "tang" and is the consistency of fudge.

The fire for these various stoves is a huge arrangement of stones and mud, with a man constantly stoking. They were making the sugar into thin strips. On a wide sort of wooden counter there was an oblong wooden frame with grooves at equal distances, along all four sides. A man spread the frame with a special kind of brown paper made from bamboo, which the Chinese use for everything, Then another man tipped a pan of hot brown steaming sugar on to the paper and with a specially shaped thin wooden "scoop" quickly spread it over. He put rods crossways into two grooves and cut along with his wooden scoop repeating this down the length of the frame and did the same lengthways with a longer rod, thus dividing it up into bars of the same size. He then sent the whole large strip to the other end of the counter where another man broke it up into the required sizes, stacked it and did it up into parcels for market.

A large number of men and women are employed, numerous actually in the fields cutting the cane, about ten men continuously carrying it in from the fields and a good many crushing it, stoking the fire, stirring the pans etc. Meanwhile the owner sits watching to make sure there is no slacking or theft etc. He was a little old man with a pigtail who has been a vegetarian all his life in the hope that he will get to heaven that way. He gave us each some slabs of "toffee" which we thoroughly enjoyed. After Mrs. Ch'u had talked to him about the Gospel we went up to the courtyard of his house where there were a lot of men and some women who listened and brought us a cup of "tea", namely rice in lukewarm sweet water and chopsticks to eat it with - totally objectionable! We saw the old man again yesterday when we were preaching by the roadside and he stopped to listen for some time.

The other day, Mrs Liu and Mrs Ch'u gave us a chicken and 30 eggs! It was so kind of them, but the chicken promptly ate all the leaves off my little wallflower plants which were growing so beautifully. I could have wept! The sooner we devour that fowl the better!

John is doing really well and having quite a sociable time in *Nanpu* with several missionary visitors passing through, including Dr Gray. Poor man, he has *such* a lot of travelling in his work, up to ten days on just one case, caring for all his patients scattered far and wide in the various mission stations, sometimes emergencies.

With love,
Ruth

Ruth
T'uch'i   December 8th

Dear Everyone
We have just finished our local four day conference which has been such a happy time and it was great to be

surrounded by so many Chinese Christians and especially nice to see Miss Allibone who has been staying for the past week. She and Lilian have been to *Sanhuei* today to look for somewhere for Lilian and me to stay when we start making visits to that outstation.

Yesterday a young woman came in to church during the service and announced at the top of her voice that someone had been bitten by a dog and needed medicine. Outside I found a little girl who had a horrid big bite on her thigh. I took her back to the house and washed and bandaged it and she was so good. In the afternoon, nine young people were accepted as candidates for baptism which was a great thrill.

December 9th

We have had a visit from the mother of the bride whose wedding breakfast we attended the other day. She brought us 12 eggs each and about 50 for Miss Allibone who has already been given about 110 and will no doubt collect some more at the next place she visits.

With love
Ruth

Ruth
T'uch'i   December 12th

Dear Everyone

Lilian and I have come up to *Sanhuei* where we are staying for a few days, my first visit to an outstation. Our accommodation is a loft on the mission premises which is quite nice but has a quaint access. There is a rickety ladder with rungs at least 14" apart going up to a little hole in the ceiling, very awkward to manoeuvre especially going down trying to carry something. I'm writing by lamplight on my bed which is the usual string-network affair, rather like an ancient tennis racquet which badly wants re-stringing. While we were having our supper up here, a row of fingers appeared at our high window, followed by heads of people who had scrambled up to have a look! We felt like monkeys in a cage!

<u>December 13th</u>

We slept reasonably well, apart from a man coming in the middle of the night to buy medicines from the caretaker, prompting a tremendous unbolting of doors and talking, and women chatting well after he had left. *Sanhuei* is quite an impressive place with many new two-storeyed buildings along the main street. We went up some steps to a large open space which serves as a recreation ground, netball pitch and tennis court on which we saw four soldiers playing. A big crowd gathered and we sold a good number of gospels. Down below a puppet show was going on and a huge crowd of people were buying and selling. A couple of men were bargaining over some thread when suddenly they started hitting each other, all in good sport!

This afternoon we went into the country and on our return had rather a shock when Mrs. Liu whispered that the caretaker at *T'uch'i* had just taken a second wife but didn't want us to know. His first wife had borne four babies but no sons. She is a bonny, cheerful soul and on the face of it doesn't seem to mind the pretty little new wife nursing her baby girl! Of course, we have not said anything to them, but no doubt Miss Allibone will when she hears.

December 15th

Lilian has stayed in *Sanhuei* and Mrs Liu and I are back in *T'uch'i*. Soon the inevitable visitors started arriving. Five women wanted to look round and see our rooms upstairs where they examined and admired everything. I played them a few tunes on the grammy and eventually they went after profuse apology for hindering us. No sooner had they gone when two women came with a baby who had some horrible sores. I consulted my home nursing book but could find no suitable remedy so gave her some *mecca ointment and dusting powder which I made up of zinc oxide and cornflour (I hope that was all right). Then another mother brought her baby boy who had eye trouble. I decided it was blepharitis because the eyelashes had fallen out, and gave boracic powder for washing it. It is very common amongst these kiddies.

Tomorrow I have to make bread, prepare for the messenger who is coming up from *Chuhsien,* get a load ready to send up to Lilian and prepare for two Sunday schools. Next Friday Lilian will be back and we are going down to *Chuhsien* for Christmas. It will be so nice to return for a few days and seem quite luxurious after *T'uch'i,* which is a haven after *Sanhuei!*

We hear that while Bishop Mowll was away from his house in *Chengtu* there was severe fighting on his compound. Not a tile was left on the roof and everything

---

*Mecca ointment** Product name of a first aid ointment used for the temporary relief of pain and/or itching associated with minor burns, sunburn, minor cuts, scrapes, insect bites and temporary protection of minor skin irritations. Contains phenol, camphor and zinc oxiden

of value was taken except the safe and the car. This is the third time he has suffered in this way. We believe that heavy fighting is still going on in *Chengtu* between the rival military factions and that hundreds have been killed.

With love
Ruth

Ruth
T'uch'i   December 17th

Dear Everyone

It is freezing this morning and I have got on a long sleeved woolly vest, three pairs of knickers two pairs of woollen stockings, the pink woolly slip you knitted me, Mother dear, my Army and Navy woolly jumper, my blue jersey coat and my brown coat and skirt – and I'm just about comfortable!

How exciting that two parcels are on their way and the lovely thing is that probably everything has been bought in Hatherleigh and handled by your hands in the vicarage so I will be able to visualise it all.

December 18th

John is safely back in *Chowkow* and is going to write to the General Director regarding the date of our marriage, which will probably be next September. I'm so longing to know where our first designation is to be. I'm listening to "God so loved the World" on the grammy as I write. The other day, I had such a fright because I thought something had gone wrong with it, but I detected some screws which needed tightening then all was well which was such a relief .... oh dear, it's gone again. Oh Mother darling, what shall I do? I can't think what's wrong with it ……….. I feel so lonely all of a sudden and there's no-one here who understands. I wish I could come to you and tell you all about it instead of writing it on this paper which will take weeks to get to you. I wish I could see John too. I know he'll be awfully sweet about it. I must write and tell him so I'll break off here………

<u>December 23rd</u>   Chuhsien

Here we are and there is a simply lovely festive feeling in the air. The Ladies, Lilian and I are sitting on nice comfy wicker chairs around a *real fire* with the little dog curled up on the rug. After a very wet walk down, we were greeted by the Ladies and all the children and servants, (and dogs), singing a carol to welcome us, then fireworks went off! I was glad to take off my sopping wet cloth shoes and stockings and wash my muddy feet. I'm back in my own nice little room and there waiting for me was a huge pile of mail!

While we were having dinner, someone turned up with a huge present for the four of us, two chickens, two legs of mutton, 50 eggs 20 oranges and flour! Then a man arrived with a present from Miss Tucker at *Tachu* to the Ladies, lovely oranges from her own garden, pomeloes, beef, chestnuts which we'll roast, red berries from the hills, all so beautifully Christmassy. It is wonderful to think that this time next year John and I will be celebrating our first Christmas together and I do wonder where we will be! I gave John a little hand-made butter knife and napkin ring. They were made out of silver dollars which the silversmith melted down and worked by hand into a pattern and produced a beautiful piece of work.

With love
Ruth

Ruth

Chuhsien   December 28th

Dear Everyone

We had a perfectly lovely Christmas. The church was packed and the singing of carols very hearty. About 160 members stayed for the Christmas feast which had been cooked the day before and only had to be heated up. Then we had another service in the courtyard with more carols, and afterwards present opening. The Ladies gave us such topping presents, including a lovely afternoon tea table made of cane and bamboo for us to take to *T'uch'i,* and for me a nice strong chair which will greatly add to the comfort of my room. From Lilian I had a length of most beautiful white silk for my wedding petticoat, made in *Kiating*, the great silk manufacturing centre in *Szechwan*. John gave me a dear little chest of drawers which he had made for me out of scented wood. So there was much giving and receiving and we were all very happy.

Another week here and then we go back to *T'uch'i*. I wonder what you're all doing now and hope you are having a lovely time at home all together. How I'd love to see you all.

With love
Ruth

Ruth

Chuhsien   January 1st

Dear Everyone

It is New Year's Day, and *this* year we are going to be *married* and I'm so happy!

Our lovely holiday at *Chuhsien* is nearly over and we are planning to return to *T'uch'i* on Wednesday. We won't be able to go visiting for a while because the people will be busy preparing for their New Year, so I'm hoping to do lots of study.

I had a long letter from Meg who was enjoying a short holiday and I'm so glad as it must be very lonely at her station with only one old lady as a foreign companion, but she never complains. John's colleague, Fred Purchas, has been told he is going to an outpost about three weeks' journey from *Kowchow*, which came as a great shock.

Miss Tucker and Lilian have been busy getting the prizes ready for the Sunday school and it looks like a gay toy shop; such an array of charmingly dressed dolls with closing eyes and elbow joints etc. nearly all sent out by friends of the Ladies. The children love bright woolly scarves and caps and look so jolly in them with their dark eyes and hair. Mother I know you and some of your friends do "missionary knitting" and wondered if you could do some for China? The children love oranges, reds, greens etc. and caps with big bobbles at the top or side. It rarely snows here, but we need to wrap up well because the cold is so damp and piercing.

<u>January 5th</u>

It has rained steadily all week and we've still not gone back to *T'uch'i* because the road would have been too awful.

With love
Ruth

Ruth

T'uch'i   January 10th

Dear Everyone

We're back, and my, it *is* cold. We have our charcoal fire, a sort of tin pan in a wooden frame which is not bad, but Lilian has just bagged nearly all the red-hot charcoal to iron with! I shall be glad when the spring comes, but wish it could always be spring and not continue into the hot summer.

The ceiling of this room is the floorboard of Lilian's bedroom above, and whenever anyone walks over it, showers of dust come down. So we decided to paper it and when we were in *Chuhsien* we bought four large packets of thin white Chinese paper. First we stuck it on to newspaper and then stuck that to the ceiling using masses of paste. The room was an absolute mess with lumps of pasty paper, unwanted strips and bits stuck on to our shoes and great sheets of prepared paper hanging over chair backs to dry. Putting it up was priceless. We stood on a table, grasped the paper firmly and got it into position then we stood on tip-toe, keeping it in place with our heads. As often as not we'd let go by mistake and down would flop the nasty damp stuff on our heads and we would collapse into fits of laughter! The end result is quite pleasing.

Another thing we did was to buy 20 cattie of pork, approximately 25 lbs. Mrs Liu removed the bones and we made the brine (sugar, salt, saltpetre and water) and cut the bacon into joints. It is now soaking for a fortnight and then we will smoke it for a day. The challenge will be how to keep it from the rats. The women hung some up on a longish string from a beam in their room, but the rats got down the string and ate it!

I have a plan! If Mr and Mrs Denham are agreeable and the roads are safe, I want to pay a surprise visit to John next month arriving *on* his birthday and probably staying about a week plus two days journey each way. I'm going to make a marvellous birthday cake and take it with me and have sent off to *Chungking* for the ingredients.

Two men have just arrived from *Chuhsien* with our new bed, table, two chairs and three chickens!

With love
Ruth

Ruth
T'uch'i   January 16th

Dear Everyone
This afternoon a coolie turned up unexpectedly with a letter from Miss Allibone advising us to go down to *Chuhsien* tomorrow and from there be ready to evacuate.

Five men have been sent up to carry us and two for our luggage, as much as we can cram in, including our bedding. The reason is that several thousand Reds have come over the *Shensi* border and are already on their way down into this province. The recent fighting in *Chengtu* amongst the Military has opened up the way for them because all the soldiers, from every direction, have been sent to join in the fray leaving easy access to these Reds.

We don't want to leave here at all and Mrs Liu and Mrs Ch'u have been in floods of tears. Alas, we bought 60 eggs and 20 oranges this morning before the markets close for New Year but they will be a surprise wedding present to the cowman who is getting married tomorrow!

I thought you would want me to tell you everything, but darlings, please don't be nervous. We know that all these things are in God's hands and I feel absolutely at peace. What grieves me is that, unless your Christmas parcels come soon I shan't be there to receive them! John is expecting to have to evacuate too.

<u>January 17th evening</u>   Chuhsien

After a prayer, when Mrs Liu and Mrs Ch'u broke down again, we left at 5.30 a.m. and had a good but freezing journey arriving in time for the cowman's wedding feast. There is no panic but in a few days' time Lilian and I will probably go to *Kwangan* which is well protected. It is about 90 li away and we will go about a third of the journey on the river and walk the rest. The Ladies will send frequent news and if necessary will join us after a few days. We may be able to return to our stations after two or three weeks – I *do* hope so.

With love
Ruth

Ruth

Chuhsien   January 20th

Dear Everyone
   You will see we're still here, and except for a suppressed feeling of excitement and the coming and going of messengers you wouldn't know anything was amiss.   Miss Edwards is coming over from *Tachuh* today as she doesn't want to be left behind.   We hear there is a place about two days' journey from here where about 27,000 men are amassed, the rich have fled and the head of the local militia and other officials been killed.   A messenger will come immediately anything happens and the Ladies have plenty of good friends who will do all they can to help us, so you see all precautions are being taken.   I'm amazed that I'm not feeling frightened.   I sleep like a top and can concentrate on study and letter-writing etc.   I am sorry for the Ladies as they have experienced so much of this before, but at least they have one less anxiety now that we are down here and not half a day's journey away.   They say this is far less worrying than former occasions when the feeling was national, whereas this is merely local.

<u>January 24th</u>
   Yesterday I got a big budget of letters which had taken seven weeks to get here.   What a lovely way to start my 23rd birthday!   I had such a happy day and John gave me a lovely *p'uk'ai,   In the afternoon Lilian and I went for a walk and wandered around the boys' school at will because no-one was there. It is a fine stone building with

---

*p'uk'ai   An extra light very warm quilt made of silk "cotton wool" covered in bright patterned material

a huge assembly hall with galleries and beautiful white ceilings. The courtyards have a similar layout to college greens at home except with typical Chinese yellow wood and whitewash. We returned to a very nice Chinese dinner and a delicious birthday cake.

February 4th

Big News! My dear fellow-worker, Lilian, and Billy Simmons are engaged!

Several women and children have evacuated from two of our stations, very sadly with the loss of a 12 month old baby boy who had bronchitis and couldn't stand the change of temperature to an open boat. My heart aches for those poor parents. We have also had news of another fellow missionary who drowned in a steamer which sank.

This afternoon a lot of soldiers arrived and wanted to spend the night in the school but thank God they were deterred. Then we received a telegram in our CIM code "British Consul strongly urges removal to *Kwangan* and if necessary to *Chungking*". It was the first time I'd helped unravel CIM code! So the day after tomorrow, Miss Edwards, Lilian and I will leave by boat with as much luggage as possible, and have a two day journey to *Kwangan*. The Ladies will probably join us later.

With love
Ruth

Ruth
as from Kwangan   February 8th

Dear Everyone

Lilian, Miss Tucker and I are all aboard a nice roomy boat with two boatmen, the wife and baby of one of them and our church door-keeper who is helping them row and Mrs Lo, our housekeeper. We are surrounded by a mountain of luggage, which will have to be rearranged before we can spread ourselves out on the floor for the night. We have rigged up a little curtained-off "bathroom" and a couple of small boxes for a table, not the most comfortable mode of travelling and we wish we had wider boards to sit on, but it could be worse. Now the family are sitting on their heels having their dinner, rice etc.

Yesterday we spent all day getting ready and I iced John's cake which, with a hamper of all sorts of exciting things, will go by special messenger to arrive on his birthday. The Ladies have been so kind and thoughtful packing up provisions for us and will send some bread with the post next week.

Next Day

Here we are tearing down the river at break-neck speed! The night was priceless! We hung up a blanket to make a makeshift "cabin" and the three of us lay side-by-side on the uneven boards covered with all the bedding we could muster. After a somewhat sleepless night we set off as soon as it was light and it was lovely to be on the river so early. The women lit the fire (an old broken caldron lined with cement) and prepared the boatmen's breakfast. Then Mrs Lo fried some rashers of our *T'uch'i* bacon and two eggs each with bread and butter, and while we were eating we got into a most awful rapid and suddenly the boat shivered to a standstill on some rocks. The boatmen had to jump into the icy water and by Herculean effort managed to free the boat, jump in and off we went again. It was quite alarming, but they are used to it.

A bit further on we had to get a pilot to help us through another difficult rapid with the aid of ropes and long bamboo poles and I was filled with admiration at their navigational skills. Now the men are rowing us steadily down the river. We won't arrive tonight so it means another night on board!

I suppose just now you're all sleeping sweetly, never dreaming that we're evacuating with a Bible and a toothbrush! We do wonder what the outcome of all this will be and where John and I will have our first longed-for home together. Next month it will be four years since we became engaged.

Next Day

We're nearly at *Kwangan* and Lilian has gone ashore to walk the last 10 li, but I've stayed aboard because there are lots of bad rapids and I enjoy shooting them. We have just come over a huge one, going nearly as fast as a car and the current wound like a Devonshire lane between the huge rocks, awfully dangerous! I clenched my hands and prayed for safety – and enjoyed it to the full! Oh Boys, you would love it!

Later

We are settling into the mission house at *Kwangan* where there have been no foreigners since 1928. Lilian and I are sharing a nice big room which is gloriously light and airy and I think we will be very comfortable. The road is below our window and I have just seen a bus which did bring a lump to my throat because it reminded me so much of the "Adams" bus of Wethersfield days!

Still no sign of your Christmas parcels and no letters since I last wrote. I'm so longing to hear from you.

With love

Ruth

Ruth
Kwangang   February 16th

Dear Everyone

Your marvellous Christmas parcels have arrived and I simply don't know how to thank you. But I know where to begin, and that is with the beautiful cardigan, my Ma, which I love and just had to hug because you'd done it for me. There were so many other wonderful things and it was especially thrilling to have the apples from our own orchard and some real Devonshire wheat which made me imagine fields of golden grain. Everything was so full of home and even the white cloth in which all the parcels were wrapped I have washed and made into a much needed table-cloth.

The situation here seems to go up and down like a see-saw. Today we hear that another place in the *Paoning* District has been taken by the Reds and that 2,000 *Szechwan* troops have deserted to them, which is the greatest danger, of course. The resident warlord General Jang-Seng, who controls *Chuhsien, Chowkow* and *Kwangan,* is totally opposed to the Reds and anyone found working for them is effectively dealt with. I have seen him twice on horseback looking very smart, firstly in plus-fours and then in khaki military uniform just like King George!

Kwangan is an ultra-modern city and speaks so much of the West. We have just seen six young men dressed in nice overcoats, trilby hats, leather shoes etc, who would go by unnoticed in a London street. The girls are also very well dressed and groomed and cigarette smoking is not uncommon.

It's not wise to return to *Chuhsien* yet and the Ladies are all packed up and ready to go at the slightest warning. I do hope you are not worrying about me because you know we're taking the utmost precautions, but above all we are trusting in the Lord.

The other day we were invited to a concert in the General's newly built town hall. The children from his various marriages were lined up from the tallest to the shortest, and the first half was all "foreign". They sang songs in English including "The Last Rose of Summer" and played little pieces on the piano and violin. The second half was purely "native" with singing by two glamorous young ladies and shrill, monotonous wailing accompanied by instruments, which we hardly knew how to sit through! One of the infants in his nurse's arms started to cry and was fiercely banished by his father!

<u>February 23rd</u>

I am thrilled to hear that Mary and Robin are officially engaged and how I wish I could be with you all to share in the joy.

Any day now John should be hearing from the General Director about our future, though so much depends on circumstances. We hear that one of our evacuated mission stations is now occupied by the Military and another has been completely looted, floors and windows pulled out and used as firewood and a whole new street of houses destroyed.

<u>March 4th</u>

We have been here more than three weeks and nothing much seems to be happening. Truly we have need of patience!

On Wednesday, Lilian had a letter from the Ladies asking her to go down to *Chuhsien* because Billy was coming to see her. Imagine her excitement! On Thursday the coolie came bringing provisions from *Chuhsien* and a letter from the Ladies written on Tuesday night saying they had just been warned that an attack was expected that night and they had been advised to leave the city. So they were packing up their bedding and going to their Christian friends in the country. Meanwhile Lilian had set off yesterday morning, was staying the night at an inn and hoping to arrive at *Chuhsien* today. I am wondering what happened when she got there.

Yesterday the General's Foreign Secretary came to ask if I would teach the *t'ai-t'ai (the General's 17 year old bride, the latest of his many wives) instead of Lilian, who had been going on alternate days. So I went, and after a very nice game of tennis when soldiers fielded our balls and the scores were in English, we proceeded to the "Book Room" and spent an hour on "English as she is spoken". The t'ai-t'ai is a dear girl, very small and looks so nice in her modern, well-tailored "foreign" clothes. After the lesson I was escorted home by a young soldier as it was getting dark and I didn't know the way. He led me on and on, and eventually I discovered he had no idea where we were and thought I was leading him!

John and his colporteur are away for nine days, staying at a market town, preaching on market days and visiting other neighbouring towns, so he will be having a pretty strenuous time.

With love
Ruth

---

*t'ai-t'ai   Official ladies

Ruth
Kwangan   March 11th

Dear Everyone

I have just watered down my remaining thimbleful of ink to make it last a bit longer and by next week Miss Allibone may have been able to retrieve my huge unopened stone jar of ink which I left at *T'uch'i*. It is a very windy day and the five windows in this room, mostly devoid of glass, allow for free circulation of air.

Lilian had a lovely time with Billy. She may stay on at *Chuhsien* and not leave unless they have to. I do miss her but Miss Edwards is such a dear and it is good to get her ideas about the work.

Yesterday I went for a nice walk, apart from the cursing and horrible names called after me by some and embarrassing invitations to sit and have a smoke and a chat at nearly every house I passed! I found a lovely patch of violets and picked a bunch which are now arranged in an empty butter tin.

Today I went to teach my t'ai-t'ai and was able to have a lovely talk with her about the Gospel. Mrs Lo came too and waited with the servants and preached to them. She said they were very willing to listen. Miss Edwards brought a very nice new Chinese New Testament with her and we are going to give it to the t'ai-t'ai.

We hear today that aeroplanes, provisions and ammunition have been sent to the *Szechwan* soldiers. A leading family in *Chuhsien* was plotting with the Reds and planning an attack on *Chuhsien* last week but the Military reached the city in time and the man concerned has had his house burned down. He fled and the country is being combed for him and his accomplices. That was the night the Ladies were warned not to sleep in the town and they went to their Christian friends out in the country.

With love
Ruth

John
Chowkow   March 14th

Dear Friends and Supporters

I returned from my convalescence in mid-December and resumed my study determined to catch up, and took my second language exam last month. I then went on a week's visit to a market about ten miles away accompanied by a Chinese colporteur and one of our "enquirers" who carried my load. We stayed at an inn and during the day we preached on the streets and visited other markets which could not be reached from *Chowkow* in one day. Everywhere people crowded to hear the preaching and bought gospels with great enthusiasm.

On two evenings the proprietor of a teashop allowed us to hold a meeting in his premises, so for two hours the colporteur and I preached to a crowd of at least 100 people standing in the shop and overflowing into the street. I guess it was partly the novelty of seeing and hearing a foreigner but we believe God was working among them and when we returned to the inn five of the men followed us right into our room to hear more. The next day the teashop proprietor invited us to hold a service in his upstairs room, and the fact that a total non-believer should open his shop like this for the preaching of the Gospel was thrilling. I am going there again next week with Mr Purchas, our last outreach together as sadly he is moving to another station. As new missionaries in China we have battled with the language together, preached, prayed and relaxed (sometimes!) together and it will be hard to separate.

In January, the military situation in the west of the province became very serious, worst of all in *Chengtu* where a day-long pitched battle actually took place in Bishop Mowll's compound while he was away. The victorious army systematically looted his house and did great damage to his property, though fortunately none of the Chinese Christians or the missionaries came to any harm. Then, taking advantage of the absence of the local soldiers in the civil war, a horde of at least 10,000 Communists crossed the northern border from neighbouring provinces and began marching southwards and westwards.

Many troops were sent to confront the Reds. Most of them had been taken by force from their homes and farms to fight for the local war-lords and were badly fed, clothed and paid. It is reported that the Reds then allured them by saying *"Do not shoot us, we are your friends; we do not want to harm you, we only want to kill the officers who oppress you. When you are commanded to fire, aim over our heads and come over and join us"*. Many of the soldiers succumbed and often the Communists were as good as their word. They gave each one $10 and if they captured a regiment they would behead the officers, pay the soldiers $5 for their rifles plus a bit of extra "pocket-money" and send them back to their farms and homes to spread the propaganda.

The Communists captured several towns including *Pachow* where one of our CIM stations is located. The missionaries and hundreds of Chinese people had to flee in thick snow, whilst hundreds who remained were plundered and killed. Other towns were threatened and many CIM lady workers had to evacuate and go south, escorted by men who then returned to their posts expecting to have to flee at any moment. Even Miss Rossiter and her fellow-worker were recalled from *T'uch'i* to *Chuhsien* and then sent on to *Kwangan*. Several parties passed through *Chowkow* by boat, which made us realize how serious the situation was and we heard all sorts of rumours and were ready to flee at a moment's notice. I believe that nearly all the missionaries have been able to return to their stations now.

    Yours sincerely
    John Carpenter

Ruth

Kwangan   March 17th

Dear Everyone
    Time flies, in spite of being in exile still at *Kwangan*! Being here has actually been a blessing in disguise as I have been able to make real progress with my study and hope to take the exam before the end of the month.
    Dad, thank you so much for your letter of January 31st enclosing a sprig of hazel catkins and a daffodil bud. They were lovely. I expect by now all the banks are covered with masses of primroses.
    News has been better this week. The Reds have been driven out of *Pachow* and are said to be entrenched

near *Tahsien* but this is connected with *Chuhsien* by river and road so the danger is not past yet. There are 700 or 800 wounded soldiers in *Paoning* so Dr Gray is being kept extremely busy.

I had a great treat on Wednesday – I played a few tunes on the General's piano and had rather a large audience, i.e. the piano master, violin master, Foreign Secretary, one of the General's daughters, and the General himself came in! Afterwards he produced a copy of "The Christian Herald" for the t'ai-t'ai's English reading and stood behind her chair while I taught her.

I can hear the soldiers having their daily singing lesson which sounds quite good. There is also an excellent band which plays twice a week in the bandstand on the hill and it reminds me of the Hatherleigh band and flower show days!

The other day a child was knocked down by a car and killed. The mother wrapped it up and took it to the General and he gave her $20 compensation. I saw her in a rickshaw with the child on her lap, face covered. Crowds followed and some overtook the rickshaw and pulled the cloth aside to have a look. The poor mother was wailing with grief. The next morning I saw the funeral procession go by, not very big because they were poor people. In front went the "band" (men banging gongs and playing a sort of flute), then the mother dressed completely in unbleached calico carried in a hua-kan with a lighted stick of incense on her lap. The coffin was decked out with coloured paper.

March 24th

We have been here six weeks and still don't know when we will be able to return to *Chuhsien*, but the news of the Reds is better so perhaps our exile will soon be over. We have found quite a lot of stores left by the missionaries when they evacuated in 1928 including 15 lbs tea, ten little bottles of lemon essence and two tins of butter which we had to throw away, but the cornflour and the cocoa are perfectly edible.

The other day the General's Foreign Secretary accompanied me back from my lesson with the t'ai-t'ai and asked what salary I wanted! I assured him I didn't want any money and that it was a pleasure to teach her.

This week there has been a wedding on this street. The presents went by all laid out, then such a gay procession with bright flags, umbrellas and lanterns led by a "band". The "music" kept up incessantly for 1½ days, the same tune played over and over again on instruments rather like bag-pipes only louder and shriller accompanied by beating of gongs, if you can imagine it!

How lovely the lawns must be looking at home. I would love to see a beautiful green meadow surrounded by hedges with cowslips growing among the grass. Here the trees are looking beautifully green.

With love
Ruth

Ruth

Chuhsien   Saturday April 1st

Dear Everyone

On Monday we had a letter from the Ladies saying that things at *Chuhsien* had calmed down sufficiently for us to return. When I told the t'ai-t'ai at the next lesson she told the General who immediately said we must go back by his car. I explained that we had lots of luggage but he insisted and said he'd send the big car (bus) for us. I was awfully bucked as it meant getting back in half a day instead of two.

On Thursday we were busy packing all our clothes and everything but the kitchen sink, when an amazing present arrived from the General - 12 tins of Quaker oats and 12 large tins of apricots and cherries which I will keep for the wedding breakfast.

When the car arrived yesterday we found to our dismay that we couldn't get everything in and sadly had to leave six baskets behind. The "bus" was already full of luggage and four other passengers who were probably not supposed to be there at all! Somehow we squeezed in and set off watched by large crowds.

We started at a good pace, or so it seemed after nearly a year without motorized transport. The road was not as good as a "B" road at home and got worse and worse – deep ruts everywhere so that we bounced right off our seats and all the luggage kept slipping so that I had to cling on to it with one hand and hold the door shut with a piece of string with the other! Twice the radiator boiled like a jolly kettle and we had to stop for water (filthy stuff from the rice fields) and a minor repair was carried out with a piece of wood and wire and eventually we reached the half-way house. It was market day and at once we were enveloped in a dense crowd. While Mrs Lo preached a young "show-off" got into the car and began fiddling about with the controls and starting up the engine, pronouncing the car to be *very* poor (true).

We continued and all was well for the next 50 li until the car stopped and refused to budge. "Get down" said the driver, so down Mrs Lo and I got – but Miss Edwards, a somewhat large lady, was stuck between the box and the seat. There she had to wait until they brought a bit of wood and levered her leg out! Well, we were glad to get out and walk a bit until our chariot caught us up and we rolled along again. About 8 li from *Chuhsien* there was another long stop and one more within sight of *Chuhsien,* at which point the car finally died. The mechanic told us we would need to arrange for men to come so while Miss Edwards and Mrs Lo stayed to look after the luggage I carried on to the mission station as quickly as possible and in no time the head coolie had collected a band of men to go and rescue the stranded ones. Now four men have gone to *Kwangan* to collect the loads we had to leave behind. This was Mrs Lo's first experience of a car journey and she hopes it will be her last, though I enjoyed the experience!

It is great to be back again and seems so civilised after seven weeks of roughing it. We will probably return to *T'uch'i* as soon as Lilian has finished her exams.

With love
Ruth

Ruth
Chuhsien   April 8th

Dear Everyone
Miss Edwards has now returned to *Tachu.* She will feel lonely on her own again. Time is going so quickly and I'm beginning to think a lot about wedding

preparations. How I wish you were going to marry us, Dad, and that you were all going to be here and Mary a bridesmaid. I know the Ladies will do all they can but I do feel the need of my dear Ma to do the things that most girls' mothers do at such a time, and I'm worried things won't arrive in time and that I won't be able to make my frock nicely. Did I tell you that I'm also to be Lilian's bridesmaid?

I'm thrilled because a special messenger has just arrived from *Chowkow* inviting me there for Easter. I'm starting out on Tuesday and will stay about a week with two days journey either end. It will be very nice to meet Mr and Mrs Denham and see Mr Purchas before he leaves.

The news is not quite so good today and it is rumoured that the Reds have again taken *Pachow*. I do hope Lilian and I will be able to get back to *T'uch'i* after Easter until we go to the hills for the summer. There is so much to be done there and in the surrounding district.

<u>Tuesday 11th April</u>   An Inn, en route to *Chowkow*

We have come 130 li today, of which I walked 38 and sat in the chair for the rest. I am now spending the night at this inn and have quite a jolly room with a bed like a shop counter which takes up half the space. The head man is looking after me so well. He swept the bed, made it up with clean sheets and got me boiling water. On the bed I spread the little white cloth which was wrapped round my Christmas parcel, unpacked my picnic basket and had a lovely supper of new bread, fresh butter, cold chicken and cake with nice hot tea. The inn-keeper's small daughter is very intrigued with this curious being and keeps running up and asking me questions.

<u>April 16th Easter Day</u>

I am having such a happy time with John and we have been able to talk a lot about the future and make plans for the wedding. It has been a lovely Easter Day. At breakfast we had boiled eggs and when I chopped the top off mine it looked very strange, all dried up and white and I thought it had gone off. But when I looked more closely I saw it was paper, and inside was the dearest little silver filigree-work brooch, an Easter present from Mr and Mrs Denham! They were so kind and such fun and it was interesting to see something of the work at *Chowkow.* John has had his exam results and he got 97%! Mr Purchas starts his long journey to *Longan* soon and Dr Snowball is coming in his place so I'm glad John will have a companion.

<u>April 22nd</u>

I got back yesterday having spent the night at a gospel hall which was nicer than the inn, although I was still glad of the *Keatings! I was just about to get into bed when I heard the head coolie at the door. He'd just remembered a letter which John had asked him to give me - a lovely long one which I did enjoy reading!

With love
Ruth

---

*Keatings Powder Kills with ease, Bugs and Beetles, Moths and Fleas

John
Chowkow   April 22nd

Dear Friends and Supporters

At Easter we welcomed to their first Communion four men whom I had the privilege of preparing and three more were baptised. It was a particularly happy time because Miss Rossiter came to stay for a week, the first time we had met since last August. Our wedding will probably be on September 6th at *Chuhsien* at the kind invitation of the two senior lady missionaries there. We have not yet heard where we are to be designated.

We have been able to rent premises over the river in *Pengan City*, including a preaching hall opening on to the main street and two or three rooms where a worker could stay for a few days to save coming back to *Chowkow* late at night.

As far as *Chowkow* is concerned, the church members have now found some very suitable premises. They are currently in a state of disrepair because they have been occupied by soldiers, but the owner has said the church can have them rent-free for six months and has also offered to pay a good proportion of the cost of repairs. They are situated on the main street and include a very large room for a "church" which will easily seat 100, a preaching hall and other rooms for guests, workers etc. The church knows that it is *their* church for which *they* are responsible and while we as members are glad to support them individually, we cannot apply to the CIM for any funds.

Yours sincerely
John Carpenter

Ruth
Chuhsien   April 29th

Dear Everyone

The Ladies have been away for a couple of days making arrangements about the bungalow at *Chiu p'an shi* where we will be going again in the summer. While they were away Lilian and I took their classes, and I had those recently baptised, most of whom were old ladies from a local charitable institution who were blind, deaf, lame or very frail, but they have something which "not many wise or not many mighty" have seen, and that is Jesus, their Saviour. So it was a pleasure to talk to them and lovely to think that they have the hope of eternity when they will be rid of all their frailties and given new beautiful bodies.

We also met three young military wives at the preaching hall. Later on they came to the house with five of their friends and Lilian preached using some vivid gospel posters.

Lilian and I will probably return to *T'uch'i* next week. Meanwhile, we are both working on our trousseaux and are busy sewing. We also paid a tailor to make various garments including a frock each which he stitched most beautifully by hand. Lilian and Billy are getting married at *Chuhsien* just before us, so I will be a bridesmaid and a bride in the same week!

With love
Ruth

John
Chowkow   May 10th

Dear Friends and Supporters

Just before Mr Purchas left, he and I went on a trip to replenish our stock of provisions and books and on our return we found Mr Denham ill in bed with what seemed suspiciously like typhoid. Dr Snowball, our new worker, was on his way here to replace Mr Purchas, so I rushed off to meet him and ask him to do the last two days' journey in one and on his arrival he immediately confirmed our fears.

The refurbishment of the new premises is in progress so I have the responsibility of overseeing the workmen and am finding that trying to communicate about mud walls, windows, floors, chimneys etc. requires a different vocabulary from preaching! We have been rather discouraged to find that some of our new church members were gambling and selling opium. I was able to speak plainly to them but felt very weak and longed for the presence of a senior missionary.

Yours sincerely
John Carpenter

Ruth
Chuhsien   May 13th

Dear Everyone

You will be sorry to hear that Mr Denham is seriously ill with typhoid fever. Fortunately Dr Snowball has arrived but John will have a great load of responsibility on his shoulders for a good time because when Mr Denham gets better he and Mrs Denham are almost certainly moving on.

We have just seen a little tortoise walking down the stone gutter, such a dear little thing about 4" long.

I wish your next letter would come, my Ma. I don't know what I'd do without them because you give me all the detailed news of home and seem to enter into the life out here so much. How I wish you could all come and see for yourselves what it is like.

May 19th

Today the four of us were invited by Lady Ch'en to a feast and Lilian and I were the Guests of Honour because it was a sort of "Goodbye" for the two brides. Lady Ch'en belongs to an old aristocratic family and is one of the old school t'ai-t'ai. Nowadays this title is given to many young officers' wives who are rather looked down upon by the aristocracy.

The feast was amazing! We had about 16 different dishes, shrimps and bamboo, fish-tripe, chicken pounded and cooked with white of egg, steamed chicken, cold chicken in sauce, hot chicken meat balls in dough, cold thin slices of sausage, tongue, ham etc, sweet rice pudding, stewed fruit etc. There were two tables of ten in our room and the hostess sat with a few other guests in another room. Our room was very nice with a proper ceiling (a rarity) and a cement floor. There was a neat bed with satin covered bedding rolled up on it in approved Chinese style, various chairs, stools, a large clock on a table with an array of bottles and vases and a large spittoon.

You would have laughed to hear the dinner guests teasing us and calling us the "brides" all the time. We protested that it was too soon and we were shy but to no avail! The Chinese love teasing. They think it strange that we don't go in for any red at weddings and asked if they could see our trousseaux. I showed Miss Tucker all my special things the other day and she was very interested.

May 20th

We have been very busy getting ready for four new lady workers, Pauline Morgan, who will be staying here and three others who are passing through. It really does look as though we will be going back to *T'uch'i* on Monday.

With love
Ruth

Ruth
T'uch'i   May 26th

Dear Everyone

We're back at *T'uch'i* at last but before we left we very much enjoyed the visit of the four fellow-workers. They were in the same situation as I was a year ago - speechless! What a difference a year makes, but there is still much to be learned as far as the vernacular is concerned and, as for the classical and written language, I have barely touched the surface. Pauline has a little organ with four octaves, just like John's, and I enjoyed playing on it.

We travelled by chair to *T'uch'i* because the road was so bad. Mrs Liu was here to greet us and had to borrow some food as the man with the stores was a long way behind. After lying empty for four months the place was filthy with dust and traces of rats everywhere, winey jam and green ginger. But two days' work has put that right and it is beginning to feel more like a home than a pigsty. There are lots of caterpillars which I'm told drop from the ceilings and sting badly.

Later

Quite a few visitors have been to welcome us back, and yesterday we went to visit the Chao family. We stopped at the house where we went to that wedding a few months ago and were so pleased to find the young wife looking happy and plump, compared with the poor miserable soul she was on her wedding day. At the Chao's house we were invited to "drink some tea and have some hot water". After a bit of humming and hawing, assuring them we wouldn't eat anything, we all moved towards the table and after a few more polite refusals to sit down in any but the lowest seats, we seated ourselves. Our "boiled water" was a horrid mixture of rice boiled in sugary water with an egg poached in it. The sugary rice tasted of wine as they use a kind of fermented rice for this particular dish. Somehow I managed to get most of the egg down but just could not make the watery stuff disappear; I hope they weren't offended at my leaving it!

Then they showed us their oil-crushing apparatus and explained how the seeds go through about eight different processes before the oil is extracted. The seeds are about as big as pinheads and are first roasted in a big iron pan, then ground in stone crushing things, then put in a drum which has a crushing wheel in it and a buffalo or cow walks round ceaselessly crushing it to powder. There are big stones tied on over the wheel to make it crush harder. It is then mixed with water and steamed and put in a frame and mixed with straw which is sort of woven in and pressed down to form flat round cakes about 1" thick and 15" in diameter. These are trimmed and the flat cakes piled. They are put in an immense crusher composed of various great wooden blocks and iron rings. There is a sort of battering ram attached and two men take it in turns to swing it backwards and forwards accompanied by loud wailing and a terrific hoarse shout and a "bang" as two iron surfaces meet with enormous force so that the wedge which is forced against the oil cakes is banged even more tightly.

When we were at *Kwangan* the oil plant was in full bloom, rather like yellow flowering cabbages, a beautiful sight and lovely scent. The chief activity in the fields now is planting out the rice which has been growing in "mother fields", a beautiful vivid green. Everywhere men are wading in the rice fields, deftly putting it in precisely straight lines, plant by plant.

But I digress. Walking home we met a young woman from another Christian family who invited us in. Here we were brought exactly the same foul dish as we had just had! To have declined would have offended. I felt as though my last moment had come, but managed to get the egg down. We simply couldn't face eggs for supper that night!

Mr Denham is definitely better but John is awfully busy though I think he is enjoying the experience.

With love
Ruth

Ruth
T'uch'i   June 1st

Dear Everyone

Sunday was the Fifth Moon Feast and there was much merry-making and exchanging of presents. Because everyone was busy preparing for the festivities not a single person came to Church apart from those on the compound but afterwards we had crowds of visitors who had all come to watch the sport on the river. There were lots of boats, and the chief attraction was to set a duck free in the water and for two boats to chase it, each with eight or nine men paddling with tiny oars at full pelt. When they were near enough one man dived in and captured the poor frightened creature.

On Monday we had a very worthwhile day visiting on the main street. One woman invited us in and yelled to all her friends and neighbours to come and listen and later Lilian attended to several people who had come for medicines.

And now I'm writing from *Sanhuei*, where Lilian and I are spending a few days. This is the outstation we visited just before Christmas and we are occupying the same two rooms in the loft, accessed by a ladder through the trap door, with the same rats playing around overhead. Do you remember that yellow and red check square you gave me, Mother? Well it is coming in very useful as we have nailed it firmly top and bottom across the lower part of the window giving privacy from the little row of heads peering in. It looks so bright and cheerful and helps us forget the dingy walls, dank muddy floor and abundance of cobwebs!

June 2nd

This morning, a woman invited us into her home and called all her friends and strangers to come and listen. Then we went up a steep alley way between houses and a young coolie stopped us and asked us to go to his house, leading us through a back path to a wretched hovel made of bamboo poles and mats with many holes in the roof. On a bed covered with a much stained curtain sat his very sick father, the brother of the man who takes the Sunday services at *T'uch'i*. His wife was very bright, but what a struggle life must be. It wrings our hearts to see the poverty and sickness and not be able to help, but we shall try to get that boy to carry one of our loads down when we go back.

With love
Ruth

Ruth
T'uch'i   June 8th

Dear Everyone

Sanhuei is not a nice place because salt used to be stored here so it is always damp. The roof in our loft leaks and in some places I have dug about an inch deep of mud off the stone floor! The air is somewhat unsavoury but we have quite refreshing walks by the river, but even there awful whiffs waft across the breeze and it is said that there is a dead unburied man somewhere along there.

There was much excitement the other day when ten boats arrived from *Pachow* carrying "tow-lan-dy", i.e.

those who are running away or escaping from calamity, wealthy people, of course – the poor do not get molested.

June 9th

The Reds have retaken three cities which they held before and have been reinforced with men, money and ammunition. We had planned to stay here till next Thursday but may leave straight after the weekend and are awaiting Miss Allibone's advice. Isn't it strange that as soon as we get back trouble starts again! What a time *Szechwan* is having! General Liu Hsiang, Szechwan's most influential warlord, is sending aeroplanes up to *Paoning* where there is a great feeling of unrest.

June 16th

We are back at *T'uch'i* and the messenger has brought up some lovely letters from home written just after Easter. You ask what makes *Kwangan* so progressive. The answer is that General Jang Seng lives there and every day makes a tour of the town followed by his bodyguard and preceded by his topping Alsatian. Does he want to widen the streets? Then down with the houses that are in the way; never mind about compensation. Does he want to build public baths or a new town hall? Then carry on collecting taxes and forget they have already been charged until 1940 and ignore the fact that people don't know where to turn to pay, let alone buy food and clothing.

Next week we are hoping to go for four days to a small market town on the road to *Chuhsien* and we should have time to give everyone a chance to hear the Gospel. There are many other markets we would like to visit but can't because it is too dangerous.

The other night we were sitting on a rock by the river when we saw a boat full of people and various lights were burning, gongs being beaten rhythmically and songs being chanted by some priests. Every now and then bits of paper were dropped on the water and it was fascinating to watch them burning for quite some time. Someone explained that a man had drowned there and that although his body had been found, the people feared his spirit was still in the clutches of the river spirits so this was their offering to propitiate them.

I wonder what the country is looking like now at home – foxgloves, wild roses, dog daisies and honeysuckle all out, I expect. Oh for a peep at it! Next month we shall be on the hill and rejoicing in masses of huge white lilies.

With love
Ruth

John

Chowkow   Monday June 19th

Dear Everyone

Last week news reached us of a new Communist push in the north of the province as the troops had once again gone back to *Chengtu* and were quarrelling among themselves. Meanwhile we heard that some bandits were about to attack *Chowkow*. These bandits call themselves "divine soldiers" and are reputed to drink some potion before going into battle which they believe makes them invulnerable; the result is that they are very fierce and the soldiers are scared stiff. One of our Church members kept coming back and reporting that they were getting nearer and nearer until they were only a mile away, and that soldiers with arms cut off were being carried back.

What could we do? Mr Denham had just been allowed out of bed for ½ hour a day and was certainly not fit for a journey except possibly by boat, but all the boats had been ordered over to the other side of the river to prevent the bandits getting across. I went to see if I could get a boat and found there was nothing like the panic I expected. There was a crier in the middle of the street calling out for every house to produce a man and military weapons, which meant anything from a toothpick to a machine gun. A few men were cleaning up rusty rifles or sharpening ancient scimitars on the pavement with children playing around them and women carrying on with their sewing in front of their houses and shops, all boarded up ready for flight. By the time I returned the danger seemed to be over. The next day we heard that the brigand leader had been caught and his legs broken and he had been taken over to the city where he was tried and beheaded.

This incident made us feel that *Chowkow* was no place for a sick man and so we managed to hire a boat and after a busy weekend packing, early this morning we saw Mr and Mrs Denham off to the safety of the CIM station at *Shunking*, a day's journey downstream, accompanied by Dr Snowball. Another complication was that the previous evening Dr Snowball had received a letter from a colleague whose wife is expecting a baby in July, wanting him to go there in good time; he had sent along three coolies to make sure he went! However Dr Snowball felt his priority was with Mr Denham, so he took the coolies on board and off they all went together!

So here I am alone holding the fort in the strangest circumstances, with instructions not to stay in the event of danger.

A few hours after the others had gone there was a knock at the door and in walked three lady missionaries! They had fled from *Paoning* and confirmed that the worst rumours were true. In five days the Reds had recaptured what it had taken the soldiers about three months to get back from them after the last advance. The city was practically empty as both the soldiers and the people had panicked and our friends had to flee without anything but hand-luggage. We had a cup of tea and then I accompanied them down to the boats where I spotted some other refugees who had passed through at the recent evacuation. I expect they will get at least half way to *Shunking* tonight but have to stop at recognized places because of bandits.

Despite all that is going on around, I really feel quite safe, in fact more so than I might have done with everyone here had we needed to beat a hasty retreat. Besides this, *Chowkow* is full of soldiers on their way to help fighting against the Communists. There is a crowd of them staying the night spread all over the floor of our new church, but we can't stop them, especially when they have come to save us and are tired after a long day's march and are off again tomorrow. But I must say it did seem a bit much last night when the cook and I found a couple of Samsons carrying off our front doors to the teashop opposite and setting them up across benches to do for beds! We managed to retrieve them and our "boys" put them up again.

Evidently the Reds are advancing westwards and when they get to *Paoning*, their next move may be towards *Kansu*, or if they are bold they may attack the *Chengtu* plain. This is a very rich area and it is said that one of the generals is Red at heart and has already got his flags ready to "change sides" when he meets the Communists. The Reds are unlikely to come this way but if they do I have a couple of legs and don't depend on a boat or even a coolie.

I was up at 4.30 this morning and it's been a long day, and now for my first night as "missionary-in-charge" of *Chowkow*.

Next Morning

At present we can get no reliable reports of these bandits. The market is full of soldiers who say they have come to save us from them. Apparently the other day the soldiers surrounded them in the two valleys and pressed in on them but then didn't know what to do next so they fled! It seems that what actually happened was that they closed in on them and then found no one in the middle! They then set to work searching farms and houses and the following day we saw long processions of soldiers and roped-up prisoners marching though the street past our front door and were told they were the inhabitants of these two valleys who were going to be cross-examined. I expect they will kill a few on some pretext just to prove their capability and not to lose face for having let the brigands go.

It looks as though Ruth and I will be going to *Yingshan* when we are married, the very place we want to go to, although it will only be temporary. Pastor Wang has been working alone since the last missionaries left and, in accordance with CIM's new policy, he is to be regarded as the head and pastor of the church, which pleases me because I feel far too inexperienced to take on that responsibility. I hope we work well together. There are six outstations each with Mission premises, and my main duty will be to visit them regularly. *Yingshan* is the county town of its own county, much bigger than *Chowkow* and *Pengan* put together and more modern. Ruth will be delighted because we have been waiting so long.

After all yesterday's excitement I am having a quiet day today and getting the house back in order.

With love
John

Ruth

T'uch'i   Wednesday June 21st

Dear Everyone

Last Saturday there was a good deal of excitement because of the arrival of soldiers on their way to face the Reds. They were supposed to stay the night but were suddenly called off and were on the march again. The next day we had a letter from Miss Allibone saying we must go down to *Chuhsien* on Tuesday morning. Then today a man arrived with another letter telling us that things were calmer so we need not leave after all.

We had dinner, started unpacking and getting used to the idea we were not going, when another messenger came with a letter "Come down immediately – very disquieting rumours – rich people leaving the city". What a business having to pack all over again. The next morning we got up at day-break, left our empty house, and set off. So here we are at *Chuhsien* once again!

With love
Ruth

John
Chowkow   June 26th

Dear Everyone
    The cook has just come in to say that the Military have killed 17 of the prisoners who they were leading past here the other day, I suppose for complicity with the Reds and the Red Lantern Brigands.
    On Wednesday evening a little company of Chinese Christians arrived, refugees from the district to which the Reds are advancing. Their boat was packed, standing room only, so they asked us to put them up for the night and we managed to squeeze them into various rooms. A few days later another party arrived from further north, having passed through a series of evacuated mission stations and finding no fellow-missionaries until they reached *Chowkow*. They also continued to *Shunking*, apart from a few who decided to stay on our premises to save going further and are still here!

River at Chowkow

Then we had a party of over 100 children from two CIM orphanages in the north of the province and their teachers. We offered them our new premises where there are a lot of rooms but no beds, but the soldiers refused to allow them to leave the river bank. It was after 10 p.m. when the cook and I got down there and found them sitting, lying and sleeping on the bank as they had nowhere else to go. Poor tired little mites. We finally managed to get permission for them to leave and they all lined up and off we set. The river-bank walk was dark and slippery with several gullies to cross where the recent rain had rushed down. On we tramped through the streets of *Chowkow* with me leading the way with a lantern and a wee blind girlie on my back. We finally reached the premises at about 11 p.m. We put down mats and made chairs and benches into beds, and soon they were all asleep.

It was nearly 11.45 p.m. by the time the cook and I started for home. We were challenged by some soldiers who said we were out too late and they wouldn't allow us to pass. We carried on and they shouted again and we heard them loading their rifles. We stood still and remonstrated with them and at last got it across that we were "foreign" people and then they were most apologetic and ushered us past most politely.

I despatched a letter by special messenger to *Shunking* to say the children were here and ask whether we should send them on at once or what we should do. Meanwhile, we kept them over the weekend until the messenger could get back with the answer.

On Saturday the children had plenty of visitors although I didn't have time to go round myself as, believe it or not, more visitors turned up - three lady colleagues escaping from the most northerly station in *Szechwan*. They had come through one empty town after another, but saw no sign of the Communists which made us wonder if the panic was necessary! Several times their boat had been ordered to stop and once a soldier fired a bullet over their heads. They had to go ashore at night and in some places were held up but their boat was never commandeered and somehow they managed to get through.

When they arrived they said it was the first inhabited city they had seen since they set out. They came up for dinner, but then found their boat could not go on that day because there was such a gale so they decided to stay here for the week-end. It would have been against CIM rules for me to put up ladies, so we found alternative accommodation and they spent all Sunday here and said how nice it was to have proper meals again and comfy chairs to sit on. They enjoyed the gramophone which Ruth had just returned and it was good to have this time of fellowship.

On Sunday morning the church was packed with about 500 people and it seemed that the whole population of *Chowkow* had turned out to see the children! The evangelist led the service, Mr Liu preached and there was plenty of singing by the kiddies. Another refugee evangelist gave a very interesting talk about the history of the orphanage and what it does now. In the afternoon the crowds came back for more singing by the children and I preached. The people were thanked for welcoming them and I think the whole experience was quite an eye-opener and that they benefited by feeling they had been able to do something to help other Christians.

The messenger turned up on Sunday evening to say they were ready at *Shunking* for the children, so we packed them off the next day. Also the ladies left this morning though the river had suddenly risen overnight and there was a delay until it fell again but they should reach *Shunking* in record time with the river still so high and rapid.

With love
John

John
Chowkow   June 28th

Dear Everyone

I was about to start writing when I heard voices in the room next door, and in walked three soldiers to have a look around. I asked them please to sit down and had a little talk to them and gave them each a gospel. They seemed quite interested.

I have tidied up the Denhams' things which they left around in their hurry, screwed up their organ in its case and wrapped up eight piles of their loose coppers and locked them in a cupboard with labels to say where each had been found.

This week we have had two refugee evangelists and their large families staying here, hoping they will not have to go any further down river. On Wednesday the cook invited us all to a Chinese dinner and about 16 of us sat down at two tables in our dining room and had a meal together. The next day one of the guests repeated the invitation and I am wondering whether I shall be expected to return the compliment!

It occurred to me that we ought to give these two evangelists something to do as they were getting lazy! So the pastor, Bible-woman and I decided to have two special evangelistic meetings on Friday and Saturday evening. The teacher wrote invitations in ink, using a brush for some and a steel nib for others, and then we duplicated 200 copies. Just before dark we made a tour of the streets led by a lantern-carrier followed by someone carrying a banner while the pastor and I handed out tracts and handbills. When we ran out I started playing my mouth organ which collected quite a crowd and we ended up at the new premises where the two evangelists were waiting for us. It was quite a good meeting with about 200 drifting in and last night we had the second meeting without the procession.

I told you about the troop of soldiers from the two valleys where the brigands had apparently evaded the Military. The latter had taken all the population for examination as some were supposed to be confederates. The results were announced this week and in their "deep anxiety for the safety of the city" the soldiers found that quite a lot were guilty and killed 29 including a 12 year old girl. The females were shot and the men beheaded publicly at the entrance of the market. You see how our "valiant, brave soldiers" are looking after us. One of the execution notices is still posted up on the door of our new premises.

We hear that the Reds have taken a city 120-li from *Paoning* which is still empty. A colleague has been informed it is in danger and advised to go and rescue some of the luggage they left behind in their haste to flee. The informant is a Christian military official who has promised to have two boats ready so he can make a quick get-away if necessary. Nothing is certain and it may mean a more general evacuation.

I only have about a month more here and then will be spending August with Ruth in *Chiu p'an shi* again. Then before we know where we are it will be our wedding! It seems incredible that we can plan holidays and weddings with brigands within three days' march of us. God has been very good.

With love
John

Ruth

Chuhsien   June 29th

Dear Everyone

I hear from John that we are to be designated to *Yingshan* and I'm simply delighted as it's the very place we had hoped for and is 1½ days from here and ½ day from *Chowkow*. I do hope nothing will prevent our going there. Foreigners have lived there fairly recently and (oh joy) there are ceilings, board floors, nice glass windows and a foreign stove.

Lilian and I spent last week-end at a small outstation a few miles up-river. We stayed on the mission premises and slept and ate in one room with newspapers lining the ceiling and a glassless window. We had a very hectic but happy time with visitors morning, noon and night. The military powers are trying to raise standards of cleanliness and hygiene and at this place the town crier goes through the streets beating his gong and announcing that each family was to bring 30 dead flies to the officials every day and that failure to do so would result in a fine! I saw one old shop-keeper with swatter in hand and a very earnest look on his face, ready to spring on any unsuspecting little beastie that landed on his merchandise. Yesterday we footed it back, leaving as soon as we could see our way and arriving in time for breakfast, much to the Ladies' surprise.

The stores have arrived, seven huge wooden boxes all nailed down. I prised them open, carefully extracting the precious nails. There are lots of things for the two weddings, e.g. jellies, ox tongues, tins of fruit, cream crackers, icing sugar, ground almonds, cherries, orangeade etc. and household equipment for our new homes. Fancy having a *home* of my own after living in other people's houses for so long!

Troops have been sent to *Paoning* and the generals have set aside their differences and are co-operating against the Reds. Our workers in *Paoning* had an awful time leaving in an absolute panic, unable to get men or boats and taking only a suitcase, but the evacuation seems to have been quite unnecessary and some have already gone back. The latest is that *Chiu p'an shi* is unsafe! It may only be an exaggeration and somehow I don't think we shall be stopped from going up there. Meg is joining us and staying on for the weddings and John is coming for August.

<u>July 6th</u>

John is still on his own at *Chowkow* but doesn't seem lonely. He has done some packing up for our home but our crockery is still at *Wanhsien*. I am simply bubbling up at the thought of having our own home at *Yingshan* and hope the Reds won't make us move on again.

Meg should be on her way here by now and I'm going to *T'uch'i* to meet her. I'm so excited at the thought of seeing her and glad she will be meeting lots of young folks, namely all Lilian's and my wedding guests.

July 13th

On Monday I got up early and set off for *T'uch'i* by chair and then went down to the river to meet Meg. At last her boat arrived, and there she was, dressed in a Chinese gown and looking very fit. It is lovely having her here and I'm so glad she's having a break from *Wentangching* which is so rough and not at all a good place for lady workers to be. We have so much to talk about and it seems quite like old times. She is much further on with her studies than I am and has a much wider vocabulary and is so good on tones.

It is sweltering hot here but we don't know when we will be going up to the cool of the hill yet as apparently it is not safe at present and Miss Allibone is going up later this week to see for herself.

With love
Ruth

Meg to Ruth's Mother
Chuhsien   July 13th

Dear Mrs Rossiter

I have been here two days now and everyone is so kind. I had rather a long journey through roads reported to be bandit-ridden. A Christian woman and two very good coolies were with me and we spent the weekend at *Tahsien* leaving on Monday for a long hot day's journey by boat. We arrived at *T'uch'i* at dusk, and Ruth came tearing down the bank to meet me! It was great to see her again and I don't think she has changed much and seems as lively as ever! We did an awful lot of talking as you can imagine and arrived at *Chuhsien* the next afternoon. It is much more modern than I imagined, with wide and comparatively clean streets and I'm still getting over being able to go out without an old woman trotting after me, such as I have to have in *Wentangching*.

The house is so pretty and there was a vase of flowers in my bedroom with "greetings to the bridesmaid"! The Ladies are lovely and it is so lively, especially after what I'm used to. I recognize many of Ruth's things from *Yangchow* days and she has shown me all the lovely things she has had made and wedding presents she has been given.

With love
Meg

John
Chowkow   July 16th

Dear Everyone
    On Monday I was unwell with temperature of 101.5° and Gordon Aldis, who has been here for the past week, kindly stayed on for a couple of days. It has been very hot so I brought my camp-bed down to the dining room and have been living here day and night, in front of the big wide-open "French window". It is quieter because rats have no bamboo-matting roof to scuttle across, the street noises are further away and I can't hear the baby

next door being continually cursed and thrashed. I have been trying to study, but the heat isn't conducive and being "in charge" there are many distractions. Every visitor has to be seen, whether they want cash, medicine, talk, gospel or just to sit.

On Wednesday I am hoping to go for a night to our new home at *Yingshan* to assess what needs to be done, finding someone to do it and fixing a price. The following week I will return to supervise the work, and as soon as it is finished set off for *Chuhsien*. The Denhams have very kindly said we can take their cook who is a keen preacher as well as a splendid handyman and very good with foreigners. He will be coming with me and will be with us in our new home.

Later

I am not going to *Yingshan* after all, because two groups of soldiers have been casting their eagle eyes on our front rooms; the first planted a three-cornered military flag on our front doorstep, just to show they'd "bagged" the place. We returned the flag with thanks. Next, I was informed by the evangelist's children that two more officers had strolled in declaring what a nice roomy place it was, big enough to sleep a "lieu" of soldiers, i.e. nominally 126 men, though usually fewer. So I dare not leave the place at the moment and hope and pray I shall be able to keep them out. We haven't had soldiers for quite a time and I don't know who these are or what they want. Both our preaching hall and guest hall are being slept in every night by various members of the evangelist's family who fix up chairs, benches and tables and pull down a door every night to make beds.

<u>6.30 p.m.</u>

There are now flags all over the place which must have been planted by an advance guard. No doubt the others will be upon us soon – then the fun begins!

With love

John

Ruth

Chiu p'an shi   July 20th

Dear Everyone

A messenger came from Miss Allibone to say it was quite safe to go up to the hill, so here we are enjoying the good gifts around us, not least the temperature being 20° cooler than in the city. The scenery is grand and it is just marvellous to be in the open country again. We are enjoying a perfect sunset and a passer-by has just given us a lily with seven heads on one stalk. Mrs Lo has brought up some wild herbs tied in a bundle which have been drying in the sun and are now smouldering at one end and surrounding us with a cloud of sweet smelling smoke to ward off the fierce mosquitos.

John is coming in August after he has taken his third section exams. I am bucked to think he's got on so splendidly, so much better than his "stupid thorn" (a Chinese name for one's wife!) Then we will be up here again on our honeymoon which I'm hoping will be fairly short as I'm longing to start normal life with John at *Yingshan*.

<u>July 27th</u>

On Saturday I am returning to the city to take charge for the second fortnight, relieving Miss Tucker to come up here. I am glad to have the chance to do something to help. Last night we went for a walk right to the top of "Pisgah". It was glorious and we could see the river in great silver curves miles away and high up on a hill top flashed the white walls of a temple shining in the sun. On Monday we saw two long processions going on a pilgrimage to the temple led by men with red umbrellas or red and white flags followed by about 100 people, mostly women, walking very slowly on their small feet and chanting.

The plan is that after our honeymoon we hold the fort at *Chuhsien* to allow the Ladies to come up here for a much needed rest. Then we'll go to *Yingshan*. There are about 19 members of the Pastor's family living on the premises at present, overflowing into the guest halls, which is fine while there are no missionaries but when we go we shall need the guest halls for our work. We pray for tact in handling the situation as apparently they are rather touchy!

With love
Ruth

John
Chowkow   July 23rd

Dear Everyone

I was finally able to make the trip to *Yingshan* to inspect the house and engage a workman. Considering how long it has been empty it is surprising that hardly any repairs are needed. I plan to leave *Chowkow* for good on Tuesday, spend a week at *Yingshan* and then proceed to *Chuhsien*.

<u>July 30th</u> Yingshan

Here I am "at home"! The workmen have been doing an excellent job, far exceeding their contract for no extra payment. Meanwhile I have been tidying up the house after previous incumbents. What hoarders some missionaries are! Also I have had several good talks about the work with Pastor Wang who is in charge here, and in general we seem to be in agreement over the fundamentals.

Now I am ready to leave for *Chuhsien* tomorrow, a day earlier than planned. It is a two day journey and I hope to arrive in time for breakfast on Tuesday. Ruth has already been on the hill for two weeks but has had to come down to take her turn in minding the city premises for a fortnight, so after being with her for only a day I shall have to leave her again and go up to the hill to join the others.

<u>August 3rd</u> Chiu p'an shi

It was lovely to see Ruth again though sad that we had to separate so soon, but right that she should take her turn in looking after the mission station. I am now on the hill after a 4½ hour walk (20 miles) this morning.

With love

John

Ruth

Chuhsien   Saturday August 5th

Dear Everyone

I returned to *Chuhsien* on Saturday and imagine my delight when John arrived on Tuesday, three days earlier than expected. We had a couple of lovely days together before he and Miss Tucker set off for the hill on Thursday. Since then I have baked lots of cakes in the sweltering heat and the cook has made bread and biscuits to send up to the hill. I am responsible for organizing the bi-weekly load of bread, eggs, cakes etc. which have to be bought or cooked in the city and sent twice a week with the coolies along with the letters and laundry. There are seven of them on the hill so it is quite a big party.

It was lovely to get your letters. They make me so nostalgic for the days when we were all youngsters together. How I would enjoy a play on the piano and a bath in the big *white* bath, and what wouldn't I do for a plunge in the deep rocky pool then a scramble for blackberries and a quick walk or bike ride home for tea! I hope the 300 cabbage plants you put in are doing well, Dad. I wonder if every time you write you would think six months ahead and give me a gardening tip, e.g. on such-and-such a date you should plant lettuces, or set potatoes, or now's the time for gladioli etc. It would be a great help as we are both awfully inexperienced in gardening.

August 9th

Last night the messenger brought back a lovely pile of letters from the folk on the hill. It is pretty hot even up there. Our cook is proving very helpful and doesn't seem to mind roughing it. Four weeks today is our wedding day! It is good that John was able to go to *Yingshan* and get all the work done in readiness for our arrival. There is huge amount of furniture and I'm looking forward to sorting everything out and beginning to use some of our nice things. The garden sounds like a wilderness with quite a lot of self-sown flowers.

The ground here is as dry as a bone and the rice needs moisture so much. I am looking after the garden for Miss Tucker and am watering extensively every morning in the hope of keeping the "wedding flowers" alive. Thank you so much for all the things you have sent, including the sprays of myrtle and service sheets which are simply lovely.

It seems very quiet here in the city on my own but, apart from feeling rather devoid of energy because of the heat (up to 103°), I don't mind and am finding plenty to do including trying to study and preparing the baskets of provisions to be taken up the hill etc. I shall be changing places with Miss Allibone on Tuesday and am sorry she has to come down to this heat. I shall feel quite bewildered being surrounded by that crowd of young, merry folks on the hill. I expect John will come and meet me.

With love
Ruth

John

Chiu p'an shi   August 9th

Dear Everyone

I am having a lovely holiday enjoying the company of friends, studying in the morning, going for walks in the afternoon, playing games in the evening but I'm thinking of Ruth alone in the city and am longing for her to come up and join in it all with me. I have been trying to make myself useful by mending the handle of an old iron with a bit of wire, unblocking a teapot spout by blowing it clear and showing someone how to rope a bed. The Ladies are having one made to leave up here to save having to bring up camp beds every time. Four weeks today is our great event! It all seems so amazing, almost too good to be true after our long wait.

<u>August 13th</u>

I have been thinking of Ruth sweltering in 100° or more down below but despite the heat she writes cheerfully and says she is enjoyng the task of looking after her "family" up here on the hill. Tomorrow Miss Allibone will be going down to relieve her and I am actually going with her to give Ruth a surprise, starting at 5 a.m. in the cool of the day!

<u>August 14th</u>

We had a good journey down. The idea was that I should hide for a few minutes and then stroll in, but things didn't quite go according to plan. One of the guard dogs, who I had been warned were not partial to strangers, suddenly appeared, at which I point I took flight and made a rather more hasty entry than intended accompanied by a loud bark, which made Ruth jump and turn round to see me!

I have just had a pair of shoes made for the wedding using an old pair of leather ones as a pattern, white canvas with leather soles, so smart and a lovely fit. Most of the men wear ordinary cloth lace-up shoes made to measure on the street locally. They cost about 8d. or 9d. a pair, last for months and are comfy for these long walks and journeys.

Today I have had a letter from Head Office saying that the Bishop has asked Mr Denham to stay at *Wanhsien* until the end of the October and they want us to go to *Chowkow* until he returns. This is not only very disappointing but very inconvenient in many ways, but we are under orders and have to accept it is God's will for us. *Yingshan* does, of course, have a pastor who has managed well for two years so another few weeks or so won't make much difference to the work, whereas *Chowkow* really needs an ordained man. One definite advantage is that it will give me the opportunity to have a long talk with Mr Denham to clarify exactly what my responsibilities are to be at *Yingshan* before I actually start. On a happier note we are to spend a few days at *Chuhsien* after our honeymoon to give the Ladies a chance to come up here for a real rest. They will certainly need it after the Bishop's visit, hosting two weddings each with its Chinese feast as well as putting up a houseful of guests. They are so kind and it is the least we can do.

With love
John

Ruth
Chiu p'an shi   August 17th

Dear Everyone
On Monday I had a busy morning making cakes to take up the hill and getting ready for Miss Allibone's return. She arrived quite early looking hot and sunburnt, and then the dogs started barking and in walked John! He had come down to meet me and take me back the next day! It was *such* a lovely surprise.

It is great to be back here, enjoying the fun and fellowship. Bishop Mowll and his wife are making their final itineration of the diocese before leaving and spent last night with us. They were tired after their travels in the heat and enjoyed the cool of the hills. They are so friendly, full of fun and interested in us all. They have given Lilian and me a lovely set of Chinese silver teaspoons each, mine engraved with pagodas. The Bishop conducted a lovely Communion service and their presence was a great encouragement. This morning we all got up very early to see them off, just as the thin moon was setting with the faintest hint of daybreak but no light except the stars and our lanterns. While we were waiting we put Lilian in Mrs Mowll's two-bearer chair and took turns in carrying it around. It was such fun but I've still got a sore shoulder from carrying the pole.

Sadly Mr Denham is not well enough to come to the wedding, but we will be married instead by our good friend, Theo Benson, who is also marrying Bill and Lily. Then a bombshell - we are to live at *Chowkow* until Mr Denham can get back, probably not until the end of October. So we shan't be settling in our own home just yet.

August 24th

The days are fairly flying past and we are due to return to the city next week and then will be frightfully busy getting ready for Lilian's wedding. Four people are coming from *Tahsien* so we will be a big crowd and it should be great fun. Then it will be our turn! I'm afraid we'll only have about five people apart from us but maybe one or two of Bill and Lily's guests will be able to stay on. It is good of dear Meg to come all this long way.

With love
Ruth

John
Chiu p'an shi   August 27th

Dear Everyone

Last week Ruth, Meg, Pauline and I went to see Miss Edwards in Tachu. It took 4½ hours and we had a most enjoyable day. On the way back Pauline had one hua-kan and Ruth and Meg shared another. Ruth had first turn intending to go only a few li but the chairmen refused to put her down or even to stop when she slipped down on purpose between the poles, so she had to scramble back again.

On the road

At each little group of houses we passed we were convinced the others must be waiting for us there, but no! On and on we went, in the heat of the afternoon sun with Meg having developed a blister. Finally, after 20 li, we found them waiting for us and we were *not* pleased when we heard about the chairmen's behaviour. However, Meg got in, just at the bottom of some steep steps, the most difficult part of the way, so she had her rest and Ruth and I had our walk back together.

<u>Monday</u> Chuhsien

This morning Ruth and I had a lovely five hour walk down from the hill, leaving at 5.45 a.m. We hear that four armed bandits have been living openly and unrecognized in the village all the month, even paying us a visit once, their object apparently being to rob wealthy travellers. Now busy preparations are underway for Bill and Lily's wedding on Thursday.

With love

John

Ruth

Chuhsien   August 30th

Dear Everyone

After we arrived back we were in a whirl getting ready for Lilian's wedding, the "girls" making and icing the wedding cake, baking, laying tables etc while the men decorated the church using the large armfuls of pretty leaves, grasses, small branches etc. which we gathered on our last night on the hill and brought down on our loads. The men were also blissfully happy taking two organs to pieces and putting them back together again, and repairing the Ladies' gramophone.

Lilian made a charming bride and was duly given away by Miss Allibone, with me the bridesmaid! Finally we saw the happy pair off in their chairs, bound for the *Sueting* hills.

September 3rd

Meg and I started right away on our wedding cake and John iced it. He got a tinsmith to make four little tin funnels with tips cut out in different shapes for the icing and cut out calico forcing bags to fit on them. He made six little pillars to hold one tier on another, using camera spools and their boxes filled with tallow from a candle which he covered with silver paper. He finished it off with six sweet little silver bells which he got on the street (see opposite) and a tiny silver vase of flowers on top and it looked absolutely splendid.

September 5th

After Bill and Lily's wedding all eight guests stayed on and two others arrived, so you can imagine what a jolly party of young people we are and great week we have had! Everyone joined in the preparations, the men decorating the church, decoding telegrams, making confetti from cut-up coloured catalogue pages while the ladies were finishing their dresses, cooking, preparing the wedding breakfast etc. So we were all in it together which made it so special. Miss Allibone and Miss Tucker were our very kind hosts not just for the day but having all our friends to stay for the week.

With love
Ruth

Wednesday, 6th September 1933
John and Ruth were married at Chuhsien

 ****

Chiu p'an shi   *Wednesday Evening*

My own dear Mother, Father and Dorothy

It has all come true! Here we are, Ruth and I, beginning our honeymoon after being married this morning (just after mid-night your time). We had an early start, a very happy service and reception and set off for here in the midday heat arriving at dusk. We have just been reading through your special wedding letters and feel we mustn't go to bed without saying a big thank-you, and for your telegram which arrived yesterday.

How we would have loved you all to have been with us. Apart from that it couldn't have been a happier wedding.

Your happy

John

My own Dear Mother, Father, Mary, Jock and Jack

I am married to John! The longed-for has happened at last! It has been such a wonderfully happy day and I'm still in my seventh heaven! This morning Miss Allibone gave me your letter which was followed by your telegram so it was lovely to feel you so specially near. Now we are up on the hill, tired but happy after a perfect day and we felt we must write short notes home before we turn in.

How we would have loved you all to have been with us. Apart from that it couldn't have been a happier wedding.

Your happy

Ruth

****

John

Thursday

Ruth looked beautiful and it was a wonderful moment when she joined me and the service started. Twice we were pronounced "man and wife together", once in English and once in Chinese. The service itself was in English though the closing hymn was sung in Chinese for the benefit of the Chinese congregation.

The wedding breakfast was a wonderful spread of chicken jelly, tongue, salad, fruit salad, jelly, cakes etc. and the wedding cake. Finally came the speeches, drinking our health in lemonade and the telegrams. Three of the men had carefully decoded yours and at first it came out as "so terrible was the sight that Moses said, I exceedingly fear and quake"! The correct version was, of course, Hebrews 13 v.21 which reads "Make you perfect in every good thing to do His will".

It was rather a long haul up the hill, partly because we had to start in the heat of a hot day, and partly because we were tired after all the excitement. Finally we arrived just as it was getting dark.

Friday

Today it is raining and very cool and we are right up in the clouds, but we have had a long drought and do need the rain and we are just far too happy to be bothered. It feels wonderful to be a married man at last after the long years of waiting. Miss Allibone and Miss Tucker have been simply splendid and such fun and they couldn't have done more to make everything go smoothly. We are so grateful to them.

With love
John.

Ruth

Thursday

The church was pretty full, mainly with Chinese folk, and had been beautifully decorated. Pauline had made lovely bouquets for Meg and me and buttonholes for the men. Meg looked perfectly lovely in her pink-mauve frock. My long white dress was trimmed with the Honiton lace you sent, Mother, and the wreath was made of Granny's orange blossom and myrtle. Both the groom and best-man were dressed in white.

It was a truly ecstatic moment when I walked up the aisle and reached John looking so wonderful! Mr Benson took the service beautifully. Waiting outside were crowds of the Chinese and we were deluged with confetti followed by a deafening volley of fireworks.

The wedding feast was in the church premises and had been prepared by our wonderful friends. There were about ten tables of guests and others waiting for the second sitting. We went from table to table bowing to the guests and thanking them for their gifts and inviting them to start eating, and they bowed to us. We sat in special chairs draped with the Union Jack and had the meal, speeches and toast and finished by singing Auld Lang Syne and the National Anthem. There was such a warm atmosphere and many of our Chinese friends gave us the most exquisite hand-embroidered articles.

To the ear-splitting sounds of more crackers, I was carried through the town with my bouquet tied to the side of my chair, an old shoe tied to the back with a tin crashing and banging behind. John was accompanied by the other three men to the boat where we set off on our long hot journey to the hills.

Friday

We will probably go back to *Chuhsien* next Wednesday to allow the Ladies to come here. I can't tell you how wonderful they have been, not least putting up with such a noisy party of young people, all with such good humour. Meg has been a marvellous bridesmaid, so unselfish and capable, and it has been lovely to see her enjoying everything so much. I hope she won't feel too flat after all the guests have gone because she is staying on to take her exam but after that she will be going straight to her new station which will be so much more suitable for her.

With Love

Ruth

Ruth

Chuhsien   September 14th

Dear Everyone

We have just arrived back in the city having had a most glorious honeymoon which was over all too quickly. Now it is the Ladies' turn to have their well-deserved rest on the hill.

September 23rd

Today day John took his first Chinese funeral. It was of a little girl who only died in the morning. We had to walk quite a long way and wait an hour before the coffin arrived. It was very heavy and the road too narrow for the four bearers. As the earth was scattered the mother started wailing and weeping "my child, my child – goodbye". It was heart-rending and I could have wept myself. When we were nearly home the rain began and people started dancing and yelling out with delight.

The Ladies are planning to come back on Monday and we shall probably leave three days later although there is some hitch about *Chowkow* now as the folks are getting worried about the Communists and are preparing to leave.

<u>September 29th</u>

The colporteur has walked over from *Chowkow* to accompany us back so we plan to set out with him on Tuesday. He tells us *Yingshan* is quite clear of the Communists.

<u>September 30th</u>

Oh! What a life! Since writing yesterday we've had a perfectly hectic time..........

(see John's letter below)

With love

Ruth

John

Tachu

October 4th

Dear Friends and Supporters

On September 29th, nine days after returning to the city, rumours came of a fresh Communist movement this time in the direction of *Yingshan* and *Chuhsien*. Ruth was packing for *Chowkow* and I was taking the last paper of my third language exam when there was a sudden alarm and I could hear excited voices and people coming and going outside. We were told that the soldiers had been defeated and the Reds were about 20 miles away and that we would have to get out that evening and sleep over the river for safety. Then word came that the soldiers had won another victory and we could stay.

An hour later there was more frantic rushing about and we were told we must leave AT ONCE. We grabbed a few hasty mouthfuls of supper and hurried back to our rooms to collect a few clothes and our bedding while the Chinese tried to find coolies to carry our things. Within an hour we were off, by which time it was quite dark.

We shall never forget that evening, the streets crowded with people rushing hither and thither, mainly down to the river, some carrying bedding, others without even that. The Lord provided us with a very real friend in need in the person of Ruth's Chinese teacher, once a potential bandit-chief, but now a very real Christian. It was he who first brought us the news, urged us to hurry, helped us find men, accompanied us down to the river and there succeeded in finding us a boat, though the first two he booked were commandeered by soldiers when his back was turned. We finally clambered on with such luggage as we had been able to bring. This quite filled the small boat which lurched dangerously as we pushed off from the bank, but we got across safely and the teacher led us to his brother's house where we found two rooms already prepared for us, also refreshments which were very welcome after our half-eaten supper.

The next morning the Communists had not arrived, but there was no question of our going back, and Pauline, Ruth and I were asked to accompany five Chinese girls and head for the next CIM station, *Tachu* about 30 miles away. This is normally quite an easy day's journey but we had a fairly late start, the Chinese girls were not good walkers and we could not get enough men for more than one chair and the ones we *did* get turned back half way. To crown it all, it poured all day, and the first 18 miles were up hill. So nightfall found us, very wet and weary, at the hill bungalow where we decided to stay the night. By mistake, the coolies had brought the wrong loads, so that instead of our normal bedding we found ourselves with a lot of our best new linen, wedding gifts etc. Fortunately there were also some extra winter blankets which saved the day because we were high up and it was very wet and cold. We feasted on some Chinese dough-strips which we bought on the street.

The next morning we hired a hua-kan and with the girls taking turns we managed to get down to *Tachu* the other side of the hill. Just as we were entering the city we met a crowd of people coming out of the gates looking very excited and I heard someone say "shah ren" (kill man) and realized we had arrived just in time for a public execution. We only just had time to get off the road when a troop of soldiers marched out of the city, the two criminals walking among them, easily recognised by the white, spade-shaped labels fastened above their heads, bearing their accusation – probable complicity with the Reds. As they passed us, two buglers blew a blast but we pressed on as we did not want the Chinese girls to see it. The procession had hardly passed us when we heard two rifle-shots and then a third and the soldiers began to line up ready to march back. Ten minutes later we entered the Mission premises and found the folk in the middle of a service – it was Sunday morning!

We were given a warm welcome and much to our relief our other loads arrived the next day.

Yours sincerely

John Carpenter

Ruth

Tachu   Friday October 6th

Dear Everyone

I was so glad to get your letters and the nice picture of Princess Margaret Rose.

We arrived here on Sunday morning and the Ladies turned up on Monday evening with several more Chinese. They had been back to the city to collect some more things and were able to get some men to carry their chairs. They had only gone about 10 li when they met some soldiers who told them there was no need to flee because they were coming to protect them, so they went back to *Chuhsien* where they were told they only had the word of a few soldiers and they should leave immediately and not run any risks. It was nice to feel they were all here and we are quite a big party, and still the Chinese keep coming!

We are told a large group of soldiers passed through here a few days ago on their way to protect *Chuhsien* and that several big cannons and lots of ammunition have been taken there too. So yesterday Miss Tucker decided to go back with the coolies who brought the wives of the cook and cowman, chiefly to keep out any soldiers who might think the compound an excellent place to billet a hundred or so men.

Yingshan is said to have fallen to the Reds and *Sanhuei* is in great danger, and the soldiers who went to protect *Chuhsien* are staying on *this* bank of the river rather than crossing over to the city. A fine way to defend it! We don't think Miss Tucker would be able to get across and we shall not be surprised to see her back here today. The cowman and the cows are here so we have milk and butter which is a help to Miss Edwards in catering for such a large party.

Miss Allibone has been considering the possibility of us younger ones going on to *Liangshan* before there is any panic here. It is two days' journey away, over two high mountain ranges, a beautiful road. I am all for it as I don't want to stay here indefinitely and am sure *Yingshan* will be out of the question for some time. You can imagine how disappointing this is after we had longed *so* much for our home together.

Every afternoon Pauline and I go to the little chapel to see the Chinese girls who are sleeping on straw mattresses spread out neatly on the floor. They seem fairly happy although their future is very unsettled, poor dears. This province is having a terrible time and even if the Reds don't come the people still have to leave their homes, land and businesses and their means of livelihood is cut off. It must be very galling to have to pay exorbitant taxes ostensibly to support a marvellous army, but one which utterly fails to protect them. Furthermore the soldiers who have gone to "protect" *Chuhsien* are not the General's men at all but belong to a rival warlord who owns *Tachu*. *Kwangan* has fallen and *Tahsien* is under threat.

<u>October 7th</u>

This morning we were told we four "youngsters" should be ready to leave as soon as possible and 15 coolies were organized, but today we were told it wasn't necessary! It's like a seesaw, one moment violent haste to leave and the next no need after all, no danger. We do wonder if we will be here ad infinitum or whether the powers-that-be will designate us elsewhere.

Today a messenger came from *Chuhsien* bringing some more of our precious things including several wedding presents and some stores which Miss Tucker had packed up, but alas, nearly a trunkful of groceries and medicines worth about $200 and all my books are left behind. Miss Tucker is sticking it out, staying with friends this side of the river and going across to our house every day, but Miss Allibone has advised her to come back.

With love
Ruth

Ruth
Liangshan   October 15th

Dear Everyone

With further bad news, it was decided that John, Pauline, Amy and I should go to *Liangshan*. With John walking and the rest of us in chairs we had a good day's journey despite our coolies being opium smokers. We stayed the first night at the same inn where I stayed when I first went to *Chuhsien*, a filthy place but at least fewer flea bites this time! We spent the next night at a market where we met a friend who was on a preaching visit. She lent John her horse and groom so the next day he rode the first 15 li on horseback. He looked topping and rode nicely but Chinese horses are very small and he couldn't get his feet into the stirrups properly. The groom then turned back and John walked the rest of the way, about 90 li, over two mountain ranges noted for being brigand-infested, and we were certainly glad when we arrived safely.

There are three buildings here at *Liangshan*, the church where all the Chinese live, the ladies' house outside the East Gate occupied by five lady workers, and the hospital occupied by Theo Benson and the Lamberts. Bill and Lilian met at their wedding. It is not actually a hospital but one of ladies does dispensing work here. We have been given a large upstairs room which we have made look pretty and homely with all the things we brought with us. I wonder how long we will be here to enjoy it. I have been asked to oversee the washing, ironing and cleaning which will leave Mrs Lambert more time to see to the cooking and her baby.

So here we are for the time being, taking a day at a time. What a strange life it is and we feel so useless and yet the Lord must have a purpose in our coming over here, although it's hard to hang on to the fact that all these wanderings are fulfilling His plan for us. One good thing is that there will be opportunities for John to help with preaching on the street and me with classes. Also it will be easier to get to *Yingshan* if and when the time comes and an added bonus is that my old *T'uch'i* teacher is here and I am able to read with him.

With love
Ruth

Ruth
Liangshan   October 22nd

Dear Everyone
It was wonderful to get letters from home after such a long gap. They were written at the end of August and

had been chasing around the province trying to find me, hence the delay. It was lovely to be linked up again.

At *Chowkow*, Liu, the evangelist, very kindly took a boatload of things belonging to John, the Denhams and Dr Snowball to the CIM at *Shunking* but unfortunately quite a lot of things were left behind. The Reds took two loads of medicines and told the people to help themselves to crocks, jam etc.

The Ladies have been advised to go to *Chungking*. *Tahsien* has fallen and people are fleeing. Probably Lilian and Billy and many Chinese will be arriving here soon and John and Theo are going to meet them on the road tomorrow to cheer them on their way and take food and chairs for the weary. Some from here will have to go on to *Wanhsien* to make way for the new influx.

October 24th

John is somewhere miles away with Theo, having set off yesterday to meet Lilian and Billy and all the *Tahsien* refugees and we're expecting them when we see them.

October 26th

Yesterday our two wanderers returned after 2½ days on the road. They didn't meet any foreigners but *did* meet a Christian from *Tahsien* who was escaping with his little girl and he told them the foreigners had gone to a nearby town and were going to stay there awhile. So they turned back and let the little girl ride in one of the chairs. The road was full of refugees carrying all they could get hold of as they left.

Today I was unexpectedly called upon to preach at a children's class. In the middle there was a commotion in the compound and an advance party of coolies and cooks had arrived and commandeered rooms in the compound for the night for about 60 soldiers, and had started getting their supper ready! This is about the fifth time passing troops have used our premises but they haven't caused any problems so we can't begrudge them a night's lodging - after all, they *have* come to protect us! There are masses of soldiers in the town at present and aeroplanes constantly flying overhead and landing on the big drill ground.

John and Theo have been out preaching and have been much encouraged by the eager response of the crowds. John has also been asked to give the sermon next Sunday and is so pleased to be getting into the work again after having had little since he left *Chowkow* at the end of July but we do long to be settled.

Tahsien has had a rotten time and Bill and Lily, Fred Skinner and Bill Clarke were hoping to be here on Tuesday, roads/brigands permitting, but today is Thursday and they haven't turned up yet.

With love

Ruth

Ruth

Liangshan   October 28th

Dear Everyone

In the end, Lilian, Bill and Fred Skinner turned up at *Wanhsien* after four days on the road. Fred had gone to *Tahsien* to see if he could help but when he was nearly there he met someone who told him they had already left. While having a break, his hua-kan and his men were taken by retreating soldiers and his cook ran off to hide. Two more coolies turned up with Lilian and Billy's loads and one of them also ran off! Fred and a boy stayed at an inn in a market which was practically empty. Suddenly some soldiers rushed in and told them the Reds were approaching and they must leave by midnight. Fred and the boy divided his remaining load and carried it on their backs, about 60 lbs each. They spent the night at a farmhouse with no beds and very cold. The next morning Fred found his fugitive cook in the same farmhouse, having also taken refuge there!

Later Fred heard that Lily and Bill were still in *Tahsien* and hadn't got out after all, so back he went to help them. He was nearly there when he met the CIM cook and family who told him that Bill and Lily *had* left, so he turned back, and what a mercy because that very day the Reds took the city.

Fred had many other adventures, including spending half a night huddled up with several coolies, the cook and his wife on an oil sheet in a ploughed field. They had to "ta ko chin" ("strike an embrace") to keep warm! Finally they arrived yesterday with about 100 *Tahsien* Chinese refugees who are lodging in the vacated orphanage next to the hospital. The 40 resident orphans and staff had only just left for the comparative safety of a hill resort.

It is getting quite cold and John hasn't much in the way of warm clothing, but if he gets desperate he can have a wadded garment made and dress Chinese-style.

Did I tell you Meg is getting a horse? She is having much more open-air and recreation with Miss Scarlett and is all the better for it. This place isn't much good for walks as it's difficult to get away from the streets.

We see a lot of beggars lying on the streets, such a pitiful sight. They are indescribably filthy and some have the most awful deformities and one wonders what sort of government it is that can allow such things. I'm sure some could be cured with proper treatment.

With love
Ruth

Ruth
Liangshan   Friday November 3rd

Dear Everyone

This is probably your Christmas letter and I do hope you'll have a lovely time. I wonder if it will be a real old-fashioned Christmas with snow and a nice thick layer of ice on the ponds. How I would love to see all you dear ones! This evacuation business has upset our plans and I expect Christmas will be a bit of a non-event. Still no more home letters but no doubt they are in a circle of redirection.

The Ladies and Miss Edwards have left *Tachu* and gone to *Chungking* as advised. Apart from ourselves and Fred the rest of our group were directed to *Wanhsien*. They took some of our stuff, so that we now have only our bare necessities and have luggage in six different places! No doubt the remainder of John's things at *Chowkow* have gone to the scavengers by now.

After they left the three of us moved across to the lady workers' house outside the East Gate. The gatekeeper was supposed to be taking our luggage and stores but was afraid to go and come back through the town by himself so John went with him while I waited here, then we went over together. The Lamberts left a load of food to be used up which we are gradually consuming.

<u>November 4th</u>

A huge budget of letters has arrived and I feel absolutely overwhelmed with joy. It is lovely to have letters addressed to me under my new name! I loved hearing how you celebrated our wedding day and how I wish I could have heard the peal of bells - and had one of the ices! I love the photo of you, Mother and Dad, and what a posh hat, my Ma! In my Christmas parcel I have sent you my fan which I used on my wedding day, a present from one of the Chinese ladies, but oh I could weep with disappointment about the wedding snaps, especially for your sakes.

With love
Ruth

John
Liangshan   November 5th

Dear Friends and Supporters

Here is a resumé of the state of affairs at present:-

Out of 24 CIM stations in the *East Szechwan* C of E district, 20 have had to evacuate because of the Reds. Not all of these have fallen into their hands but it is impossible for most of the Chinese to return and certainly not the foreigners.

Chowkow We were encouraged to hear that the church members had continued to run the services even when the town was captured by a band of Communists.

We hear that it has now been recaptured by government troops.

Yingshan is still in the hands of the Communists who have made their local headquarters there.

Chuhsien has not yet been taken but the Ladies have left and gone southwards to *Chungking*. We only hope that the defending armies will not use the premises and take the opportunity to help themselves to anything they can find.

The Communists are still active and news varies from day to day. Many soldiers are being sent up to the front, and during the last fortnight aeroplanes have been assisting, making *Liangshan* their base.

The evacuation has, of course, upset our plans completely and since we married two months ago, we have stayed in six different houses, not any for more than 16 days. As for *Yingshan*, our longed-for first "home" and sphere of united service, it is still in the hands of the Reds and seems further away than ever. We are sure we have lessons to learn through these experiences and are trying to make the best of our time in exile and there are a few opportunities for work.

We want to testify to the perfect peace God has given us in moments that might otherwise have been anxious and together we have been able to share the excitements, disappointments and all the other experiences of this evacuation. We thank God for his guidance, not least as regards the date for our wedding. Had it been earlier, we would almost certainly have moved to *Yingshan* and had to evacuate leaving most of our belongings to the Reds. .

Yours sincerely
John Carpenter

Ruth
Liangshan   November 17th

Dear Everyone

The big news is that Pauline and Fred are engaged! They are so happy!

John has been going out every day with some Chinese men to preach to the crowds on the street. I am taking the opportunity of doing a lot of study because I'm very keen to complete my third section. Our cook stays on, making himself useful, but I do wish he could get news of his wife and family who were in a district overridden by the Reds.

Some more soldiers have been trying to get in and live in the compound but after several efforts they have given up and gone away. News from *Chuhsien* is better and the school has reopened with about 20 children but it is still not safe enough for us to return.

November 25th

We have heard today that *Yingshan* has been retaken by the troops so that is more hopeful.

This morning I went to the funeral of an old Christian woman which took place in her house, an unbelievably squalid place. It seemed a rather casual affair with the huge black coffin, lid not quite shut, perched on two small benches right across the small room nearly blocking the door leading on to the street. There was a good bit of arguing about the price the coolies were to be paid for carrying the coffin to the graveyard followed by a short service. This afternoon I have been round countless streets with a Chinese woman, inviting every woman we saw to church tomorrow.

<u>Sunday</u>

John took a class for English speaking Chinese students this afternoon and I helped with the Sunday school. There was a huge crowd as all the girls from the girls' school have to come. We are glad to be able to take part in the ministry in these ways.

<u>December 4th</u>

Mr Hannah, the sub-superintendent of *Szechwan*, has just been for a long week-end and it has been so refreshing to listen to his talks in English and hear about England from one who has so recently returned. He is such a nice man with years of experience in China and we so much enjoyed the presence of an older foreigner as we are all young here. We had an interview with him about the work at *Yingshan* and he thinks we should be able to go there soon as the news is much better.

The church here runs regular campaigns at a temple to help men to break away from opium and bring them to the knowledge of Christ. They last about a month and the Christians who run them have been much used. One is starting today and John has gone to help and two Chinese refugees are doing the catering which will pay them a wage for a while. The temple is in beautiful countryside and has a well which never goes dry.

While John was out we visited a woman in her "house" i.e. a roof with two walls and the rest open to the elements. She was quite nicely dressed and was sitting on the bed making shoes. We threaded our way back through the crowded streets and when we got back found a refugee in tears. She said she was going to have to abandon her baby girl as she had no money and didn't know where her husband was and although she had the offer of work, the employer wouldn't take children. We are trying to help people who are destitute and Fred is going to talk to her.

Yesterday there was a dead or dying man lying on the street emaciated and covered with flies. He's gone today but a new little beggar has appeared. He has no feet and rolls over and over in the middle of the crowded street so that people nearly tread on him. He shouts and is wearing just a ragged top and a loincloth. It's simply terrible.

John had a letter today from the *Yingshan* pastor who said that all the foreigners' things have been taken and some of the doors of the house have been removed and burnt, so it won't be a very inviting home to go to just yet.

With love
Ruth

Ruth
Liangshan   December 8th

Dear Everyone

Christmas is coming though I haven't been able to work up a Christmassy feeling at all, and don't even know where we will be. This touch of uncertainty creates an element of surprise! It is now more than three months since we were married and still we are *kay lu. How we both long for our home together.

---

*kay lu   visitors/guests/strangers/pilgrims

December 11th

Now there *is* a Christmassy feeling in the air which came when a friend brought some very holly-like leaves and berries from the hill so I have suggested we have an expedition to see if we can find some more.

December 16th

I was glad to get your letter today as I have been feeling rather homesick. Presents are a problem and I was so looking forward to our first Christmas in our own home. It is disappointing that there is no prospect of this in the foreseeable future but so lovely to have John and we are so happy together. I'm going to try and brighten our room up a bit and tidy away the previous occupant's papers and get rid of the hideous greenishgreyishbrownish old curtains and make more space. At present we only have one long drawer and two small ones for us and our linen.

Sunday

John and I are sitting in the garden in a lovely patch of sunshine. It is very cold in the shade but gloriously warm in the sun. Someone has just brought along some sweet little puppies which were born last week, an aeroplane is flying over, a woman is weeding on the hillside chatting, gnats are flitting about, the leaves of the palm trees are swishing back and forth and the other leaves are swaying gently in the breeze.

When you wrote on October 31st you were just beginning to hear about the renewed troubles in *Szechwan* and I expect we will soon have replies to our letters written at the time of the evacuation! My poor Ma, getting such a shock when the telegrams arrived.

With love
Ruth

John to Ruth's Parents

Liangshan   December 17th

Dear Mother and Father

We have now been here ten weeks and are "making a move towards making a move", i.e. we have permission, when eventually we can leave, to go via *Chungking* for Ruth to have some dental treatment and me to have my earache seen to. How we long for our own home but are afraid the Reds have wreaked havoc on the *Yingshan* premises. It seems strange that we are just receiving letters from you in answer to our wedding ones, and you were addressing them to *Yingshan*, completely unaware of our evacuation.

It is good to have opportunities for ministry here and this morning I preached at the main Chinese service. I prepared one of my English visual-aid addresses translated into Chinese. I cut out the diagram, a refugee Christian tailor sewed the hems on his machine, the pastor wrote the characters and Ruth made the gadgets to hang it up.

We have just had fun buying and making Christmas presents for our China friends. They have all been so kind to us and many of them have lost or had to leave behind far more than we have.

With love
John

Ruth

Liangshan   December 24th

Dear Everyone

The Chinese folk have been very busy making all sorts of decorations, and at the hospital, school and church building they have erected huge archways, about 16 ft. high, made of bamboo covered with fir sprigs and coloured paper flowers. Also there are many lanterns of all sorts of shapes, e.g. aeroplanes, cabbages, rabbits, fish etc. and the whole place looks very gay. We have also decorated our room with paper-chains and even a little Christmas tree.

<u>Boxing Day</u>

Despite my misgivings it really has been a wonderful Christmas with colleagues from several other evacuated stations. It started with carols in the garden, then opening stockings, breakfast, giving presents to our servants, a long Chinese service in a packed church followed by a Chinese feast. Our cook gave John and me a topping pair of slippers each which he'd had specially made. Then we started our own celebrations, exchanging presents between the ten of us and finally John and I opened the two huge parcels from his parents, packed in cardboard boxes and sewn up in sacking. They were full of an amazing array of things, ranging from shirts for John and silk stockinette petticoat for me to mending wool and scouring pads. It was such lovely way of making me feel welcomed into the family. And it's lovely to know that your two parcels are on their way.

Today we put on an entertainment for the 80 or so Chinese Christian refugees then went to a very select feast at the pastor's house and now one of the workers has gone up the hill to help the orphans have a good time.

<u>December 30th</u>

This week's letter from you was written when you had just heard of our thrilling evacuation to *Tachu*.

That certainly was an adventure but somehow, because we were carried along by the adrenaline and necessity of it all, it didn't seem too hard to cope with. It's this continuous waiting, uncertainty and deferred hope which is difficult to endure patiently. "When do my wanderings cease? I am here a little, there a little"!

The *Tahsien* missionaries have come off very badly. The houses have been left mere shells, doors taken, floors pulled up, ceilings battered down, windows smashed, furniture destroyed, possessions removed, books torn up and chucked into the garden. *Yingshan* and *Chowkow* have also fallen, but so far *Chuhsien* has escaped.

With love
Ruth

Ruth
Wanhsien   January 13th

Dear Everyone
    You will be surprised to see this address! We are staying at the Mission station for the weekend on our way to *Chungking* for some dentistry. We left *Liangshan* yesterday and got here in one day walking much of the way, stopping for a funny dinner at a filthy inn and completing the journey on a very crowded bus. We were so relieved when our cook and two other coolies arrived with the rest of our luggage which we'd had to leave by the roadside.
    Very regrettably we have had to pay off our cook. As you know, the intention was for him to come with us to *Yingshan* but we simply could not go on paying him when there was no work for him in the foreseeable future.   However, much to our delight, one of our colleagues has taken him on temporarily.
    With love
    Ruth

Ruth

Chungking   January 20th

Dear Everyone

After 2½ days on a Chinese steamer we reached *Chungking*. This is a major CIM station with plenty of comings and goings apart from the permanent staff. There are 20 of us, mostly refugees like ourselves, and it is especially good to see Miss Allibone, Miss Tucker and the Denhams again. You can guess how our tongues wagged after so long!

When John and I left *Chowkow* and *Chuhsien* respectively we had to leave behind many of our possessions which we hoped would be sent here for safe keeping. Unfortunately we have lost quite a lot, but John was delighted to be reunited with his typewriter, gramophone and huge Chinese dictionary and most of my things of sentimental value were also rescued. Amongst the missing things were about $300 worth of stores and medicines. News of *Chuhsien* is very good so it is possible the Ladies may be able to go back soon.

Chungking is a big river port and a great mixture of old and new. We have to go through a lot of very dirty narrow streets to get to the main streets which are wide and clean with continual streams of motor cars, sedan chairs, bicycles, rickshaws and pedestrians all jostling each other for room. There are many fine big buildings, some very modern, and beautiful shops with huge plate glass windows. On our steamer there were some enormous steel windows which took about 20 men to unload. Shoe shops are in abundance. Chinese women and girls have very small feet even when they have not been bound and many of those whose feet have been bound wear big shoes padded out with cotton wool.

There is electric light but not as far out as the CIM station yet. We have very good lamps with mantles like the one John had but which is now sadly in the hands of the looters.

<u>January 28th</u>

This week I have had one letter from home, dated September 4th. In it you said "we do feel for you in the heat" but if you could see me now you'd feel for me in the cold. I'm sitting in our bedroom wrapped up in thick underclothes, petticoat, thick frock, overcoat, mittens and thick rug!

As you know, one of the reasons for our coming here was to have some dentistry, and I duly visited the dentist on my birthday. He gave me half an hour's agony, using the drill far too freely for my liking and tells me that it will take another month to complete all the work. Much to his surprise John was told he needs six stoppings, so he is in for more than me. The dentist is a Canadian missionary and has a well-equipped room with a porcelain basin with hot and cold water like we have in the bathroom at home.

We have spent a lot of time going through our things which we left here on our way to language school three years ago. We have had to decide what to take and what to leave as we have a good deal more than we will need.

I suppose it will be almost springtime by the time this reaches you. How I would love to see the orchard with all the primroses and daffodils!

With love
Ruth

John to Ruth's Parents
Chungking   January 28th

Dear Mother and Father

It has been wonderful to be together for all these evacuation experiences but we long more than ever for a home where we can get on with the work. Here there are few opportunities for work, and sometimes we are tempted to think we could be of far more use at home rather than living as visitors among a lot of foreigners at a big Mission station. However, we do not forget that, although we can't altogether understand it, this indefinite wandering is part of His purpose for our lives. One obvious gain is that we are able to devote time to language study in a way that wouldn't be possible were we in charge of a busy station. On the other hand, increased knowledge of the "bookwork" is of little use when we get so little chance to use it.

With love
John

Ruth
Chungking   February 4th

Dear Everyone

First of all we must tell you the exciting news that you are to be grandparents in October!

Thank you so much for the woolly caps and scarves. They arrived in perfect timing for the arrival of three little orphan girls who had had most of their clothes stolen. They looked so bonny in their lovely bright caps and new clothes which a colleague made them, and came down to give us a bow. Please tell the ladies who made them how much they are appreciated.

Today by the river, we watched the longest, gayest, most extravagant funeral procession you could imagine! There must have been well over 1,000 people. First came an outsize coffin carried by 32 men, bearing the name of the corpse who was the mother of a high-ranking military official. Then several enormous idols made of thin bamboo laths covered with paper, a half-size paper elephant and other big animals. Then ten horses ridden by small children with faces painted bright pink and marvellously dressed up. One had a silver headdress and another had a huge pair of antennae. There was an enormous foreign-style paper house and two paper summer houses with gardens which were to be burnt so that the old lady might have somewhere to live. There were dozens of paper men and women and about 100 paper soldiers dressed in uniform, and two ranks of real soldiers "marching" at intervals in the procession each with a stick of burning incense in his rifle. In the middle of it all was a decorated sedan chair carried by four men with a big photograph of the deceased in the back.

The situation is becoming more settled across the province now and workers are beginning to return to their stations. *Yingshan* is said to be "extremely peaceful and quiet" and the Reds have been driven a long way back, so we hope it won't be long before we can go too.

February 11th

This week I took my oral exam which involved reciting three long passages of the New Testament from memory, reading some passages from the Bible and prayers from the Prayer Book and having 15 minutes' conversation. I am taking the written part next week.

<u>February 19th</u>

Miss Darby returned from furlough on Friday bringing your huge parcel. A big thank you for all those lovely things, especially the garments you have made and the beautiful photo of you which I love.

I wish you could look out of the window with me and see the shimmering waters of the Yangtze backed by the misty foothills and dim mountains in the background.

<u>February 25th</u>

Yesterday our dentist and his wife invited us to lunch at their lovely foreign house which had a real "family" feel and the nicest lawn I have seen since leaving home. They took us to see the new hospital which is in a magnificent position overlooking the place where the Yangtze joins the Kialing river.

As there is no further news of the Reds it seems we may be able to get away next week. The idea is that we should go to *Shunking* and then John will probably go ahead to *Yingshan* and see what repairs are necessary.

With love

Ruth

Ruth

Chungking   March 11th

Dear Everyone

The Ladies and Miss Darby are back in *Chuhsien* and are very busy but say they are missing Lilian, Pauline and me very much. We have had a letter from Mr Parsons, HQ, asking us to delay our departure. I wonder what this means and whether we shall be sent somewhere else temporarily. Miss Allen and Miss Warren, who are to be with us at *Yingshan,* left for *Hochow* last week and will have to wait there until they get the go-ahead.

March 18th

The other day I had a pleasant surprise - a wedding present of a beautifully embroidered table cloth and six matching napkins from Mr and Mrs Lamb who I met coming up the Yangtze when I first arrived. He was high up in the shipping company which owned the boat.

I have passed my exam with 96%, and have now started to study for the fourth and final section; the huge pile of books is somewhat daunting. John is getting on so well but, being a man, has to take two more sections.

I shall be so glad when my dentistry is finished. I hate going out on the streets here. The city is so smelly and noisy and I miss the country very much. I often imagine myself wandering by the lovely "still waters" of the river at Wethersfield and the joy of picking cowslips and forget-me-nots and standing on the white bridge and watching till a kingfisher flashes by or a water-rat swims along the bank. What wonderful childhood memories.

Our superintendent has written to say he doesn't think married ladies should return to their stations yet and that John might have to go alone. This is most unwelcome news and we will miss each other terribly but we feel it has to be the right thing. Our party is dwindling fast as our co-workers continue to return to their stations. John has been asked to take the Easter services here and the service at the Canadian hospital next Sunday so we do hope he will still be here. The other day I went on a day's preaching with another colleague and two Chinese women to a branch church.

March 25th

It's Sunday again and a lovely spring day with the sun shining, a gentle breeze blowing and sparrows twittering all around.

John and I are almost certainly starting on our ten day river journey to *Shunking* the Wednesday after Easter where we will stay until we can proceed to *Yingshan*. Mrs Stibbs and her baby and cook are also coming and it will be nice to travel with her as she knows the ropes and it will be fun having the baby to help look after (good practice for October!). Mr Stibbs has already gone on ahead. I am so glad I won't be left behind and it will be such a relief to get away from here and feel we are one step nearer our own home, geographically at least.

The Ladies have been asked to take charge of the Mission house at *Shanghai*. I *will* miss them.

With love
Ruth

Ruth
Chungking   April 1st

Dear Everyone

We're on our way up to *Shunking*, the last CIM station on the Kialing river which has not had to evacuate during these months. We have about 40 pieces of luggage which have all gone under the floor. Our part of the boat is covered with bamboo matting over an arched framework and the men have both ends of the boat for rowing, cooking, eating and sleeping etc. We have three camp beds, the baby's cot, three chairs, two small tables and a little bit has been screened off for a "bathroom". At night we put up curtains at both ends of the arch and a coconut mat in the middle as a screen so it's divided into two quite private little sections. Mrs Stibbs' cook prepares the most delicious food by means of burning charcoal in an earthenware pot about 6" in diameter and using some little tin pots and pans.

There are ten men on the boat including the master and his brother and a man who spends all his time punting off rocks and shallows accompanied by a great deal of shouting and cursing and occasionally smoking opium. He also prepares their food, five meals a day. Seven men spend most of the day "tracking", i.e. walking along the bank pulling the boat by a rope attached to the top of the mast. When it is more expedient to row they come on board and ply the oars full lustily, singing their strange song "oh-ay-ay-oh". Yesterday, when conditions were favourable, we went quite a long way under sail while they uttered loud shrill cries for the wind to come and fill the sail.

We have been able to have two lovely evening walks along the sandy bank and on one occasion collected quite a big crowd and John was able to speak about the Gospel and sell some books. Last night just as we were mooring the boat, the cook told us that last year a boat was robbed by bandits and 11 people were killed! Why do they like to tell us these cheerful details just as we are reaching a place rather than after we've left!

We are just drawing into *Hochow* where I can post this and we will take up a box of stores to the mission house and they will give us a supply of bread and a cooked chicken to help us on our way.

With love
Ruth

Ruth
as from Shunking   April 15th

Dear Everyone

This is our second Sunday on board, and very early this morning we reached a little town where who should appear but Mr Stibbs! He had come to take Mrs Stibbs and the baby the rest of the way to *Shunking* by chair, a short distance by land but 1½ days by boat because the river winds so much. John has just gone to speak to some officials who yelled after us wanting to see our passports. We have had no customs men on board for several days and thought we had finished with them.

The other day we saw three men in three little boats, so small that they could pick them up and carry them inverted over their heads. Each man stood and paddled along rapidly using both ends of a long bamboo. In each boat there were two or three cormorants which were put into the water and every now and then would disappear and resurface with a fish in their beaks. A ring round their necks prevented them from swallowing their prey and the boatmen were kept busy going from one bird to another, picking them up on the end of the pole, extracting the fish and putting the cormorants back in the water, all the while scolding them for not keeping nearer the boat.

<u>Sunday April 22nd</u>

We arrived at *Shunking* last Monday but I am now a grass widow as John left yesterday to spend the weekend in *Chowkow* before proceeding to *Yingshan*. As soon as he can get the Military out I will join him which *will* be joyful! I don't like this separation and feel awfully lonely as we have been together so very much since we were married. Miss Allen, who will be working with us, is here and we will be travelling together.

Meanwhile, I have been able to teach an enquirer here and have been invited to speak at the preaching hall this evening, so it is nice to feel I can be of some use. The other day I visited two CIM nurses and it was a treat to sit in their lovely garden. They took me to see the refugee orphans nearly all of whom had something wrong with them. One girl had very deformed hands as a result of being tied up when she married as a child into an unkind family. Several of the bigger girls were getting ready to be married and were making their own shoes and handkerchiefs etc. They all receive such wonderful care from their Chinese workers.

With love
Ruth

John
Yingshan   May 6th

Dear Friends and Supporters

At *Shunking* I had to leave my wife and come on alone to *Yingshan*. Thus, on April 23rd, just seven months later than we expected, I arrived "home"! The main premises were still occupied by the Military who let me have two rooms and the use of a small mud stove in the corner of the kitchen. The pantry was filled with rifles and ammunition and the bathroom had been used as their telephone office. Not all the windows were smashed as feared and I recovered what I could of the doors and furniture. Over the front door was a proclamation from the General forbidding any troops from being quartered here and in response to a good deal of pressure they decamped after six days. Immediately I called in the workmen to clear the mess and make the place habitable. I have an excellent handyman, my only concern being that he has worked for a missionary before and was sacked for theft so I do hope he won't steal much.

On May 4th I was joined by my wife, so here we are, full of joy that the Lord has at last brought us to *Yingshan* to live and work for Him together.

Yours sincerely
John Carpenter

Ruth
Yingshan   Sunday May 6th

Dear Everyone

I can hardly believe that we are really and truly at this long-hoped for home of our own! It is simply wonderful and we are so happy.

By last Tuesday most of the soldiers had gone, so the next day Miss Allen and I left for *Chowkow* en route to *Yingshan*. We each had three men to carry our sedan chairs and two for our loads and most of our luggage went by boat. We spent the first night at an inn and were just getting off to sleep when we heard a great kerfuffle outside and someone shouting that a runner had arrived with an urgent letter for Miss Allen. A telegram had arrived just after we left *Shunking* asking her to go to another station to be with a co-worker who was there on her own!

This was such a shock, but Miss Allen immediately consulted her map and having located the place decided to continue to *Chowkow* and then find the best way to proceed. We stayed the next night with the Denhams and Miss Allen organized three good men to carry her chair and two coolies to look after her on the road during her four day journey. She is probably a bit older than you, Mother, and I should not like to think of you having to do that long journey alone and did feel sorry for her.

I reached *Yingshan* on market day and the streets were jam-packed. It was thrilling to set foot inside the house and to see John again. The pastor, Mr Wang (the Rev. Conquer-Devil King!) and his wife, the Bible-woman and gatekeeper all welcomed me so kindly. They all live on the compound along with several members of the pastor's large family and some boarders from the Church school.

I am charmed by this house. It has one room upstairs and eight downstairs with the garden running right around. There are floor boards, real ceilings, glass windows, Venetian shutters and at least 20 doors and windows so that locking up at night is quite a business. The masons have made a wonderful imitation foreign stove with built-in oven and flues using bits from the old stove which the Reds smashed up and the cook has baked an excellent cake in it! We bought 124 catties

(155 lbs) coal yesterday for $1.70 (approx. 2/-). We have a good supply of stores which we brought with us from *Chuhsien*, a real help as we have a lot of other initial expenses.

The garden is pretty tangled but has some beautiful plants and trees and I have picked some orange blossom, honeysuckle and red roses. There are grapes, plums, figs, pomeloes, quinces and a lemon tree, a rarity in China.

<u>Monday</u>

As we were having supper last night we heard somebody outside sobbing and crying "i-yah, i-yah" followed by a great commotion. A child had fallen into the river and drowned. A crowd had collected around the mother's house to see her weep. Poor soul - a son too, so very precious in the eyes of the Chinese people.

With love
Ruth

Ruth
Yingshan   May 13th

Dear Everyone

Yesterday we had our first foreign meal and laid the table with a new cloth, table napkins, sparkling glasses, our "silver" and our jolly dinner set with a bowl of bright red rambler roses in the centre. It looked very festive and we sat and gazed at it before we started eating. The cook made a very nice brawn with potatoes and mint from the garden followed by a delicious pie with our own mulberries.

On Thursday the church laid on a welcome feast which was most enjoyable. John gave a lantern talk and the place was packed. This morning I took the Sunday school which was attended by about 75 children, all from the day-school; attendance at Sunday school and church is compulsory. We are planning to start a new class hoping to attract children from outside and I am also going to take charge of one of the women's classes.

John is splendid at managing the workmen, and is very busy doing the accounts, preaching, teaching daily scripture classes in the school, taking confirmation classes etc. It is great to be fully occupied after all these months and wonderful to be in our own home. We do hope and pray the Reds won't come and destroy everything again.

Miss Allen and Miss Warren are joining us in about a month's time and it has been nice to get the place straight before they arrive. It will good to see them and will help financially. Much as we love receiving parcels from England, we do hope friends won't send any more bulky ones because the duties are ruinous and we just can't afford them.

We thought a walk down to the river would be very pleasant, but disappointingly it was too damp, smelly and hot to be healthy and there were several men washing their feet and an open grave with all the ribs of the corpse sticking out. So we won't be going there again and will have to explore a bit more.

We're now listening to a gramophone record as a nice finish to the day.

With love
Ruth

Ruth

Yingshan   May 20th

Dear Everyone

It was wonderful to receive those longed-for letters in answer to our special news, and to know that you are happy about it. I am keeping very fit and John is so good to me and we're both looking forward to October enormously.

May 27th

We have been consulting the pastor about a feast which we, for etiquette's sake, must give the Chinese. We also had a group of people from the compound to listen to our two records of Chinese hymns which they love (but give me a pain). I have been doing some evangelistic work with our Bible-woman, Mrs Chang. There is a lot of superficial interest but then people change their minds, e.g.one woman who is not prepared to burn her idols, a teacher who is afraid of the devils he worships and his wife who fears it would affect his career. It is often this fear which keeps people back from believing. I am learning slowly to see things from the Chinese standpoint and in a way, the more I see under the surface the more I wonder whether we should be expecting them to change their ways from the culture in which they have grown up.

Thank you for your interest in all my descriptions of Chinese life. Now I am more familiar with everything to some extent the novelty has worn off. What I will never get used to are the beggars - little children in rags lying asleep on the side of the road, women sitting by the roadside with their bosoms uncovered searching for fleas and killing them between their thumb nails which are heavily stained with the blood of the creatures, the blind man going along the road on his haunches yelling out his supplications in an awful loud unearthly voice, the man with hardly anything left of his face. It is so hard to reach them because they all belong to organized bands with a "beggar king".

The other day we wrote to Mrs Liu, our house-woman from *T'uch'i* to ask if she would be willing to come to replace our present woman who is old and not up to the job. She is delighted and will arrive in about ten days' time. She's such an efficient cheery soul. Miss Allen and Miss Warren aren't coming for another fortnight after all.

Time is going quickly and we are very happy, but how I would love to see you all.

With love
Ruth

Ruth
Yingshan   June 3rd

Dear Everyone
On Tuesday, Mrs Chang and I were invited to spend the day with a prominent Christian family in the country, quite wealthy farmers who lost much at the hands of the Reds and the husband was taken prisoner. Some of the grandchildren are boarders at the school and they came with us, such a jolly little crowd all dressed in clean clothes and carrying fans and umbrellas. They skipped ahead, dawdled behind and led us on the wrong road for fun until finally we were met by their grandparents some distance from the house with much delight all round.

We were grateful to sit down in the cool and drink lots of bowls of refreshing tea. Eight other women arrived with babies and the tables were cleared and laid with chopsticks and spoons. We sat down to quite a substantial meal of dough strips and sauce which was eaten with great noise and gusto and then Mrs Chang preached using colourful posters but it didn't seem to cut much ice. Later, proper dinner was served. Most of the women were vegetarians thus seeking to store up merit by not eating anything unclean. They sat at one table whilst we sat another and were pressed into taking the seats of honour. Very thoughtfully John had sent my chair for the way home, much appreciated in the intense heat.

We had a curious request from the taxman who sent a dollar and asked if we could provide a dollar's worth of foreign bread from time to time because he was ill and wanted nourishment and knew that our baked bread was very good! So when the cook has a baking session he makes a loaf for him. The taxman is also buying 20¢ milk per day from the pastor.

June 11th

Bishop Holden has been staying this week-end and has now gone on to *Chowkow* accompanied half way by John. It has been great entertaining our distinguished guest who was very easy-going and quite unperturbed by my many blunders. The servants did a splendid job and were delighted with the tips he left.

Thank you for the seeds, Dad. Our garden is a perfect jungle at present but it is ablaze with huge red and yellow kannas, lots of lovely dark red and tawny dahlias and a beautiful pure white flower with great thick velvety petals and a glorious scent. I have picked six vases full of flowers for the house.   We are going to get a man to help in the garden and look after the cow which we are hoping to get.

With love
Ruth

John

Yingshan   June 16th

Dear Friends and Supporters

Here at *Yingshan* there are six "outstations" connected with us, towns and villages situated between 20 and 40 miles from the city where there are Christians, churches and church premises. They have not been systematically visited for years, and the recent trouble has for some Christians quenched the remaining flicker of life whilst for others it has brought a spiritual awakening. Our coming here has enabled the pastor to visit the outstations and later on I hope to visit them myself.

Meanwhile there is the work in the city, the school, the church, preaching in the street chapel on market days etc. We have started a children's service on Sunday afternoons with an average attendance of about 120. The children love "picture talks" and choruses with Chinese tunes which they sing with great gusto if not tunefully. We very much enjoyed the Bishop's visit and he was pleased with the splendid congregations and general keenness of the Church – a tribute to the faithful work of Pastor Wang who has been carrying on singlehandedly for the past three years.

We are very conscious of the heavy burden placed upon us in ministering to these people who have been so deeply affected by the recent terrible sufferings. This is a daunting new task which we can only face in God's strength and we pray that there may be a true revival. We thank Him for all His goodness to us over the past few months, for safe travelling, wisdom in times of perplexity and unfailing provision.

Yours sincerely
John Carpenter

Ruth
Yingshan   June 18th

Dear Everyone
During the past eight days we have had three visits by a thief, rather disturbing in the middle of the night! The dogs raised the alarm and there was a hue and a cry from neighbours but each time the man got away, albeit empty-handed. Then yesterday the gate-keeper found a man sitting behind the church claiming he was picking plums but we were pretty sure he was waiting to try and break in.

The Chinese have just celebrated their Fifth Moon Feast which is a national holiday and a great time for present giving. My English pupil, the pastor's daughter, gave me a pair of beautifully embroidered slippers. We also had a lot of eggs, flour, a basket of steamed "puddings" made of flour wrapped round syrup or meat and a collection of "rice puddings", i.e. little three-cornered packets of glutinous rice wrapped up in green leaves and tied together with reeds and steamed. We bought 111 peaches for 8,400 coppers, about 5d in English money. I have bottled some and made some jam.

I had a very nice enquirers' class yesterday morning and spoke to a church full of youngsters in the afternoon, many more boys than girls and so well-behaved.

<u>June 24th</u>

Yesterday the pastor, Bible-woman, John and I were present at the burning of the Lew family's idols. We had a hymn and a prayer and the pastor addressed the large crowd inside and outside the house. Then Mr Lew got to work with ladder and axe and soon the four beautifully gilt carved wooden figures, incense bowl and paraphernalia were in a pile on the ground. The wood was carried outside and set fire to where all could see and the Bible-woman preached to the crowd. During the preparations there was a bit of a diversion when two small girls started boxing each other. One finished up with a nose pouring with blood, but we mopped her up and nobody took much notice.

Later John and I went for a walk and passed two beggars crouching over the remains of the "idol fire" trying to get warm. The temperature has dropped drastically and we have had some big rains, much to the delight of the people as it was desperately needed.

<u>June 26th</u>

Once again it is sweltering and I hardly know what to do with myself.

<u>July 2nd</u>

Now it is cold and wet again which is much better, but these extremes are not healthy.

In the end Miss Warren came alone which has given John the opportunity to visit some outstations. He set out early this morning and expects to return on Saturday. There was a huge congregation at church yesterday including quite a lot of new people. Miss Warren is getting ready to open a dispensary and I shall be glad to learn some things from her. She has bought a huge quantity of lard as a base for ointments. Already several patients have been to see her as she has quite a name here as "doctor" though she has had very little medical training and what she knows she has mainly learnt on the job.

July 8th

It is lovely to have John back and he is writing separately about his escapades.

The thermometer has risen to 90° and it's an awful effort to write in this heat. We go on day after day getting drenched and always bathing and always changing. Ironically we've been buying coal for the winter which gets increasingly expensive and it is hateful to feel one is being diddled every time.

With love

Ruth

John

Yingshan   July 9th

Dear Everyone

Last week I visited several outstations accompanied by our new colporteur. The main purpose was to report back to *Shanghai* especially regarding the schools.

<u>Monday</u> Our first port-of-call was *Tien-Ch'-Dz'* (Heavenly Pool), where, equipped with camp bed and mosquito net, I stayed a couple of nights in the small CIM premises.

I was invited to the house opposite where there was a room with a huge millstone which would normally be turned by a cow or buffalo. Fixed across the top was a pole with a sort of straw collar at each end. A man came in led by his wife, followed by their little girl. He was completely blind and his wife had sight in only one eye. After leading him to his collar the woman harnessed herself to the other, and together they started circling round and round. He told me that if they worked from dawn to dusk they could make the equivalent of 3d. per day, and his face lit up as he spoke of the joy in his heart because the Lord provided the grain for them to grind and make a living. It was so moving to see these two Christians, blind and poor yet full of heavenly light and riches.

<u>Tuesday</u> We made a vain attempt to walk to the next outstation 12 miles on. After trudging through pouring rain along paths that were streams and wading through small rivers we finally came to a large river where the stepping stones were quite submerged and we could go no further. We saw what I think was a dark grey otter with her baby in her mouth. When she saw us, she dropped the baby and ran off but the colporteur managed to catch the baby. It was a bit like a large kitten, but with a long pointed nose and black and white ringed tail, a fierce little creature which the colporteur returned to the rushing stream and it swam off to find its mother. Then back we went along this lonely, waterlogged route to *Tien-Ch'-Dz'*.

<u>Wednesday</u> The river was lower today and we got over the stepping stones and three bridges quite easily. Then, what a climb! We thought we had reached the top but the road petered out and we had to follow a path up and up until eventually we reached a small temple at the very top. We followed a road across a

long narrow ridge with very steep slopes on either side. Apart from being extremely muddy the rest of the walk was quite pleasant, finishing with a long steep descent down stone steps into *Ba-jiao-wan*. There is no regular Chinese worker there now so the people gather themselves together for Sunday worship. At the school I gave a scripture lesson and discussed school affairs with the teacher because the CIM wanted a report from me before continuing his grant.

Thursday We walked to the third outstation. The first part of the journey was fairly flat but then became very hilly. After crossing a river by ferry we climbed a long steep flight of steps and at the top followed the path through the scattered village. Once again we were welcomed by the Christians, 20 of whom had recently been baptised by the pastor and confirmed by the Bishop when he was passing through. The premises comprised a compact bungalow with schoolroom, two guest rooms, kitchen, a room for the church and a room off where the women sit for services.

By dusk, my coolie still hadn't arrived and I imagined him struggling up that last hill after an already hard journey. Two men went in search of him but had to give up when it became dark. At 10.30 p.m. he turned up in a very bad temper having started his day at 5.30 a.m. and taken 17 hours to do 25 miles. Later we discovered that he had only carried the load for about nine miles and had then hired helpers for the rest of the way. We had specifically checked with him before we set out that he could do the journey.

Friday Before leaving I interviewed the schoolteacher, took a service and visited a family who wanted to burn their idols. I found a rather grumpy old man with one idol and a tablet in his shrine complaining that someone had taken the others away. Everyone except him seemed to know that his wife was the culprit. Through the bedroom window, the local colporteur proceeded to exhort her loudly to be at one with her husband and allow us to burn the rest of the idols, but she declined.   So we left as we were not prepared to burn only some of the idols, especially as the family was divided. However the colporteur came running after us saying the wife had relented and returned all the idols so would we go back and witness the burning. We then set off for home, a very hot, hard 22 mile tramp, arriving just after dark. How good it was to be home again and to see Ruth.

Love from
John

Ruth

Yingshan   July 23rd

Dear Everyone

By the Chinese calendar, today is supposed to be the first day of the "Great Heat", though in fact it is only 76° after 94° last week! We have now been joined by Miss Allen and she and Miss Warren are such nice ladies and splendid fellow-workers.

August is nearly upon us and rice is cheaper because the folk are afraid they won't be able to sell their old stock before the new is harvested. The school is about to break up for its month's holiday and most of the meetings will cease because of the great heat. As a result of the rain a large piece of the garden mud wall fell and workmen have been here all week putting up a temporary fence to keep out dogs and thieves. I wish it was going to be permanent because it looks so pretty, but of course it lets in the smell as well!

John is at a church council meeting which promised to be quite tricky because the pastor, a very independent man who doesn't seem to recognize any authority but his own, has been appointed to *Nanpu* and is refusing to go.

August 6th

This week John had a fever and a temperature of over 102° and we feared it might be typhoid again but mercifully he soon recovered.

August 12th

The other night we heard a lot of bangs and people shouting and screaming. The sky was red and just across the little river a house was blazing furiously and we watched it collapse and burn to the ground. Now I can hear the banging as they put it up again. These houses are mostly timber structures with lath and plaster walls and tiled roofs so it won't cost much to repair, but they are mainly occupied by the poor and, of course, are not insured. It brought home to me the terror of fire and to add to the tragedy, only last month three of the five members of that household died.

We have had part of the garden cleared so it isn't quite such a breeding ground for mosquitos. The back is still very overgrown, partly with huge rambling marrow plants all over the ground and climbing up trees - a huge pumpkin hanging in a mulberry tree looks quite comical! We have had some gigantic pomelos and there are also about 40 quite large lemons on the tree.

Your new kitchen sounds very pretty and somewhat different from ours with its funny earth floor, paper windows, mud stove, zinc oven stuck round the edge with newspaper to keep the draught out and old tiles to cover the holes in the top, a tin kettle and a huge oilcan of water which serves as our "domestic boiler"! But I have four nice sparkling saucepans so they are a redeeming feature!

To answer your questions, *Yingshan* is about the same size as *Chuhsien* and is under the same General. So far I haven't discovered if it has any special industry, but probably silk because that is common to all these towns. The church is about 40 years old and our team is made up of the Misses Allen and Warren, Mr. Wang the Chinese pastor, his wife who helps with the women's work, his daughter, son and daughter-in-law who are teachers in the school, a fourth teacher, the gatekeeper, the Bible-woman, a voluntary Bible-woman and ourselves.

With love
Ruth

Ruth
Yingshan   August 9th

Dear Everyone

Thank you for your lovely letters which are always such a joy. You are doing the biggest thing you could by writing so faithfully and interestingly.

John is still not a hundred per cent fit but he keeps up the same pace and is always so loving and good to me. The other evening we were sitting on the veranda when we saw a snake two yards below us waving its head furiously! We fixed it with a light and houseboy came and killed it with a big stick. It was about two foot long and an inch in diameter.

<u>August 26th</u>

We have been packing up some of our loads ready for *Shunking* where I am having the baby. We leave in about four weeks' time, then John will return and come back to *Shunking* at the beginning of October to welcome the new arrival.

<u>August 27th</u>

There has been some disquieting news from *Tahsien* and we hear that all the town people have fled and there is much *larfoo.

<u>September 1st</u>

I am at *Chowkow* en route to *Shunking*, a few days earlier than planned because the Reds are advancing. *Yingshan* isn't in any danger yet but one never knows when panic might set in and coolies would be impossible to get, so we felt it was better to leave while the going was good. Apart from the chair-bearers dropping me once, I had a very comfortable journey in my lovely new chair which the Ladies gave me as a wedding present. John has gone back to *Yingshan* for the weekend but will return on Tuesday and then we will proceed to *Shunking*. He is a good walker, but I don't like to think of him trudging back 60 li or so in this awful heat.

All the *Tahsien* folk have had to leave just taking what they could. As you know, Lilian is also expecting her baby soon but she managed to walk 20 li and then they were able to get a boat to *Chuhsien*.

With love
Ruth

---

*larfoo   Impressing men for coolies or soldiers

Ruth
Shunking   Sunday September 9th

Dear Everyone

John duly returned to *Chowkow* and we set off for *Shunking* on Wednesday. The water was very high and we did the journey in eight hours, whereas the same journey upstream can take three days. We were greeted warmly and have met Dr Parke and the nurse who will be with us for the birth, such pleasant people, so I shall be well looked after.

Shunking is a sort of "safe haven" for missionary evacuees and there has been a stream of comings and goings. Bishop Holden has been here to support us at this time of unrest and it was a great help to have his cool judgment. He came by car with his secretary and they had a terrible journey because so many bridges were down due to the heavy rains and periodically they had to hire about 50 coolies to help them through rivers. He carried on yesterday by foot to *Paoning* where there are five ladies and one man, mostly old and frail.

September 16th

This week has been very eventful. John had a telegram from Miss Allen calling him back urgently as the situation is getting very bad again because the Military forces have retreated and people are fleeing from *Yingshan* and pouring into *Chowkow*. I had a post-card from Mr Denham yesterday to say John had arrived safely having walked all the way, 120 li (36 miles) in 12 hours. He was going on to *Yingshan* the next day to collect Miss Allen and Miss Warren and returning as soon as possible.

I have a feeling John and I will be here for a good while, but I hope not and that we will soon be able to go home. What unsettled times we are living in.

With love

Ruth

John

Hochow   September 24th

Dear Friends and Supporters

Having returned to collect Miss Allen and Miss Warren, we and ten others from *Yingshan* proceeded to *Chowkow* where we picked up more folk and the next day set off by boat for *Shunking*, plus mountains of luggage.

It was a miracle that we could get a boat because virtually all of them had been commandeered by the Military and there was just one solitary boat by the bank, bearing a seal stating that it was engaged by the "Gospel Hall" and forbidding anyone else to take it. One of the *Chowkow* workers and I stayed on board all night and with us an army officer who seemed to fancy the idea of commandeering the boat. At about midnight he was joined by some friends who took it in turns to go down below and smoke the boat-owner's opium, the rest squatting around on top talking until daybreak when they finally drifted away and we were left unchallenged! This was September18th.

Before leaving *Chowkow* we saw a bridge of boats with planks laid across from one bank to the other, each end guarded by soldiers. All day long there was a steady stream of people urgently crossing over to

Pengan as rumour had it that the Military would not allow them to leave the next day. There were men carrying loads of newly reaped rice, women with baskets containing the family bedding and a few belongings, often with babies on their backs, and little children. Many were very weary having already trudged 18-20 miles through the mud in the pouring rain. Some may have been hoping to take refuge with friends or relations but many had no homes to go to and nowhere to buy food. As evening drew on, the swarming crowd seemed to increase as the inhabitants of *Chowkow*, as well as the travellers, were all anxious to get across the river before the soldiers broke up the bridge and cut off their escape.

We only stayed briefly at *Shunking* and then, in order to relieve congestion and move further away from the danger zone, we have come another 2½ days upstream to *Hochow,* a much quieter and safer place for our baby to be born. We are accompanied by Dr Parke, the nurse and our cook and his two children.

Yours sincerely

John Carpenter

Ruth

Hochow   September 24th

Dear Everyone

You can imagine the shock of having to uproot from *Shunking* at this juncture, just when everything and everybody was ready for the birth, and to move to a completely strange place where we know nobody and have no idea how long we will be. And of course all this has incurred considerable extra expense, but we trust in God's provision.

There is pessimism abroad that the *Szechwan* troops will be unable to combat the Reds due to lack of unity and training, while the Reds seem fiercer and more determined than ever. Our hearts just ache for the people who have laboured so hard to get back on their feet since they were able to return to their land and had just gathered in a splendid harvest which now looks in danger of being snatched away. Apparently the German Consul takes a very serious view of the whole situation and it is possible that all foreigners will have to be evacuated from the province.

<u>September 30th</u>

We are settling down in this new mission station which is run by two German ladies, Baroness von Reiswitz and Nurse Lorch, both of whom are kindness itself and such fun. It is a lovely stone-built house and so much more private and suitable for the birth of our baby than the rickety house where we expected to be. These missionaries are supported entirely by senior girl students in Germany and at present it's difficult to get money out. This is tough on them as they have to pay for everything out of their personal remittance, rents for the house and preaching hall, workers' salaries, dispensary etc, whereas we only have to use our remittance for personal needs. They do get more than we do but it is a lot for them to be responsible for and it is not an easy place to work in.

With love
Ruth

<u>October 8th</u>   Our daughter, Margaret Ruth was born

Ruth
Hochow   October 19th

Dear Everyone

This is my first letter since Margaret was born since when I've had a slow recovery and today is only the second day I've been allowed up. Margaret is a very good baby and John has been marvellous looking after me and doing so much for her, and the two German ladies could not have been more caring. Dr Parke had to leave suddenly today to attend another sick colleague. He has been so kind and friendly, taking such an interest in Margaret and even bringing my meals sometimes, yet always very professional.

We hear that General Jang Sen plus body-guard and retinue are in our house at *Yingshan* and have turned out all our stuff which is now sealed and locked up in the pastor's study. Presumably the General will keep the house clean as he's frightfully strict on hygiene. In peaceful times, towns in his jurisdiction have frequent inspections, each home thoroughly examined by soldiers armed with flashlights who search under the beds etc. and then paste either a green label with characters for "clean" on the lintel, or a pink one labelled "unclean" for all the world to see. Then at the next inspection if you have earned a good mark, your previous disgrace can be covered over with a nice green ticket!

<u>October 28th</u>

I am feeling much better and am able to do much more for Margaret but Nurse Lorch keeps a strict eye on me and I may have to go *Chungking* for some hospital treatment.

General Jang has written in reply to John's letter, gushing with congratulations about Margaret (he has about 15 children of his own!). He commented how nice and clean our house was and how pleasant the garden and assured us that he would vacate the premises if we return.

With love
Ruth

John to Ruth's Parents
Hochow   October 28th

Dear Mother and Father

It is almost three years ago since Ruth and I arrived in *Shanghai*. It has certainly been a very eventful time and here we are with our precious new baby. It was sad that we had to evacuate again at such a crucial time, but we feel so thankful we have come here and are so blessed in having such wonderful hostesses. It is also reassuring to know that it is only about five hours by launch to *Chungking* where there are doctors and hospitals in case of need.

Much to my delight, there is a good deal of work for me here, and I have been helping with the Sunday services, children's meetings and street-chapel preaching. I have also been going with the evangelist to a small town about five miles away to preach to the many who flock to market, uphill work but we believe worthwhile.

Neither *Chowkow* nor *Yingshan* fell and some people are beginning to return. However, although the Red advance has been checked no decisive victory has been gained by the soldiers. Indeed, we rather feel that we are waiting for them to advance again.

With love
John

Ruth
Hochow   November 4th

Dear Everyone

Margaret is doing well and I'm feeling very fit and getting back into normal life. I'm going to take over Miss Lorch's household responsibilities which will give her more time for her Chinese work. I'm glad to say the medical treatment will not be necessary which is a great relief as travelling with such a tiny baby would have been difficult and dangerous. Oh how I wish you could see your granddaughter/niece!

Weigh Day (German scales)

November 11th

Armistice Day! How strange to be spending it with the German ladies, to whom we owe *so* much and have grown so fond of, but for whom this is a poignant day. I have been making cakes in their lovely foreign kitchen. It is a dream to see a white ceiling and boarded floor with nice tables, cupboards and aluminium pots and pans after what we've been used to.

This week Miss Lorch has been running the dispensary again after devoting all her time to Margaret and me for the first month. The other day she was called out to a very poor woman who was in labour. The two Chinese midwives were beside themselves with fatigue. The woman's face was smeared with chicken's blood and feathers, offerings to the gods, and there was mirror fixed up to scare off any visiting devil that might look in it. The woman herself was slumped on the mud floor, propped up against a bench and absolutely exhausted. Miss Lorch asked the people to remove the idolatrous things then got the woman on to the bed. Fifteen minutes later the child was born, but alas was dead, the previous five babies having suffered the same fate. The people were most grateful to Miss Lorch for her help and the nurses and neighbours turned up at her enquirers' class.

One day a woman arrived at the dispensary carrying an enormous bundle wrapped in a black and yellow striped cloth like a tiger-skin. Layer after layer of thick wadded blue and black garments were removed to reveal a very large unhealthy baby boy, with many spots, a bleeding sore, ulcers on his lower half and a hoarse, low, wailing cry. He was the fifth baby of a wealthy family and the victim of a terrible hereditary disease from which the other four had died. With a few deft touches, he was treated by Miss Lorch and was again encased in his heavy, stuffy wrappings and carried home. He hasn't been again and we can only wonder if he has joined his brothers and sisters, in spite of the "tiger-skin" which is supposed to make babies grow into strong men. He is only one of many who come daily for treatment, and who, of course, will always hear the Gospel.

November 25th

Most of my time has been taken in looking after Margaret but we are all well and happy. The biggest thrill has been the arrival of all your letters written after the news had reached you and it has been so lovely to hear all your comments.

December 3rd

"Chill December hath set in" and there is a real Christmassy atmosphere. The German ladies start their decorations on the first Sunday in Advent and the rooms are so prettily adorned with evergreens, red candles etc.

Yesterday I introduced Margaret to the women's class. One young mother was super-polite in trying to find out whether "it" was a boy or a girl and I hastened to inform her, in humble terms, that "it" was "a female". I didn't say she was a "cabbage stalk" or a "visitor" as the *Chuhsien* people call their girls. Boys are always "master of the house". All the women were most interested and I'm so glad to have this new link with them. There are few unmarried women here but these are regarded with great respect and a woman certainly goes down a peg or two when she marries.

Ruth and Margaret with young onlooker

Today John approached the Custom's Officer about the illegal taxes the Ladies were having to pay on parcels. There are three waiting to be collected but the Post Office was demanding $5 or $6 before they would release them. With passports and a British Consul's card John was able to reason with the officer who signed and sealed a statement that the parcels were to be delivered free of duty. So tomorrow the coolie will go armed with this certificate to claim the goods.

With love

Ruth

Ruth

Canadian Mission Hospital   Thursday
Chungking   December 13th

Dear Everyone

We have had to come to *Chungking* for medical attention after all and arrived yesterday. We were up at 4.30 a.m. and walked to the launch through the dark still streets with lanterns, Miss Lorch carrying Margaret. We had to go down masses of slippery stone steps, across a long narrow wooden gangway with no railings and wait in a jostling crowd until we were let on. There we sat on hard wooden seats for over three hours before setting off on the six hour journey to *Chungking*, 50 people all tightly packed in one small cabin. This was followed by a slow trip in an open boat during which poor Margaret yelled most of the time. Finally we had a longish steep ride up to the hospital, Margaret with me in a chair with John walking. Very soon we were having a refreshing cup of tea and a bath in a *real* long white bath – gorgeous!

This is a superb new hospital in a beautiful situation on top of a high hill overlooking the place where the Kia-ling River flows into the Yangtze. The Kia-ling is "our river", i.e. *Hochow, Shunking, Chowkow, Nanpu and Paoning* are all on it. Margaret is with me and John is staying with a very kind couple from the Canadian Mission.

December 17th

Ordeal over and I am feeling very fit and being discharged tomorrow. John has been an absolute tower of strength. Initially we will stay at the CIM Mission house the other side of the river which was our "home" for the first three months of this year. John has been asked to take several services over the Christmas period.

So we take a fresh step into the unknown and do wonder how much longer this wandering, uncertain life is going on. God has guided us all along up to the present so there is no reason to suppose that He will not do so now!

With love
Ruth

Ruth
Chungking   December 23rd

Dear Everyone

When I came out of hospital I was greeted by the most terrible news that John and Betty Stam had been murdered by the Reds. Betty was at language school with me and I only heard from her just before Margaret was born to say she had had a baby girl, who thankfully is safe and sound. The bodies of her two young parents were found on the battlefield. The news has cast a shadow over me and somehow made me feel different about life and work in China. I couldn't get rid of the picture of that poor little baby, left to cry, no food, no mother to care for her. But I know how good the Chinese are and I'm sure some mother took pity on the mite and looked after her until she could be taken to her Granny, who also lives in China.

I sometimes feel I couldn't come back to China after furlough, and yet I feel the need. If only we could get on with the work without being chivvied about from pillar to post. This existence makes me feel so terribly useless and I often feel I could be of much more use at home. So many people are interested in us and pray for us, and yet what are we doing in spite of all this prayer backing? And I'm so afraid that I am a hindrance to John though he insists I'm not and is such a comfort and support.

Oh my dears, you can't think how I yearn for you both and how I would love to see the old grandfather clock and Dad come in with a big bunch of holly. I'd like to go and strum on the piano, wash up the dishes with a hot tap and lots of soap flakes in the jar, and I'd like to see Margaret playing about on the lawn and rolling on the grass (when she's a bit bigger). I hope you don't mind if I let off steam like this - it helps to do so sometimes. On a brighter note, Meg is coming on New Year's Eve for dentistry and we are hoping to arrange Margaret's baptism while she is here as she is her Godmother. It will be simply wonderful to see her.

<u>December 30th</u>

Christmas seemed rather strange this year, but we had a really happy time and of course it was special being Margaret's first. We have officially been designated, at least "pro tem", to *Shunking* which we both feel very happy about. Geographically it is in a good position and less likely to be endangered by the Reds. Moreover we will have a doctor and nurses on the spot. My job will be chiefly to run the house for quite a big family which I shall enjoy, and the type of work being carried out there is after John's heart. The only drawback is the long journey at a bad time of year.

With love

Ruth

John
Chungking   January 2nd

Dear Friends and Supporters

We are staying at the CIM home in *Chungking* with fellow refugees and workers from other missionary societies in the city. The CIM has a big business department here and a Mission home, but the local Church is run entirely by a Chinese pastor who, while glad of occasional help with preaching etc. naturally cannot provide regular work for visitors.

This week we have received instructions to proceed to *Shunking*, to hold the fort while the workers go on furlough. We shall probably be taking the eight days' journey up-river in mid-February. It is a big step towards *Yingshan* though the latter is still unsafe, at least for ladies, so for the time being we shall concentrate on the work at *Shunking*. My wife is looking forward to the responsibilities of home-keeping again and also more regular work among the women while I shall enjoy the evangelistic work and studying the Bible with Christians and non-believers.

Once again the Reds seem to be breaking out in new activity in some directions.

Yours sincerely

John Carpenter

Ruth

Chungking   January 18th

Dear Everyone

1935 started well with Meg arriving in time to be Godmother at Margaret's baptism on New Year's Day. Margaret becomes more and more fascinating and is, of course, a most engrossing topic of our time, thought and conversation!

This morning we were to have started our journey to *Shunking* stopping first at *Hochow*. We got up very early and Meg and another woman went ahead to book our tickets on the launch and bag our seats. We were all ready to leave with our luggage but the coolies were very late. When we eventually got down to the launch we sat down in our seats but the crew flatly refused to take our luggage, so there was nothing for it but to come back. The whole performance will have to be repeated tomorrow and meanwhile you can imagine we're in rather a state with everything packed.

<u>Later</u>

We were in the middle of supper when a telegram arrived from Headquarters:- "Carpenter – advise delay". So now we know why we couldn't go this morning! This bomb-shell gives rise to a number of complications. Our main luggage has already gone ahead to await us at *Hochow*. It contains 1½ loads of our stuff (approx. 60 lbs) including a store order for the Denhams. Also we left one load on the launch here this morning so it will have to be fetched very early tomorrow. However, I'm quite relieved as Margaret has got a nasty cold and I was not relishing the prospect of a cold, tiresome eight days' boat journey.

January 19th

John managed to retrieve our luggage from the boat this morning and we have unpacked again. Most of our clothes are on the river at *Hochow*.

Now a big thank you for the thrilling Christmas parcel which has just arrived and contains such an abundance of wonderful surprises and treats for Margaret and ourselves, including all the beautiful garments you have made.

January 26th

I wish you could see us now on the veranda, me scribbling on my knee, John writing sideways at a small oblong table because he can't get his knees under, and Margaret in her cot gazing at the pretty pink sky which forms a grand background for the British flag waving proudly from the very impressive looking Consulate. We wait on indefinitely as it is felt unwise for the baby and me to go to *Shunking* at present, though there is a possibility John might have to go alone. I *do* hope not. Apparently there are five parcels waiting for us there! Meg is still here continuing her dentistry. Her presence is a true bonus.

With love
Ruth

Ruth
Chungking   February 3rd

Dear Everyone

Tomorrow is Chinese New Year, or the Spring Festival as it is now called, and there is a general holiday feeling abroad, different from Christmas when all the big shops are looking at their worst with stocktaking and sales on.

I wonder if you heard about the Chefoo School children and their teachers being captured by pirates. The British Navy did a brilliant job scouring the seas and discovering the ship within six hours of the alert being raised that it hadn't arrived at *Shanghai*.

February 10th

We are expecting Miss von Reiswitz here for dentistry soon and she is going to bring our load of things which landed up in *Hochow* last month which we shall be glad to see. We now have a very good woman working for us and she has made some beautiful little clothes for Margaret. This morning she mended John's flannels but unfortunately there is still a very thin patch where he sits down. His old bags for patching were left at *Yingshan,* but to my great joy a colleague was willing to swap a new yellow duster for a piece of his old "flannels" he had wrapped round his Bible. He reckoned he'd got the best of the bargain but John thought not because he said he couldn't patch his trousers with a yellow duster! Mr Denham has been able to rescue our belongings from *Yingshan*, including some treasured wedding presents, and they are now safely at *Shunking,* for which we are profoundly thankful.

John has been asked to preach at the English service on Sunday and we are pleased that he is now getting quite a few opportunities to help. He has just come back from the dentist after a rotten time having a wisdom tooth out.

We hear that the Reds have left this province and gone to *Shensi*, which is bad news for them but very good for *Szechwan* and we are expecting to be called to our station fairly soon. Meg is still stranded here because she hasn't been able to get a cabin on a steamer yet.

With love
Ruth

Ruth
Chungking   February 19th

Dear Everyone

There is still no word to proceed to our station and generally we seem to be at a standstill and almost despair of things ever being settled.

The latest craze here is for aeroplanes to fly over the city dropping leaflets. I caught one as it fluttered down and it was advertising the "New Life Movement" which is a sort of moral reform that the Government is trying to carry out – no opium dens, no wine etc.

Yesterday was John's 30th birthday and everyone rallied round to make it good fun.

Miss Von Reistwitz has arrived. She is very tired and enjoying the rest and freedom from responsibility of running her busy station. Meg has gone and I do miss her. It has been lovely having her here all these weeks.

<u>March 4th</u>

We continue to live in a constantly changing family household and several have left to return to their stations while others have arrived, including two who have come back after an abortive attempt to return to theirs as it was unsafe. We are disappointed that we still haven't been given permission to travel to *Shunking*, but we believe our superintendent is much more wary now after the re-evacuation that had to take place when he sanctioned the return of workers to their stations twice before.

March 12th

There was great excitement the other day at the arrival of Madame Kiang Kai-Shek. The streets were cleared and only those who had tickets were able to go and see her. Kiang Kai-Shek himself had been the previous week to set up his Central Government in this city.

Margaret is full of beans and gives us so much pleasure, but I'm afraid letter-writing is tending to take second place as she needs so much attention. Your letters keep coming and I do love to hear every detail of what is going on at home.

March 19th

Today John and some colleagues went to see General Kiang Kai-Shek who had sent out a special invitation to all missionaries saying he wished to meet them. When John was walking there along a narrow street he saw a bundle of rags lying on the cold wet stones - it was a dead new-born baby.

March 24th

There have been more comings and goings and one unexpected visitor was Mr Robinson, CIM Superintendent of *Kweichow* Province. General Kiang Kai-Shek had been visiting there and his aeroplane was "returning empty" to *Chungking* so he offered to bring Mr Robinson back so he could see his friends here! He didn't know he was coming until the last moment so didn't even bring a toothbrush. The Generalissimo left today with 12 of his staff and Mr Robinson has been down to the aerodrome nearly every day to see if he can get a flight back. John and I walked to a place where we could see the aerodrome and one or two planes landing and taking off. It was thrilling to watch them go up and up till they disappeared over the tops of the mountains. You would have enjoyed it Dad!

Yesterday John spoke at a meeting attended by some business people and refugees from another province. He said they were all very rich and posh. One lady asked him "Is your God a selfish god? If not why do good people who don't believe go to hell and bad people who do believe go to Heaven?" Another man, a soldier, who was in great sorrow because he had just lost his only son, was comforted by the message and said "your doctrine seems just right for me. I want to believe in God".

With love
Ruth

Ruth
Chungking   March 31st

Dear Everyone

There is no further development as far as *Shunking* is concerned, but meanwhile we are going to relieve the folk at *Hochow* for a month's much needed holiday which will give us a welcome change too.

April 7th

News of big advances by the Reds on all sides has come through and several mission stations have evacuated to *Chengtu* (the capital) which itself is not altogether safe or well protected. *Paoning* and *Nanpu* have also been taken and they are now on the *Shunking* side of the Kialing River. Fifteen ladies have left various stations and should be here on Tuesday so it will be a big crush! I shall try to keep Margaret quiet and away from people as much as possible otherwise she will get far too much attention. It is very difficult bringing up a baby in a natural way in this sort of community environment and I do hope we shall not have to be here for much longer, though the whole situation is looking quite pessimistic at the moment.

John has to go to *Hochow* tomorrow, the second trip in the past fortnight. All this travelling to and fro is very upsetting as he is trying to prepare for his exam. We have a nice bedroom but only a minute table at which it is impossible to study or write, and all our writing has to be done on our knees. If you use the dining room it means carting the paraphernalia over there and you can be sure of interruptions. John does need a study. He had such a nice one at *Yingshan*. Oh dear, this is turning into a grumble and I don't mean it to be because we know how good the Lord is to us. He has given us such a wonderful baby and having her and each other is far better than the loveliest house!

<u>April 9th</u>

I was expecting John back from *Hochow* today but he has sent a wire saying he has to stay to help with about 70 orphans and 10 nurses who are expected there soon to take refuge.

Meanwhile life continues as normal here in this big modern city which is full of contrasts. We see the cheery old-fashioned country women with tunics well above their knees and long blue cotton trousers tied in at the ankle, hobbling along on their small feet. Then there are the modern young ladies, with 3" heels, silk stockings, long silk or satin gowns over beautiful long loose trousers, earrings, sleek bobbed hair and elaborate make-up. (Bobbed hair has just been forbidden by Kiang Kai-Shek.) The coolies are nothing but skin, muscle and bone wearing just a pair of blue cotton trousers and walking along with knees bent under the huge weights they carry. Every now and then they stop and rest on their bamboos and wipe the sweat off their gleaming backs and brows.

You would be astonished to see the scowling, angry, unshaved face of the armed policeman in black cotton uniform, heavy truncheon in hand, standing on a stone pedestal in the middle of the street and "directing the traffic", i.e. mainly swearing at rickshaw coolies and chair-men. But if you were sitting next to me you would hardly know you were in China except for the coolies chatting down below and some shabby wood and plaster houses with bamboo clothes lines stuck out of the windows. Apart from that I can see mostly foreign houses, the British Consulate and behind that the French Consulate and a big Roman Catholic building.

With love
Ruth

Ruth
Chungking   April 15th

Dear Everyone

We have received the five parcels from *Shunking* which the folks kindly brought when they had to evacuate. They contained a wonderful array of gifts including beautiful home-made clothes for Margaret. She looks so sweet in them and thank you for all for the time and love you put into making them. She is such a happy baby, always bouncing for sheer joie de vivre, completely oblivious to all that is going on around her, of course.

Today a telegram came from *Chengtu* to say they will probably have to evacuate - *Chengtu* of all places – that's bad.

This morning there was an enormous fire about a mile away. We went to see the ruins and my, what a dreadful sight! Hundreds of homes have been destroyed in a huge area just outside the city wall down by the river, a poor area where most of the houses were small and very over-crowded. Everywhere was still smouldering as groups of people were scraping through the debris to try and salvage what they could. Others were hurrying to the site of their demolished homes with big bundles of matting and bamboos to erect makeshift shelters and make claim to their plot of land. Sadly several people lost their lives.

With love
Ruth

John
Chungking   April 17th

Dear Friends and Supporters
    I have had a few opportunities of work recently including leading a community service for foreigners attended by officers and crew of the British gunboat in

port, conducting a service at the Canadian hospital, preaching during the great Chinese New Year holiday to a large gathering and addressing about 700 people at a weekly Gospel meeting.

On one occasion I went with two fellow-workers for a day's preaching to the river-bank settlement, a most interesting place. Every winter when the Yangtze is at low level, several quite large villages, almost towns, spring up on the flat sandbank which becomes exposed. The houses are simply frames of wood or bamboo with bamboo mats for walls, and roofs made of bamboo, thin planks or straw thatch. They have no fronts or doors, just single rooms in which people eat, sleep, buy and sell. In April, when the water begins to rise again, there is a scramble to get their belongings safe on to the bank again, and invariably some houses cannot be rescued in time, and sometimes people are lost. I walked down a street at least ½ mile long with houses touching all the way. It was full of sedan chairs, pigs, dogs, chickens and butchers, cloth-shops, tailors, teashops with the usual heavy benches and tables and even a Post Office. It was a privilege to spend a few hours among the people preaching on the sandbank behind the houses.

Another unique opportunity was the invitation to teach English to some Communists which I accepted on condition that there should be an opening to preach the gospel. The venue was a government prison, strictly guarded by soldiers, where men who were convicted, accused or suspected of Communist propaganda were interned. There were 80 or 90 men, many quite well-educated, who were kept in good conditions with daily lectures and games. About 20 of them formed a class where I was able to teach English three times a week, never without a definite Gospel message in their own language, which seemed to interest them as much as the lesson. The Lord knows where the seed sown has fallen and what fruit it may bear.

Among the refugees here is our superintendent who has informed us that our designation has been changed to *Paoning*, when it was safe to go there. It is still further north and is one of the oldest CIM stations and the cathedral town of our district. There are schools and a big CIM hospital there. But here is the challenge! *Paoning* has withstood repeated attacks from the Communists during the past 2¼ years, but during the last few weeks has been captured by the Reds who have also crossed the river from east to west and have been ravaging quite a new area of the province. As I write they are getting so near the capital, *Chengtu*, that the Military there are preparing for a three months' siege and have ordered all foreigners to leave at once. Some missions have even engaged special aeroplanes to transfer their ladies and children to *Chungking* as evacuation is expected. The situation is far more critical than it has been since the Reds entered the province at the end of 1932, and humanly speaking, *Paoning* was never a more hopeless proposition.

Sometimes we think it is only a matter of time before the Consul orders all missionaries out of the province; at other times the thought of this new designation seems like a challenge. We pray that the Lord will make us ready for whatever work He calls us to do and meanwhile give us patience. We have already been here longer than we were in *Yingshan*.

Yours sincerely

John Carpenter

John
Chungking   April 30th

Dear Friends and Supporters

Since I wrote a few days ago the news has come that the Communists have left *Paoning* and gone on to the extreme west of the province where it is said they are much weakened by disease and the barren nature of the country. So the way is now clear for missionaries to return and I have been asked to go there with a few other men with a view to reporting back on the situation and to encourage the Christians who have suffered so much from the Red invasion. The Chinese refugees who have returned to the city report a sad story. Though buildings have not been destroyed, everything has been looted or smashed including the Cathedral organ and a valuable library. The Reds were not driven out but apparently they had business elsewhere. Sadly I will have to leave my wife and Margaret as there is no question of them coming until at least after the summer.

I have just completed my fourth language exam leaving two more to go. My wife is also studying for her fourth but Margaret keeps her busy!

Yours sincerely
John Carpenter

Ruth
Chungking   May 6th

Dear Everyone

It is Jubilee Day, quite an exciting day for the foreign community even here in *Chungking*. This morning

I went with some others to a celebration on board HMS "Peterel" while John kindly stayed in with Margaret. A posh motor launch transported us to the ship where there were many business people as well as missionaries. We gave three cheers for the King and champagne, lemonade or water was served. The Consul gave a short speech and read out a telegram from the King to all the British subjects in *Chungking*. Then we drank to His Majesty's health, followed by 20 men firing 100 volleys in five relays which was most impressive.

In the evening John and I were invited to supper and a wireless entertainment by the wealthiest Chinese family in *Chungking*, bankers. We were greeted by a young English-speaking host and ushered to straight-backed black wooden chairs with red cushions arranged in rows. We were served with cups of Chinese tea and were given nice clean little towels rung out in hot water to wipe our hands and faces. Meanwhile we listened to the wireless but unfortunately missed the beginning of the service. However, we heard the trumpets at the very end and the hymn "The Day Thou Gavest", Auld Lang Syne and the National Anthem. It was the first time I'd heard a wireless in China and it was positively thrilling to hear something that was actually going on in England and I almost shed a tear. Supper was served cafeteria-style. We each took a plate, bowl and chopsticks and helped ourselves from the many dishes spread on the large table. Everything was delicious. Unfortunately, the King's speech was so late that nobody could stay for it. Still, we really did join in the King's Jubilee celebrations, and wonder if you were listening in too.

May 7th

John had a very early start this morning as he had to catch the boat to *Hochow* where he has been invited to help at a week of special services. We have officially been designated to *Paoning* now, though I don't give much weight to mere prognostications as our actions seem to be dictated so much by sudden circumstances rather than to any plans.

With love

Ruth

Ruth

American Methodist Episcopal Mission   May 16th
Chunking

Dear Everyone

It has been a hectic week because we have moved into a spare ground floor flat at the American Methodist Episcopal Mission with Reg and Eileen Bazire and their two boys. The reason was to relieve congestion at the CIM premises and also to allow the Bazires a more congenial family life. At the CIM Mr Bazire and one boy were sleeping on the ground floor and Mrs Bazire and the other boy were on the second floor underneath the eaves where it was like an oven. When the influx arrived, the whole family were asked to move up to the attic which would have been unbearable for them.

Here we have five big rooms and several smaller ones. There is electric light but no water laid on. Our fire consists of two oil tins cut out with a grating across and built in with clay and is about the size of a saucepan.

This is a very common method of making a fire place in China. We burn coke so don't need a chimney and the coolie carries the fire outside to light it so it doesn't make smoke in the house.

The flat was virtually bare but people are very kindly lending us furniture and helping in various ways. The Bazires' coolie is head-cook-and-bottle-washer and my helper does the washing, ironing etc. It is very pleasant and Margaret is settled and the boys are delightful. John hasn't returned from *Hochow* yet but I wrote as soon as I knew we were moving and asked him to bring stores and other needed things and I expect he will arrive tomorrow. It will be lovely to have him back and I'm sure he will enjoy his new temporary abode.

<u>Later</u> John is back and has brought all our stuff so now we are a bit more civilized.

<u>May 22nd</u>

We have had a very happy week and family life is *so* welcome after months of communal living.

With love
Ruth

Ruth
AMEM   May 30th
Chunking

Dear Everyone

Today we had a C of E Communion service here in the drawing room to which 17 CIM folk came, followed by a tea-party. I did enjoy being hostess and using some of our own things. We live a hectic life here, have very friendly neighbours and it is much more interesting than at the CIM. Reg is very clever at photography and has kindly developed a film for us. We will send you some of the photos which have come out beautifully.

Very sadly our colleague Miss Darby at *Chuhsien,* died of typhus last week. She was our colleague who brought back your parcel when she returned from furlough last year. It is possible we may be asked to go to *Chuhsien* pro tem. Being a mother with a baby it is quite out of the question for me to go to our designated station of *Paoning* at present although the latest directive is that John should go there alone immediately, leaving me behind with Margaret. We are waiting to hear from Mr Hannah, our deputy superintendent, about *Chuhsien* and I'm trying not to get too excited at the prospect of going in case he thinks we should stick to the current plan. If we do go it will mean a glorious month on the hill where we have had such happy times together.

June 9th

Mr Hannah's telegram came today confirming our posting to *Chuhsien* and telling us to proceed as soon as possible. We are thrilled! We hope to leave at the end of the week, but before then Bishop Holden is coming to stay for two days and we have invited some folk to tea to meet him and we have to pack, so it is going to be a busy week.

How kind of people to enquire after us and our work. I fear they expect too much of me as my time is largely taken up with Margaret and there has been little to do at *Chungking* anyway. I do hope I can really get down to some work amongst the women at *Chuhsien*.

With love
Ruth

John
Chuhsien   June 22nd

Dear Friends and Supporters

A few days before my expected departure to *Paoning*, once again all our plans were disrupted and we received instructions to proceed immediately to *Chuhsien* to take over the work, as the missionary-in-charge had suddenly died of typhus fever. We were very grieved at the news yet so glad to be able to return to "active service" having spent six months in *Chungking* and been absent from our station for ten months. *Chuhsien* is much further from the Reds than *Paoning*, so it meant we could go together and not have to separate.

It seems strange that after so many abortive plans for our future we should suddenly find ourselves in our old "home" and the place where we were married. My wife's health had been suffering from the heat and notoriously bad climate in *Chungking*, and Margaret was also affected. Being here in *Chuhsien* means we will be able to retreat to *Chiu p'an shi* for the summer which will be a wonderful provision for our physical needs and we will also have the pleasure of meeting up with friends. There is one other worker here, Miss Fearn, who is fairly new and we believe that she and my wife will work well together.

The main areas of our work here are as follows:-

<u>Classes</u> There are three separate classes for boys, girls and outsiders, three for baptised women, one for those who want to be baptised, a separate one for the old women who live in a sort of insalubrious workhouse, and a "hearers" class. All are taken by foreigners.

<u>School</u> The school is on the compound and has about 60 pupils.

<u>Preaching Hall</u>   On market days several from our compound go and we hope will be joined by some unpaid workers.

<u>Outstations</u>   Miss Fearn and the late Miss Darby have visited some of the outstations during the last year, but most are in rather a sad state.   Both the men who used to take the services at *T'uch'i* have died and no-one is interested in carrying on without being paid.   *Sanhuei* too has been at a standstill since two-thirds of the town was burnt about a year ago.

I have no plans for the autumn, and even if I had they would probably not materialize!   Apart from all the other work, I have to attend to the business side of things which can be very time-consuming, and often the language study gets pushed to the back.

Our little girl is fit and overflowing with good spirits but difficulties affect her welfare such as food, climate, companionship, exposure to harmful sights and sounds. There is also the danger of her becoming spoilt by too much attention as, to the Chinese folk, she is a fascinating sight with her blue eyes, fair hair and skin. We pray for wisdom in bringing her up in the best possible way.

Yours sincerely
John Carpenter

Ruth
Chuhsien   July 2nd

Dear Everyone
I can hardly believe I'm writing to you from *Chuhsien* again! The journey took seven days, three by houseboat

and four days overland by a road which was badly troubled with bandits. We spent the first night in a classroom at a mission station where John had a big blackboard for a bed. We had a wonderful welcome and it is so good to be back.

Last Thursday John went to *Yingshan* where he and Pastor Wang are doing the rounds of some of the outstations. We have had some most trying hot weather which is making Margaret very fretful and I must take her up to the hill soon. At present Mrs Lo is wheeling her about in her pram with the cook's two children running alongside which makes a jolly picture! We both miss John very much and are longing for him to come back.

I have had to take over the housekeeping because Miss Fearn, who should be doing it, is unwell. It involves quite a lot of work which I enjoy and the cook is very capable.

<u>July 12th</u>

Thank you so much for the snaps, Dad. How pretty the church looks in the snow, and how very remarkable to have snow on May 17th, especially after the perfect "summer" weather of Jubilee Day eleven days before!

Everyone was astonished on Monday when John walked in at about 6 p.m., having walked all the way from *Yingshan* in one day, 170 li – over 50 miles! It is so lovely to have him back and he looks very fit and as brown as a horse.

It is so terribly hot and Margaret, Miss Fearn and I are going up to the hill on Friday. John is coming for about a week, during which he will go almost daily to preach to hundreds of pilgrims who pay a yearly visit to a celebrated "One Thousand Buddha Temple" which is situated right at the top of the hill.

With love
Ruth

John
Chuhsien   July 12th

Dear Friends and Supporters

I have just returned from *Yingshan* after a ten day visit to the city and two outstations. I led a Communion service at each place and a service at *Yingshan* with a congregation of 200 and it was so encouraging to see the Christians standing firm despite all they have been through. I was asked to see a young man who was given to wild fits. He had just had one before I arrived and although he was calm he was still bound and his parents refused to release him until we had prayed. Observing the usual shelf with idols and incense I asked them how they could pray for his deliverance while at the same time they were worshipping idols. The mother promptly climbed up and pulled down all the idols, incense sticks, bowls, red papers and even the shelf itself. We then had a bonfire in the street with witnessing, preaching and singing to the crowds. Later we returned to the house to dedicate it to the Lord. It was a big step for a "heathen" family to renounce their idolatry so publicly and we pray that this outward reformation may be accompanied by a real change of heart for the boy and the whole family.

The Reds have not actually been to *Yingshan* since we left last year, but they came fairly near. Some of the military who were sent to oppose them appear to have done more damage to property and treated the people even worse than the Communists.

Yours sincerely
John Carpenter

Ruth

Chiu p'an shi   July 18th

Dear Everyone

I am sitting outside our lovely bungalow on a beautiful summer morning. The sun is coming up and dispelling the mists which are fleeing reluctantly over the fir-capped mountains. It is so lovely to be in the country and beautifully cool, and already after two days we are beginning to feel like different beings! Unfortunately, John will have to go up and down to the city quite a bit to take the Sunday services. Mr Clark has arrived, also Lilian and Billy with their baby but so far the two babies are not very amicable.

July 21st

We are expecting Dr Parke and Miss Wilson soon so we will then be a very happy company of nine enjoying the most beautiful surroundings. The house too is lovely now. As you know, it was completely ruined by the Military about five years ago, since when work has gradually been done and it is now restored to its original condition.

Several children I remember from former visits hardly seem to have grown at all. We had a good crowd at the service yesterday and today a number have been up for medicines. All are very interested in the foreign babies and ask if they may see them and are quite disappointed when they are told they can't because they're sleeping.

The country boys have brought us dozens of beautiful huge fragrant white lilies which they find when they take their goats and cows around the hills. How I wish I could send you an enormous box of them! This morning a man came with some venison from wild deer killed in the night, which we shall have for dinner tomorrow. We have just bought a new cow with its one month old calf. It promises to be good so Margaret will be able to have cow's milk soon.

<u>August 6th</u>

The past fortnight has been very relaxing and enjoyable. One day we walked to Pear Tree Abbey where I went three years ago, with its countless gruesome idols. We were shown around by the chief abbot, an intelligent, forceful young man, and Miss Wilson tried to preach the gospel to him but he was impervious and content with his own religion. I could see the influence he might have over the ordinary Chinese women and the visit to the temple made me realize how little I really know about their thoughts and outlook. I feel it's not so much the idols and worship which is so grim – it is the dirt and degradation of the people, the opium, immorality, ignorance, hate and violent beating of defenceless little children. That is what I feel can only be changed by the love of Christ entering individual hearts and lives. Many modern girls don't believe in idols and are often atheistic.

We hear that two senior workers from *East Szechwan* are not returning from furlough, and with two or three workers having died the numbers are dwindling. Certainly the opportunities seem to be very few in this district and workers have been sent to other parts of China. Thankfully we have a little peace in *Szechwan* now.

<u>August 12th</u>

Today a man brought along a hare which he'd just shot, just in time for dinner so we had a treat instead of the interminable eggs and it was delicious! Our new fat black cow is doing quite well and its wee calf is brown. The sun is beating down, bees are buzzing, cicadas are deafening and our houseboy has just carried in a load of water looking very hot and sunburnt under his wide straw hat. Doctor Parke has extracted several teeth for him and he feels much better.

With love

Ruth

Ruth

Chiu p'an shi   August 18th

Dear Everyone

This morning we had the largest congregation ever and they all seemed loth to go. We feel they really come to learn and not merely to see the foreigners and it would be wonderful if they could have a permanent pastor. The medical work has been a means of attracting several people.

At present we have a beggar boy living in the water cistern and he is being treated daily by the doctor and nurse. The mosquitos are awful so we have made him a net with two strips of mosquito netting, one of Margaret's thin nappies, two pieces of an old petticoat and two pieces of an old pair of aertex pants. It overlaps the edges and on the sides and corners we have tied stones to hold it down and it fits perfectly! The lad has some dried leaves in the cistern for a bed but the smell is most unpleasant.

The time is flying all too quickly. Soon the big rains will come and it will be much cooler, and I dread the myriad of mosquitos that are doubtless waiting hungrily for our return to the city. The other day we scaled a very steep cliff to the top of one of the highest hills in the area. Amongst the undergrowth we came across an old fortress, an arched gate leading to a walled-in bit which had such an eerie and exciting atmosphere and the most magnificent view of the *Tachu* plain. The descent was a thrilling half mile scramble down the steep hillside through countryside which was full of birds, flowers and wild fruit.

Last Wednesday Billy and Lilian went down to *Tachu* for the wedding of one of their workers. About 1½ hours after they left we heard some shots and later learned there had been a robbery on the road less than a mile away. A while after, someone told us he had smelled something like a corpse on his way up and it transpired that one of the robbers had been shot and dragged into a wood nearby.

I feel so remote from life at home, partly through distance and time but chiefly through things which have happened to me. I've moved in such strange circles and have missed all the interaction with the wide diversity of people at home. Here nearly all the foreigners one meets are of the same mind and China has become so much second nature to me now.

With love
Ruth

Ruth
Chiu p'an shi

August 26th

Dear Everyone

The beggar boy has died, and within an hour the dogs started to paw him. The doctor and Billy saw that he had a decent burial.

Rumour has it that the Reds have entered the *Pachow* district again, and how we hope there isn't going to be another evacuation. Also rumoured is that there is a large band of *fei about 30 li from here, and 150 soldiers have been staying for a few days because of the recent robberies.

In the city many things are waiting to be wisely planned and managed. We feel very incompetent to take over the most difficult job we've had to date and we will need much tact in dealing with the house staff and Church members.

In October the *North* and *East Szechwan* sub synod meetings are to be held at *Chuhsien* and I shall be the hostess!

September 2nd

Our party has now dwindled to five, and it's wet and misty and we're all dressed up in woollies trying to keep warm! Dr Parke did six temporary fillings and one extraction for me before he went!

This has been a simply lovely holiday after all the stress of the past year and I feel young and normal again and so much better for the relaxation, fresh-air and fun.

---

*fei   Brigands

<u>September 8th</u>   Chuhsien

We are back in the city now and this afternoon we attended the funeral of the mother of a church member in the family home. It was a typical Chinese funeral with the coffin on display and an archway of white paper on a bamboo frame, decorated with paintings and coloured paper flowers, white paper lanterns and small table with a big photo of the deceased with a few little lights. The mourners were all wearing sackcloth with beautifully embroidered white cloths on their heads, and scrolls hung in the doorway. Usually all this is accompanied by mournful droning and beating of gongs by heathen priests who "open a road" for the dead, but instead we sang hymns and the pastor preached.

With love
Ruth

Ruth
Chuhsien   September 17th

Dear Everyone

I am very busy with the work and running the home which is part of my work. Several visitors have called, mostly teachers and girls from the government schools, and of course the great attraction was Margaret!

The other day we went for a walk into the country with the house-woman carrying Margaret on her back in a bamboo basket especially made for carrying babies. Today John and I went even further, carrying her in our arms and, at nearly one stone, she was no light weight! I am having a big tussle to get Mrs Lo, her nurse, not to pick her up whenever she cries. We're very fortunate having a lovely wide veranda but I often long for a nice quiet English garden with a green lawn and shady tree where we could put her cot or playpen.

A man has gone to *Hochow* to fetch our luggage so we will soon have our winter clothes, books, crockery and gramophone. I wonder when we will be re-united with the rest of our belongings which are scattered in six different places.

With love
Ruth

John
Chuhsien   September 18th

Dear Friends and Supporters

We have returned to the city after a very happy holiday on the hills, where we were kept in perfect safety, despite rumours of many robbers in the country around.

We are so much appreciating having our own home once again with regular work and a settled life. We are blessed with a very committed team of Chinese workers, a pastor, a Bible-woman and three school teachers. Unfortunately there is a lack of commitment amongst some of our professing Christians and senior church members and they are paying only part of their quota for the pastor's salary and he has to go short. They plead poverty and yet last week, two of the leaders invited 1,000 guests to a funeral feast for their old Christian mother, with a costly funeral to follow. However, in other areas there are signs of encouragement.

At the end of October, the diocesan meetings are to be held here. Important matters are to be discussed and much wisdom will be needed.

Yours sincerely
John Carpenter

Ruth

Chuhsien   September 25th

Dear Everyone

We are starting to get ready for the synod and are expecting between 15 and 20 foreign visitors here and 50 to 60 Chinese delegates who will stay in the school. We're racking our brains as to how to accommodate everyone and manage to feed them all for so long, and what we shall put their drinking water and teeth water in! How lovely it would be if drinking water were on tap rather than having to boil it all. We will have to get another cow as this one gives so little milk.

Along with thousands of other people, we've just lost quite a lot of money in exchange because the $1 notes in circulation are being recalled and only realize 80 cents each. They will remain legal tender until November 20th and then become waste paper. Chinese currency is frightfully complicated and we gather the Generalissimo is trying to standardise it which we can only applaud.

October 2nd

A blind beggar boy has made his "home" down by the cowshed. He is called Changuping and is about eight years old. He has a straw mattress under cover where he sleeps and spends the day if it's wet. We have given him some warm clothes and are feeding him and have written to *Liangshan* to see if they can take him into their orphanage, but his age and sex may be against him. When he was five years old he was ill and given medicine which destroyed his eyesight. His mother and her new husband didn't want a useless blind boy so turned him out to beg; there's no law here against such diabolical treatment. We would love to do so much more for him and offer him a secure home, but there is a very large population of blind children in China and if you provide for one it wouldn't be long before all the children for miles around came pleading for the same treatment, and if you gave one decent clothes they would soon be ripped off his back. If only there were some sort of institution where he could go and be properly cared for.

Changuping

October 8th

Margaret is one year old today and has had a lovely birthday with lots of presents including a dear little swing in a secure frame which John made for her. We've fixed it up on the veranda and she absolutely loves it. She has become quite a magnet for visitors and we want to use this as an opportunity for outreach.

October 15th

Our visitors arrive at the end of the week so life is hectic with all the organization and preparations. It has been absolutely pouring for the last few days and the roof has started to leak in several places!

With love
Ruth

Ruth

Chuhsien   October 23rd

Dear Everyone

We are in the middle of our long-planned synod week and life is very full. We have 17 foreigners staying in the house when normally it only accommodates four comfortably but we've managed to fit everyone in. Three more are staying at the church house, including the Bishop. As you can imagine it is a lot of hard work catering for such a large party, but our cook is doing a splendid job assisted by two men. You would have laughed to see the steamed pudding he produced one day, cooked in an enormous old biscuit tin! The women helpers are working hard and cheerfully and even the two cows are performing well, so everything is going smoothly. It is a real pleasure to be entertaining such nice guests, many of whom are friends. The meetings are all held in the church.

The synod will be followed immediately by a missionary conference when three or four more guests may be coming, so I hope the stores will hold out!

On Friday as we were about to start supper we heard a terrific beating of sticks from all over the city. Earlier we'd noticed some "fireworks" being let off but didn't think anything of it because that is a common occurrence, but it turned out that a raid had been made on the house of a rich man and he had been carried off to be held for ransom. This place is not well protected and brigandage in the countryside is rife. With this and the awful weather we were relieved when all our delegates arrived safely.

With love

John

John

Chuhsien   October 25th

Dear Friends and Supporters

Present at these meetings was Mr Gibb, the new General Director of the Mission, and I was delighted to be appointed as General Secretary for young people's work in the district. It will mean a good deal of travelling and separation, but it is the work which is dearest to my heart and I have been able to do so little since coming to China, so when the invitation came, with the support of my wife, I gladly accepted. The work will involve giving advice regarding Sunday schools to Chinese and foreign workers, training teachers, holding model classes, recommending literature, methods of register-keeping and hints re prize-giving, treats etc. and if possible doing some teaching on parenting. I have very little experience in this field and as yet feel quite inadequate for the task. I will still be responsible for the work here.

Another outcome of Mr Gibb's visit was that, out of the blue, our lady colleague, Miss Fearn, was asked to go immediately to Chefoo School to teach for about 18 months. This was a great blow but appointed in her place is Meg Scorer, my wife's best friend in China and Godmother to our daughter.

We have been having financial difficulties in the church and have now organized a free-will offering scheme in addition to the weekly collections. So far 52 people have responded and together have promised over $100 for the coming year though there are some church members who refuse to enter the scheme. One of the outstations has started something similar, one of the contributors being a little boy who asked that he should forego his daily biscuit and put the money in the collection.

Yours sincerely
John Carpenter

Ruth
Chuhsien   November 3rd

Dear Everyone
    Can you believe it – for three days after the synod, we were a houseful of 23 and two babies so as caterer I was well occupied. Everyone seemed very happy and to my delight It was mooted that the synod should be held here every year.

We had a terrific "jumble sale" while the foreigners were here, a unique opportunity to dispose of a lot of unwanted things from the premises. We raised about $220 which has gone towards clearing the debit balance which we inherited when we arrived.

Now it's down to the "regular" work after a very busy period of which I've enjoyed every minute. I am very fit again now and it is lovely to have my strength back after feeling weak for so long. Poor Margaret has whooping-cough very badly. I wish I could take her away to get some sea air. She is saying a lot of words now, more Chinese than foreign and isn't a bit shy with people.

I can't tell you how delighted we are that Meg is joining us. She has just sent Margaret a pair of silver bracelets like the Chinese babies wear. They each have three things hanging on by little chains which the babies can bite, e.g. a fish, a bee or a peanut. Margaret's has a monkey and a pistol! Mrs Lo says she is a little soldier for Jesus and considers the gun on her wristlet quite appropriate!

Our gramophone records became terribly warped after the hot summer but John has succeeded in flattening them again by putting them in the oven and we are enjoying them so much.

November 14th

We have been nearly down to our last cash over the past few weeks because although we've got "plenty" (comparatively speaking) in the banks, no one will part with their silver for cheques because of the currency crisis. This morning I gave my last $2 to the cook for provisions and I don't think John has any more, except some extra good dollars which he's trying to keep till the others are no longer useable ...... *At this point* the Post Office manager arrived with a man who had $54 in change and wanted to exchange it for a cheque for that amount. So I have just completed the transaction with the help of the cook who examined all the silver to make sure it rang true. So now we shall have enough to tide us over for a while – isn't that wonderful!

With love
Ruth

Ruth
Chuhsien   November 21st

Dear Everyone

John and I are on our own for a few days for the first time since Margaret was born which is so nice. Some evenings he has been reading to me while I knit a scarlet suit for her. Our harmonium which we left at *Hochow* has just arrived. We had only used it briefly there and hope we will be able to enjoy it longer this time, though who knows if "sudden destruction" will come upon us again. The news of the Reds is vague but not good.

Our coolie is a real treasure. He carries loads, goes on two or three day journeys with messages, helps in the kitchen, lays tables, waits at table, gardens, cuts the grass for the cows and yesterday he altered a Chinese garment for me, having originally been a tailor. Everything is done with such good humour.

November 29th

Dear Meg has arrived and I feel so happy. She is looking very well and has brought Simon, her horse and her semi-foreign dog who has been most courteously welcomed by the two Chinese gentlemen dogs on the establishment. Mr Denham is here this week taking a special mission which is being well attended and very encouraging. The news of the Reds from the west of the province is concerning and we hear that some of our people have had to evacuate again.

<u>December 7th</u>

I have been introducing Meg to a few people in their homes, and tonight we have been invited to a welcome feast by the woman who kindly held a feast for Lilian and me just before we got married. Also the church laid on an evening meal to welcome the Bishop, who is visiting. Over the past few months he has walked about 4,000 li (1,300 miles) visiting different stations – quite amazing!

Margaret is much better now and has been given a lovely present by our cook of a bamboo "back-basket" for carrying her on a coolie's back. It is like a long enclosed cylinder with a little seat inside so she can stand or sit, with her head coming out at the top. We took her for quite a long walk yesterday and it was nice to have a change of scenery and a good blow of fresh air. The house-woman carried her as far as her house then Meg's groom took her. Meg wanted a last ride on her horse before she sells it in a few days' time. Margaret has really taken to her Godmother.

With love
Ruth

Margaret with friends

Ruth
Chuhsien   December 14th

Dear Everyone

Yet another week has gone by and still no letters from you! John and the pastor went away yesterday to visit two outstations.

Changuping, our blind boy, is still with us and looks a picture in the new wadding we made for him out of old curtains and cotton wool. He has a nice new navy blue cotton gown to go over it and Mrs Lo gave him an old pair of shoes so he is quite fitted up, but it is a great problem to know what to do with him.

Yesterday I had the task of going to the girls' school to call on the head mistress, a pretty, modern woman wearing a long black foreign-style overcoat. After I had been plied with questions by the staff I was shown around the school buildings. The dormitories were plain and very neat and the classrooms were very light and well equipped and the whole place was impressive. It had been two or three old temples which were made into one big building. I do wish we could get some definite religious instruction into the school.

December 26th

We have had a perfectly marvellous Christmas, joined by our friend, Reg Bazire, who declared that apart from the fact that Eileen and the boys weren't here it was the happiest he'd had in China. (They have been at Chefoo School for the past seven months.) The house looked very festive and Meg and I made all the traditional Christmas fare. We woke up to the strains of a beautiful carol sung by an English choir – Meg was playing her gramophone on the veranda. Church was followed by the usual Chinese feast, a walk, Christmas dinner, then a hilarious evening playing riotous games. Reluctantly the party came to an end and while John and Reg finished their packing, Meg and I prepared provisions for the road, cold goose, mince-pies etc. Finally we got to bed at 1 a.m. and were up again at 6 a.m. to say our sad farewells as they left for *Yingshan*.

With love
Ruth

Meg to Ruth's Mother
Chuhsien   December 30th

Dear Mrs Rossiter

I have been here a month now and thought you might like to hear the latest news of your daughter, son-in-law and grand-daughter!

I am thrilled to be here. Ruth is so much fitter than when I saw her in *Chungking* a year ago and just like her old self. She likes being here and the Chinese love her and Margaret. We get quite a few visitors who come just to see the foreign baby. They love to hold her and Margaret shows off beautifully! She is very active and hardly ever stops talking!

Everyone says how well Ruth arranged things for the synod with so many people to entertain. We have just had a very jolly Christmas together with Reg Bazire. Now John and he have left to visit some outstations, and Ruth and I have settled down to a more staid and sensible demeanour. Ruth misses John so much and longs for him to return. He works awfully hard and everyone speaks well of him and says what a good Chinese speaker and capable worker he is.

Best wishes
Meg

Ruth

Chuhsien   January 4th

Dear Everyone

The coolie has gone to meet John at *Yingshan* taking an old bath of Miss Allibone's which a colleague is going to buy. You would be amazed to see him setting off cheerfully on a 1½ day trek with this bath on his back!

This week I had to examine all the school children in Scripture repetition. They had to say the Lord's Prayer, the Creed, Ten Commandments and four psalms. Some had nearly 100% which is not bad for six and seven year olds. Next week I have to examine them in singing which should be interesting!

As you know we have been having difficulty selling cheques for silver but I'm glad to say I've been able to acquire quite a lot of change this week so have been able to pay all the salaries.

January 10th

On Tuesday I went a long way to meet John, over the river by ferry and then on in the mud. It was market day and we had to push and shove our way through the street about the width of a Hatherleigh lane. John is now up to his eyes in accounts and has to go away again next Monday. It is so nice having him at home and not good for the soul to have so many partings.

John reports on his visit to Yingshan:-

Since the evacuation at *Yingshan*, not only had the Mission day school been closed but there was no children's work so I initiated some classes for a few young volunteer teachers and we started a Sunday school. Initially the attendance was small but the average has now risen to about 50. I also called at the home of the uncontrollable boy who I mentioned last July. Sadly he is still far from well although his mother still prays for her son. After returning home briefly I set off in the opposite direction to *Tachu* where I helped with a children's outreach project during their school holidays.

Ruth January 14th

Meg and I usually knit and talk after supper and our thoughts constantly turn towards our dear ones at home. I feel so homesick sometimes – I thought I had almost got over it but find I haven't. We conjure up in our imaginations the scene as our steamer slowly draws into the dock and we try to make out the figures standing on the quay and as we gradually draw nearer they get clearer!

January 18th

Two lovely budgets of papers and magazines arrived this week. Thank you, Mother dear, for all the trouble you take in doing up these big bundles and sending them. You would have felt fully rewarded if you could have seen Meg and me at supper last night poring over the Weldon's fashion book spread out on the table between us.

With love
Ruth

John to Ruth's Parents
Chuhsien   January 25th

Dear Mother and Father

After all our wanderings, we are very glad to be settled at last and are happy here in *Chuhsien*. As you know, I have been asked to undertake the young people's work in this district which involves quite a lot of travelling and I don't like leaving Ruth and I know she feels it greatly when I'm away but always puts on a brave face. She is such a big help to me in all the work, not so much by actually taking part in it because it is nearly all stuff I have to do personally, but by her presence and support and influence in the home.

So far I have not been relieved of any of the responsibilities I had before taking on this new role and have written to headquarters about it as I can't do both jobs properly and they are hoping to send another worker soon.

Ruth is fit and strong but she has been having trouble with her teeth. She should really see a dentist, but the nearest one is five days' journey away, the equivalent of England to the South of Italy, so it cannot be undertaken lightly.

Yours affectionately
John

Ruth
Chuhsien   January 25th

Dear Everyone

Yesterday was Chinese New Year, a very busy day, and we had several hundred people coming and going throughout the day which gave a great opportunity for preaching and selling gospels which we hope will bear fruit. Today we had another 30 or 40 visitors. The streets look very gay and all the doors have new red strips of paper down each side and across the top and colourful new paper gods pasted up. All the people are strutting about in their new clothes while the poor little beggar boys have only thin rags.

Last night John read to us the old station records going back to 1901. It was interesting to see how the work received a setback around 1927 since when it has never returned to the flourishing state it enjoyed then. John is trying to write a report of the station now.

<u>January 30th</u>

Meg has gone for a month into the country to visit some outstations with about ten other Christians. They will spend the first ten days at a place where there is no church and their base will be the country home of a rich, keen Chuhsien Christian who is making all the arrangements for their hospitality etc. Then Meg and the Bible-woman are going to some other outstations which John visited just before Christmas.

We heard the news of the King's death on Sunday. He has been such a good King and it will not be easy for Edward VIII to follow him especially in this time of unrest. We also heard that Rudyard Kipling had died.

With love
Ruth

Ruth
Chuhsien   February 7th

Dear Everyone

Today a crowd of people came to see, touch and hear Margaret. Just after they'd gone a huge procession came down the street with beating of drums and cymbals, escorting "the old dragon". This was a fearsome creature made of gaudy paper with an enormous head and huge tail borne aloft on poles, and a long snakelike body made of rings of bamboo covered with sackcloth or paper. It was carried, curling and squirming, by 30 or 40 men and boys causing a great deal of excitement. There was also a smaller dragon and some men dressed up as lions and masked players parading the streets and fooling about. I couldn't resist running to the gate to see the dragon when I heard the cymbals and drums approaching!

Changuping is still here and seems happy enough, but it is not a satisfactory life and we are hoping to get him into an orphanage or a Christian home. The old gatekeeper is good to him and takes him to church every Sunday. The problem would be if we had to evacuate but there doesn't seem much fear of this at present, although we believe there is some trouble further afield.

You asked me to tell you a bit about *Chuhsien*. It is on a nice broad river so we get good water – *Tachu* and *Yingshan* were not and we depended on the rainfall for our drinking water. Here we have to clarify the water by means of a filter, i.e. an earthenware system with sand through which the water is filtered.

The streets are "wide", i.e. almost as wide as Hatherleigh streets, with mostly two-storeyed houses made of lath and plaster on strong wooden frames, with tiled roofs. On some streets practically every house is a shop, nearly all having a counter either right across the entrance open to the street, or down one side. The streets are not like the old-fashioned ones made of stone slabs with mud squelching up in between, but the surfaces are reasonably good. We owe this to General Jang Sen when he was in command here. At intervals along each side of the streets little trees have been planted.

There are pavements too but no-one thinks of walking on them - everyone walks on the road. There are no cars, horse-drawn vehicles, barrows or rickshaws and the only method of conveying things is by baskets on poles or the backs of men and women. People are transported by chair or hua-kan. The city wall has been pulled down in parts but rebuilt as there are so many local brigands. Outside the city bounds the houses are smaller and shabbier, many with thatched roofs. All around the ground is very fertile and highly cultivated and there is barely an inch of wasteland anywhere.

Chuhsien still has a lot of temples but several have been converted into schools for hundreds of scholars who all wear uniform and look so nice. They also have playing fields and excellent teachers. There are no other foreigners apart from us now the Roman Catholics have gone. There are certain foreign things we can buy such as Palmolive soap, a good many medicines, cigarettes, cheap crockery, but no wool or colourfast cotton. Nor can we get foreign foods such as you have so kindly just sent us, which are *such* a treat.

I think John told you that I have a problem with my teeth. Very reluctantly we have decided I will have to go and have them seen to and that, as it's so difficult to take Margaret, I should go alone, leaving her to be looked after by John and Meg. It will be a tremendous wrench and I can't bear the thought of leaving my dear ones but we feel there is nothing else for it and it's impossible to wait until furlough. We have applied for the permission of Mr Hannah our superintendent and should hear next week.

With love
Ruth

Ruth
Chuhsien   February 15th

Dear Everyone
I'm passing through rather a nightmarish time, simply dreading the thought of parting from Margaret and John and he is not looking forward to it either. Margaret has

been distressingly poorly recently with a cough, nasty ulcers and swelling in her mouth, fever and loss of appetite and I do hope she will be her happy little self again before I go. She loves her Daddy and he does everything so well and I'm sure they will be all right. She really needs to come to England and spend some time in lovely Devon and walk on the clean green grass, having lovely English creamy milk and butter, water to bath in that you aren't afraid will have germs, and not the continual nagging fear that someone from the street will be touching her. There is TB in many households and the people wipe their noses with their fingers just disposing of the sputum with a shake or wipe down the door post or under the bench – ugh. The children squat down anywhere to do their business and often you'll see a dog waiting to eat it. It's perfectly horrible. Why aren't we told these things before we come out here? It's more difficult than you can imagine bringing up a baby here. Margaret seems to get any germ that's going. However, she is a happy little girl and if you could see her now you'd probably say she was the picture of health.

<u>February 23rd</u>

Margaret is much better now and I will be setting off to *Chungking* on Wednesday. Oh, how I will miss my little family and hope Margaret will be all right.

It's so nice to have Meg back again after a very busy month in the country. She was a bit lonely without any English company and somewhat tired of the over friendliness of the people who never leave one alone, even in one's own room.

<u>March 4th</u>

I arrived at *Chungking* yesterday after an uneventful five day journey by land and boat with an overnight stop at *Hochow* with our two lovely German friends. I am very re-assured to hear from John that Margaret is well and happy.

<u>March 6th</u>

I have had two long sessions of dentistry and there is still more to do so I don't know when I can turn my steps homeward. John writes regularly and is looking after Margaret so well, but I do miss them so much and am longing to get home. There are only six of us here this time, a very small number compared with our previous visits. Everyone is very friendly and I was taken for a short ride in a motor car hired by two American missionaries. There are quite a lot of cars in *Chungking*, some very posh, as are the ladies who ride in them! Fashions change quickly here and now all the smartest ladies are wearing dresses which go in at the waist and down to the heels with short tight sleeves. They wear dainty high heeled leather shoes and foreign style overcoats with big fur collars. Their hair is permanently waved with tight little curls at the nape of the neck, eyebrows are pencilled, faces powdered and rouged, and lipstick generously applied. Sometimes the general effect is very attractive and sometimes ludicrously funny. That is Miss *Chungking* in 1936!

With love
Ruth

John to Ruth's Parents
Chuhsien   March 11th

Dear Mother and Father

It was a great blow when we realized Ruth would have to go away for dentistry, and the separation has not been any easier than we feared. This is the longest time we have been apart since we were married and made me realize how precious Ruth is to me and how hard it is to be without her. With the help of Meg I am getting used to looking after my little daughter and love her more than ever now I have to do so much for her. The other day she wasn't very well, and imagining all sorts of dreadful diseases I sent a telegram to Dr Gray for his advice but she was probably just teething as thankfully she soon recovered.

    With love
    John

Ruth
Chungking   March 15th

Dear Everyone
    I have had my last visit to the dentist and tomorrow I leave by launch. I had a meticulous Chinese dentist who wore a fresh white coat every day, which I could tell by the number of missing buttons!

    John tells me Margaret is well and has put on weight. I have bought a lot of things to take home, including shoes for everyone, some bananas and apples as a treat and a big tin of chocolates which I made. Our coolie got back safely with the load I sent by him but had some narrow escapes and apparently the road is not at all desirable.

    I shall enjoy the journey back because the countryside will be looking beautiful and every step will take me nearer home.

<u>March 22nd</u>   Chuhsien

I can't tell you how happy I am to be home with my dear ones again and it is lovely to see Margaret looking so bonny.   I was also delighted to find lots of letters from home with news of preparations for Mary's wedding.   All you can tell me about it is eagerly devoured.

<u>March 29th</u>

This week we gave a feast which included everyone who had invited us, i.e. all the church council members, teachers and servants on the compound, 32 guests in all. The cook excelled himself and I think everyone enjoyed it, although as soon as they had finished eating they got up, said thank you and left! Such is the custom in China where a feast is given primarily for the food rather than the social intercourse.

The other day, Mrs Wang, the wife of our pastor, suddenly became very ill about half an hour after her husband had left to go to an outstation. Meg went to be with her and found her beating her breast, clenching her teeth, moaning and crying. She poured out all her woes to Meg after which she lay still, perspired profusely and was hardly able to speak. Meg sent an SOS asking me to go up at once with some medical books, so armed with Moore Family Medicine, a medical dictionary and bottle of brandy I set off escorted by the house-woman. When I arrived I found the room half full of people and a Chinese doctor in attendance, a very nice man who seemed to have a good grasp of the situation. He wrote out a prescription for Mrs Wang containing liquor of strychnine and she is much better now.

It would appear that the pastor and his wife don't get on. He says she's got no gumption because she can't read or write, and she says he goes off to the outstations without telling her, sometimes without leaving her enough money to buy food for the five children. Two nights before she was ill they had a terrific row and he actually beat her - and this the spiritual leader of the flock here! Can you wonder that there is deadness and no real advance?

With love

Ruth

John

Chuhsien   April 1936

Dear Friends and Supporters

One of the resolutions passed at the sub-synod meetings last October was that each parish should aim to take the Gospel to one new place every year. *Chuhsien* decided that its objective for 1936 should be *Wu-chia-ch'ang*, a large market about 12 miles away. In February, a preaching band led by the pastor spent a fortnight there and the response was most encouraging. One of the first believers was the proprietor of a large teashop who not only lent his courtyard and benches for the daily meetings but also set aside a nice guest-hall for use as a temporary place of worship. Most of those who wished to believe were women and even their unbelieving relations could recognize the power of the Gospel in their changed lives. With only the help of a few local Christians they have already contributed $80.00 (approx. £5) and bought a site for a permanent church in this town.

When the Chinese school breaks up we are hoping to arrange a special effort among the young people in *Chuhsien*. It is very difficult to get them during term time as they are at school all the week and their Sundays, which used to be free, are now occupied with the "New Life Movement" activities such as Scouts and Guides. We are at a time when Young China is waking up to new ideals of nationalism expressed in working towards better education, higher morality, improved physical culture and hygiene etc. The normal government school student doesn't have an hour from Sunday morning to Saturday night to call their own and even in vacations they have holiday tasks. This comes as a great challenge to us in trying to present the rising generation with the claims of Jesus Christ.

We are expecting another worker to join us at *Chuhsien*, chiefly to take charge of the work here so I can be freer to travel to other parishes and carry out my young people's work. We thank God that, for nearly a year, we have been able to continue our work here unhindered by the Communists, though they have been active in other parts.

Yours sincerely
John Carpenter

Ruth

Chuhsien   April 12th Easter Day

Dear Mother and Dad

By the time this reaches you I expect it will be just after Mary's wedding and it will feel strangely quiet after all the excitement. How I wish I could be there and am longing to hear every little detail.

April 19th

It is terribly close and gusty which doesn't suit Margaret at all and she has yet another violent cold and tummy upset. There is no sign of rain which is much needed for the setting of the rice.

April 26th

Thank you for your concern about Margaret's health and all our ups and downs. We're on the verge of another "down" as tomorrow John leaves for ten days to go to *T'uch'i* and we shall miss him so much.

You say that some people at home imagine how worthwhile it is out here "on the front line" preaching the Gospel to those hungry lost souls, but it isn't really like that as, in reality, the majority of people *aren't* just longing for the Gospel but we praise God for those who *are* true believers and those who are sincere enquirers. Somehow I don't think China is ever going to be a Christian country like England. I think the few here and there are going to be saved and form part of Christ's church and it is our job to give as many as possible the chance of hearing.

May 2nd

Meg is back safely after her latest visit to the country and John has gone to *T'uch'i*. Everywhere is in a prize muddle because the decorator is here colour-washing six rooms using a very nice distemper made with lime, yellow mud and cow glue – all native products. He is making a good job of it and it will be a nice surprise for John. It is terribly hot and leading up to a big rain, I think.

We have had an absolute glut of cherries and last week we made 25 lbs of jam and 27 quarts of bottled cherries, all stoned, to say nothing of what we are eating. Next we shall get apricots, then peaches, plums, pears, walnuts, persimmons, mandarins and finally oranges.

Tomorrow morning I am going to the telegraph office to send a cable to Mary and Robin and hope it will be nicely timed.

Next Day

The telegraph office man tells me that it would cost $24 to send the cable, i.e. $3.95 per word which is the equivalent of £1.10.0., enough for one of us to live on for a month. Sadly this would just be too much and I am so disappointed but know Mary will understand.

With love
Ruth

Ruth
Chuhsien   May 9th

Dear Mother and Dad

Yesterday was Mary's wedding day and I do hope it was perfect in every way. I felt like a prisoner beating against the bars trying to get out, such was my longing to be with you all. Meg's sister is getting married in July with all the family there except her, so we are wiping each other's tears away.

Our big news is that Margaret is to have a little brother or sister next January!

May 17th

Meg and I continue with the women's work but there are very few new members. The seasons always make such a difference and now people are very busy planting rice and hardly a soul comes.

Margaret is full of fun and mischief and hails her Daddy with a breezy "John" when she sees him! She talks much more Chinese than English and does a lot of things which send the Chinese into fits of laughter. Sometimes I take her to the front gate and passing soldiers or schoolgirls or women stop and talk to her and she generally plays up beautifully.

<u>May 24th</u>

We have just had a sweltering week, and now it's gone down 22° and we're all in thick clothes and woollens and still shivering. It's such a weird climate. The men came to repair the leaking roofs and had just done one day's work when the heavens opened, resulting in large round yellow sagging patches in some of the ceilings.

John is not booked to go away at all at present but he is very busy here. He has been overseeing the building of Miss Darby's gravestone. It is a massive structure and two men have already spent two days sitting on their haunches polishing the headstone with two stones which they just rub up and down, pouring water over it. Then the letters and Chinese characters have to be painted and carved on it before it can be set up.

Reg Bazire has had paratyphoid and is going to Chefoo for the summer to be with Eileen and the boys whom he hasn't since they went there a year ago. We have had a mass of most beautiful roses in the garden and now it is full of huge hollyhocks. Everything grows profusely here. Apricots are in season and we bought 660 for just over a dollar and have used them for jam-making and bottling.

<u>June 6th</u>

It is hot and getting hotter, devastating for one in my condition and I'm so looking forward to going up to the hill in a month's time. It feels so free and home-like up there, not closeted in a big compound, and I love the grass and trees and rocks to sit on. Some of the other CIM bungalows are unsafe because of brigands who are rife in most areas, but we haven't heard of any trouble locally.

With love
Ruth

Ruth
Chuhsien   June 10th

Dear Mother and Dad

I can't tell you what a thrill it was to receive your letters giving me such a vivid account of Mary's wonderful wedding day! How happy everything sounded.

John is busy planning for the effort for government school boys which he is making in July. Meg and the Bible-women are running a similar one for the girls.

Margaret loves playing with the Chinese children, who call her *Mardi, and tears around so fast that old Mrs Lo, her nurse, can't keep up with her. She loves her swing which is an easy means of entertainment and helps keep her cool. There is so little playing space most of the day as the sun blazes down on the stone courtyard and

---

*Margaret became known as Mardi and was called by this name for the rest of her life.

even when it has moved round the stone is still baking. Meg has just returned feeling much better for her visit to the country and Margaret was thrilled to see her.

June 20th

The post has just come bringing the wireless notes. It looks awfully serious for China and I wonder how long before full-scale war breaks out with Japan.

With love
Ruth

John
Chuhsien   June 17th

Dear Everyone

We are sweltering in our first heat-wave, i.e. over 90° in the coolest room of the house. We are fortunate to have a *punkah in the dining room. We have received five huge stores parcels from *Shanghai*, including two which were duplicates of our December order which was looted on the way and never reached us but fortunately was insured. As you can imagine, unpacking five huge wooden boxes containing parcels wrapped up in brown paper and string, sorting out the contents into three piles for three parties, dividing the cost of postage and insurance fairly between them, which involved first weighing the things, all took up a lot of time and contributed to making this a busy week.

The work on Miss Darby's gravestone has come to a standstill as the stonemason who is going to carve the Chinese characters has been taken off to work on the new

---

*punkah   Large cloth fan on frame suspended from ceiling

road. Apparently, they are still building the bridges and we often hear them blasting away through rock in the distance. A good deal of it is passes through rocky terrain and they will have quite a lot of levelling out to do.

My language studies are continuing and I am now giving my Chinese teacher English lessons. He has an amazingly good vocabulary of words but absolutely no idea how to string them together. There is a lot of work to be done on the Sunday school lesson course and I must fit in one or two visits to outstations before the synod. With all the station responsibilities too it is difficult to keep up with everything.

I am now using the other side of this old blue typewriter ribbon, having given it a good oiling to give it a new lease of life!

With love
John

Ruth
Chuhsien   Saturday June 26th

Dear Mother and Dad

John is taking Margaret and me up to the hill on Wednesday, staying two days then returning for a week for the young people's mission. He is so busy and looks rather thin and pale and I shall be glad when he can stay and breathe the pure air. Only two more summers after this!

<u>July 3rd</u>   Chiu p'an shi

We're on the hill, wrapped up in as many warm clothes as we've brought and wishing we had more! Several of our party have arrived including Bill and Lilian with their two little girls from *Tachu*.

Ruth, Meg, Lilian and children

Since we arrived Margaret has had an awful tummy upset and fallen prey to the almost inevitable cold which accompanies a sudden drop in temperature. John is so good and the first night he got up to her five times. He has fixed up everything in our room, strings and nails to hang things on, and sorted out various boxes and shelves which are necessary as we have no furniture apart from our beds!

July 10th

Mardi is still very poorly and as well as the upset tummy she has a horrid skin rash on her legs and thighs which I think she probably got from a child in the city. She has not been easy to look after while John is away.

July 18th

John is back. Margaret is still not right but happier and I'm feeling much better. Several of us are working towards our fourth section exams and I try to do what I can but am still nowhere near ready. We hear that Miss Sanderson is to join us in the autumn and not the male colleague after all.

We are sitting on the veranda engaged in different activities with all three babies asleep. The 3½ year old son of the tenant, a jolly, grubby little boy wearing next to nothing, has a chopper and is quite skilfully splitting wood into sticks to be made into bundles for market. The two hens are scratching about on the grass, nappies are hanging out to dry and the sparrows are gaily chirping.

With love
Ruth

John
Chiu p'an shi   July 19th

Dear Everyone

Today we had quite a number of the road-building squad and the local Military at our service but none of the usual men. For many years the Gospel has been preached in this place for a month every year but there is no church yet nor are there any baptised Christians.

We have heard from *Shanghai* that our financial requests have been granted which means that the three Chinese women workers are all being provided for. Also our church has more than reached its diocesan quota without touching the ordinary weekly collections or the "sale-of-grain" money. Of course, our liabilities are increasing but we hope that our offerings will increase so that the share of the diocesan foreign money should gradually decrease and the church become self-supporting.

It is lovely to be back in this beautiful, restful place, this time with our little girl.

Perfect balance!

July 27th

The other evening we had a lovely walk through woods and undergrowth to "Pisgah", the nearest peak which overlooks the *Chuhsien* plain, about two miles from here. There is an amazing view and you can see the winding river in nine different places. It's a great place for sunsets but you have to get away quickly to avoid too much of the woody part in the dark. When we got back we found everyone on the "lawn" reading by lamplight their home letters which had just arrived.

We have been looking at the *Tachu* side of the new road which is wilder and steeper than our side and will therefore have more hairpin bends because the road is not allowed to be too steep. It has considerably altered the look of the landscape but is going to be a beautiful drive over the mountains. Great care will be needed as there are so many hair-pin bends with sheer drops and continuous downhill slope.

Motor road under construction

From our bungalow we can see the men bedding in the small stones which they had laid to form the first layer of surface. There are about 60 men tramping up and down, singing like a team of boat rowers as they pull the huge stone roller behind them on two long ropes. Down the lines and at front and back are foremen, some guiding the pullers, others whacking lazy or tired ones with bamboos. They have to pull incredibly hard as the road is on such an incline. The poor men get nothing but their food and have to work from daylight to dark with three hours rest during the heat of the day. It really is awful. Considering that, apart from gunpowder blasting, the whole road is made by hand, it is an amazing piece of work and speaks much for the Chinese as a race of hard workers.

On Tuesday I am going down to the city to do a few end-of-month jobs such as paying wages, also to attend the wedding feast of two young Christians. The man is a male nurse at *Paoning* Hospital and the girl is the daughter of the man who did so much for us on that evacuation night three years ago, finding a boat and lending us his house across the river.

With love
John

Ruth

<u>Chiu p'an shi</u>   July 31st

Dear Mother and Dad

Dr Parke and Ken Phillips have now arrived so our party is complete with four ladies, seven men and three babies. Mardi is very fit and jolly now and quite at home with all the "uncles". Before we left the city I was giving her four or five baths a day because of the heat, but now she only needs one. We are all benefiting by being here and feel so grateful for such a lovely refuge. Sad to say, after we get back, John has to go away for a month for children's work.

<u>August 7th</u>

I'm sitting up in the new "workhouse" which we have had put up this year. It consists of three trees and a stout post for the fourth corner, roofed with fairly thick planks of wood which gives protection from the sun. There is a trestle table and benches so it is a very convenient place away from the bungalow to study or be quiet, also an excellent place for the Sunday children's service which hitherto has been held in the boiling sun. There is a gorgeous breeze and all round I can hear "scissor-grinders" (cicadas) making such a noise.

Dr Parke has just done some dentistry for John, and his present victim is Meg.

<u>August 16th</u>

This week when the men were out walking, they discovered two caves. They couldn't get quite near enough the first but threw a stone down which took several seconds to land at the bottom so it must have been pretty deep and was probably the dry bed of an underground river. They explored the second cave with lanterns and torches which was exciting, except that it was very dirty and full of bats!

Another excitement was the long-awaited picnic in a lovely spot about a mile away. The cowboy carried Mardi in a basket on his back which she loved. After a while John took her back and put her to bed while I stayed and enjoyed the picnic. We had a delicious supper followed by games and songs around the fire, finishing with Auld Lang Syne and the National Anthem. We sang choruses all the way home arriving back after dark. It was such fun and all the nicer because we weren't being watched all the time.

John and Meg

The men are going down to the village to take an open air meeting tonight. Margaret is very happy and does so enjoy the company of Bill and Lilian's little girl and all these "uncles" and has a craze for a goat and a cow which live on the road nearby.

We are very disappointed because it now seems as though we may not be getting an extra worker after all as the need is greater elsewhere.

<u>August 21st</u>

John is being perfectly wonderful and really doing more than his share with Margaret, letting me go for lovely long walks with the others while he looks after her. The other day I went with Dr Parke and Ken to explore the cave I mentioned last week which was thrilling. It was pitch black and very cool with bats hanging on the roof, singly or in clusters. We had to walk very carefully along the slippery rocks, some thickly coated in bat droppings which we christened the "Axminster carpet", grabbing on to anything we could and sometimes having to stoop nearly double. It seemed never-ending and when at last we emerged, with hands completely black, it felt like walking into an oven.

<u>August 30th</u>

Our time is nearly over and we return to the city next Tuesday. It has been such a happy, healthy holiday, living an open-air life, enjoying long walks in the beautiful countryside and sharing fun and fellowship with our friends. I feel a different woman and far more able to cope. The staff have been amazing. We are so pleased that Dr Parke has agreed to be with us again for the birth in January, and Miss Wilson is going to be our nurse.

With love
Ruth

Ruth

Chuhsien   September 5th

Dear Mother and Dad

I have some lovely news. Meg and Ken are engaged! I am overjoyed for them. Ken is such a nice person, so witty, and he delights Mardi with his endless drawings. They are so well matched and I'm sure will be most happy together. They have sent a cable to Meg's parents and await their approval before making it public. It is probable that the wedding will be here in the spring.

We arrived back on Tuesday, and Mardi was delighted to see her little Chinese playmates again. She doesn't seem a bit upset by the change of temperature this time, though it is terribly hot and the mosquitos are awful.

September 12th

Meg is exuberant because she has received her parent's cable giving their official approval of her marriage to Ken. So now they can start planning.

John couldn't go on his itinerary last week because of another very painful abscess in his ear, but all being well he will leave next Wednesday and will only be away for three weeks instead of four. I have been encouraged by the number of government school girls who are coming to the Sunday class which is my bit of work and a big responsibility.

September 15th

Thank you so very much for your kind gift for Changuping which will be a big help towards his keep. The plan is for the *Chuhsien* church council to have the guardianship of him, and for us to invest with them sufficient funds to keep him for life. We need the sum of $150.00 and have already got about $34 towards it with more promised so I don't think it will be difficult to reach our goal. Your gift is a sure seal on our plan! We feel we need to make arrangements before our furlough and not burden our successors with the responsibility.

Poor Mrs Ts'u, our old Bible-woman, is dying. According to Chinese custom her coffin has been fetched and now she is just patiently waiting for the transfer from life to death and longing to see her Lord. It is lovely to see her so peaceful, though sad to see her suffering.

John is quite better and getting ready to leave tomorrow.

With love
Ruth

John

Liangshan   September 20th

Dear Everyone

I duly set off for *Liangshan* walking over the hills and stayed at *Tachu* overnight. The second day was over a big mountain range to a large market where there was a letter waiting for me saying that the Post Officials considered the road to *Liangshan* unsafe. They said they would be willing for me to travel with their mail-bags under military escort, but I must be prepared to set off early and travel fast. I got up early and called a hua-kan which took my bedding in order to lighten my load.

However, the PO must have got news that the robbers had gone as they had no military escort. There was no sign of brigands and people were travelling quite freely and after a while we went at our own pace. We had to go over a double mountain range which was very wild and lonely and there have been robberies quite recently, so I was thankful for a safe journey. I made up for the absence of brigands by reading lots of Lorna Doone and learning about the times when England was the same sort of country.

There are five missionaries here and the way has been very well prepared for the mission and there is a great sense of expectation. Over the next ten days I have a very full programme of daytime and evening meetings and services, ranging from preaching in church, visiting Sunday schools to meetings for orphans and street children.

With love
John

Ruth
Chuhsien   September 26th

Dear Mother and Dad

The cook has made about 16 lbs jam from three marrows we bought for 5,000 cash (about 3d.) We use the native brown sugar which is very dear and has to be purified first of all. It took the cook nearly all day to do this with the help of the house-woman and they extracted one handful of straw and fibre and another of sand and grit. He takes a great pride in getting it thoroughly clean and it's worth it.

The other day one of the school girls aged about 13 cut the tip off the end of her finger and I treated it. She showed interest in becoming a believer but I now hear she has run away from the father who it is believed adopted her with a view to selling her later for evil purposes. She was enticed away by some man so I suppose this means a life of misery. She can't be traced, of course, and even if she could we couldn't do anything for her.

We went to quite a posh feast at the home of one of the Christians who has just had a baby son. I was amazed to see one of the guests feeding her one year old baby with something from nearly every dish. He was heartily attacking a small piece of small *un*filleted fish when he choked on a bone about half an inch long which caused him to splutter and vomit until at last he brought it up.

October 2nd

Your letters today have made me awfully homesick and long to be with you again. Two years isn't long really, but I'm so afraid of Mardi's childlike innocence being spoiled by things she would never hear or see at home. Sometimes I feel "oh to get her out of this land quickly and never bring her back". I'm so longing for you to see her. I thought you sounded a bit desolate too with all your family having left home after the many happy years we had together.

John seems to have been away for ages and I am so looking forward to his return on Wednesday. Miss Sanderson *is* coming after all but not until the end of November.

<u>Saturday 5th</u>

Last night at about 11.30 p.m. a telegram arrived! Such a commotion and barking of dogs you never did hear and the messenger had to shout for ages before he could wake anyone up. It was a telegram of congratulations for Meg from Miss Scarlett who used to be her senior worker.

The next day the cook came to me looking very serious and asking if I'd be willing to pay the house-woman's wages for four months in advance as her husband wants to start a milk selling business and he can't afford a cow. So I have advanced $20 to her and she will just get $1 per month instead of $6. We have just sold our older cow; we needed two on the hill but only one now and we will probably have to get another for Christmas and the following months when we are expecting a lot of visitors. A Chinese cow only gives about as much as a good goat at home.

With love
Ruth

John
Tien kiang   October 4th

Dear Everyone

I left *Liangshan* last Monday and arrived at *Tien kiang* the next day, met by two colleagues a few miles out.   Incidentally one of them was designated to *Chuhsien*, but, as usual with our promised workers, never came. We have had a very encouraging time with well-attended meetings, a good response among some very bright children and useful training/preparation classes for the splendid team of teachers.

My coolie from Chuhsien has come to meet me and we start off after an early breakfast tomorrow.

<u>October 10th</u>

We managed to do the three day journey from *Tien kiang* to *Chuhsien* in two, arriving just after dark, much to Ruth's amazement. In total it was about 260 li, all of which I walked except the last 20 li when a passing empty hua-kan agreed to carry me the rest of the way, only just in time as I had tramped through my walking shoes.

We have had rather a difficult time recently not being able to sell cheques and get ready money when we need it. Everyone is so keen on the "Cash on Delivery" system nowadays and pays for their purchases through the Post Office, so they don't want our cheques and we have several times been down to only a dollar or two in the house. Recently a man wanted to send $1,000 to Shanghai so we took our chance and gave him two $500 cheques in return for cash though we don't usually like to have so much money in the house. It is going very quickly, what with repairs, mission wages and our own expenses.

With love

John

Ruth

Chuhsien, Sze   Thursday October 10th

Dear Mother and Dad

My dear husband got home safely after dark on Tuesday night having done the three days journey in two. I was absolutely flabbergasted! Now he is up to his eyes in the quarterly accounts for this station. Next week Mr and Mrs Hannah and Ken are coming to stay so that they can meet together to discuss wedding plans

Thank you for the lovely presents you sent Margaret for her birthday which she thoroughly enjoyed. We gave her a dear little pram which we had made by the bamboo and cane man, very simple and crude but nevertheless it thrilled her.

October 15th

Yesterday Ken arrived looking very fit and happy and he and Meg are in their seventh heaven! In fact, Mr and Mrs Hannah were delayed and will not be coming until next week so Ken will have a little longer than expected with his beloved.

It really does seem as though the Sino/Japanese situation is working up to a crisis and things may become very lively in the near future. I pray that if we have to evacuate it may be *soon*, and not *after* the baby is born. One never knows the way things are going to take.

Meg, Ken and Margaret

Mary does sound happy in their little home and how I should love a wee home like that with my little family. This is a hard life with so many responsibilities and worries and I do so long for furlough.

With love
Ruth

John to Ruth's Parents
Chuhsien   October 19th

Dear Mother and Father

I am in two minds about the young people's work here; I do enjoy preparing the courses for leaders and visiting the various stations and can do the clerical side of the work as well, though only have time for the essentials of both jobs. But I don't like travelling so far from Ruth especially in times of unrest and it will be harder still next year with two infants, Meg leaving and the promise of a new worker yet to materialize. Mr Hannah is here now so I will be able to discuss this and other matters with him.

Ruth is keeping fairly well but finds the climate and conditions in general rather trying, not least the servants. Today I found that, before washing one of Margaret's soiled nappies, her nurse had spread it out on a stone for the dogs to lick first to get the worst off. It's no use telling people when they don't understand our ways and that's just how they do things. Five years of this is a bit wearing, especially for Ruth, but despite all the difficulties she is so patient and faithful in her work, and always so very good to me.

Thank you for the lovely parcel which arrived recently. We so much enjoy our little English snacks. And thank you too for all the interest and love you show to us all.

With love
John

Ruth
Chuhsien   October 23rd

Dear Mother and Dad

Ken, Meg and Mr & Mrs Hannah have all left after a very happy few days together and now it is just us three. While Mrs Hannah was here we talked over the problem of Mrs Lo, Margaret's "nurse". The upshot is that we are going to dismiss her at the end of this month on the grounds of old age although we have many other reasons. I'm dreading telling her because she has worked for foreigners here for 20 years or more. We are hoping to engage Mrs Liu who used to work for Lilian and me at T'uch'i.

Dad, you said you'd like to know more about that underground stream. Well, so would we! Dr Parke found several entrances to holes leading deep into the earth all along the same chain of valleys and it seems obvious that they all lead down to the same underground river. The question is, where is its outlet? Probably half way down the mountain side somewhere but those hills are so vast that it would be hard to find it. We don't expect it will ever be explored though Dr Parke thinks that if it could be engineered it might provide a never failing source of water which, if it could be harnessed properly, could create much more fertile land and thus increase the prosperity of the people. But I don't suppose that will ever happen!

October 30th

Mrs Lo leaves tomorrow and was perfectly amenable to our faces but probably cursed us behind our backs. She has already cursed the house-woman for telling us she had taken various things, which we already knew and was part of the reason we sacked her, but it was mainly her age and need for someone quicker and with more initiative when there are two little ones.

With love
Ruth

Message from Ruth's Mother to Friends and Parishioners

October 1936

A year ago there wandered into the CIM compound at Chuhsien an eight year old blind boy. The boy's mother and stepfather had completely rejected him because of his blindness. Touched by his pitiful condition and story, Mr and Mrs Carpenter allowed him to shelter in a shed and saw that he had a small amount of daily rice and that his rags were replaced by warm garments. Perfectly content with these small provisions the little lad attached himself to the compound and here he remains.

As well as his blindness he also had a large open sore and was sent to the nearest hospital until his bed was required for someone whose need was greater and he returned to the mission station.

Now, taking into account the Carpenters' family responsibilities, the fact they will be due for furlough in two years' time and the imminent departure of their fellow worker, the problem of the little boy's future is becoming more pressing. They and their fellow workers have now devised a plan. They want to raise 150 Chinese dollars, invest it in the name of the local Chinese church and ask the Christians themselves to administer the tiny annual income for the support of the child.

Among themselves they have raised about $34 and as a seal of their plan came a gift of 10/- (about $8) from a friend at home.

Collections at meetings are not permitted by the China Inland Mission, but specific needs always arouse sympathy and interest. We therefore propose to send out in the first week of December any sums which we may have received for this special fund.

Here is a nine year old boy, blind, suffering and deserted, but learning of the love of the children's Saviour through the practical love of His followers. Can we help give this child a future?

Margaret Rossiter, The Vicarage, Hatherleigh, Devon

Ruth
Chuhsien   November 6th

Dear Mother and Dad

This past week John has been a brick looking after Mardi as I've been swotting hard for my exams next week. Every day he takes her to post and collect the letters. She runs down the street with her little basket on her back, holding the letters, inevitably collecting quite a following. They pass an old temple, now army barracks, with two large carved stone lions at the entrance which always intrigue her and she must stop and see the creatures which have not been made more handsome by being whitewashed with grey patches, big round blue eyeballs and red lips!

Mardi (Margaret) with friends

Mrs Liu started on Monday and is a real treasure and it is a joy to be able to leave Mardi in her care with complete confidence. Furthermore she and the house-woman get on very well together.

<u>November 21st</u>

The exams are over apart from the oral which includes a 20 minute scriptural address for which John will probably be my examiner! Then I hope I shall never have to take another exam.

With love

Ruth

John

Chuhsien   November 23rd

Dear Everyone

I hope this letter will reach you in time to wish you all a very happy Christmas. I wish we could be with you, but it will be especially nice to listen to your message to us on the gramophone record.

This week we have had a mason over from *Yingshan* to make us a new mud stove with a built-in oil-tin oven to replace our ancient broken one. He also brought over the bed I made years ago which will be useful with all the visitors in the New Year. A number of people will be passing through on their way to Bishop Houghton's consecration, Dr Parke and the nurse are coming for the birth and then we will have quite a few visitors for Ken and Meg's wedding.

Congregations have been rather low since the summer but we are in process of reorganizing the Sunday schools which we hope will encourage a better attendance. The numbers at Ruth's class are very erratic due to the girls often having to go to Guide parades or other school activities. The young headmaster of the boys' school has promised to become a Sunday school teacher so it is likely we shall get some of his pupils too. His father says that since his conversion, he has become a changed person and through him he (the father) has received a blessing himself and has offered to take a class.

With love
John

Ruth
Chuhsien   November 27th

Dear Mother and Dad
On Wednesday I gave the usual 20 minute address at the regular women's meeting as part of my "oral".

There was such a good attendance, including our Bible-woman, Mrs Ts'u! As you know, we had all been expecting her to die but she has made a marvellous recovery and was her usual dear old self. The women were tremendously bucked and teased her by saying that she had been lazy in doing the Lord's work and He wasn't ready for her yet. Old Mrs Lo came along too and brought a "chien" she had made for Margaret, a little shuttlecock all Chinese children love to play with. It is made of one of the old coins with a hole in the middle covered with cloth. Into the hole is stuck a bit of the bottom of a chicken's big feather cut to make a tubular holder, then into that four or five nicely coloured feathers are stuck, fanning out, so that it always falls the right way up.

Unfortunately we had to sell our cat because it was too foul, since when the rats have become bolder. One came within two feet of us tonight and the other day all the edge of the cake had been nibbled. We must get another cat.

December 4th

John has been preparing the first 12 weeks' lesson sheets and golden text cards for his new Sunday school course to send out to the stations which have ordered them. We all helped count them out and between us we did over 10,000.

We are expecting Miss Wilson, the nurse, just before Christmas in readiness for the birth. She is such a dear and I shall feel much safer when she is here. Dr Parke is arriving just before the New Year and it is so good of them both to come so far to help us, especially in the bitterly cold weather. Miss Sanderson is also hoping to get here before Christmas.

Ken and Meg are getting married on February 17th and Mardi is to be a bridesmaid. They will live at *Chowkow* where Ken is already stationed.

December 11th

Miss Wilson has been delayed which is very disappointing as it would be grim if things started and we had no qualified help here.

There has been a tragedy at one of our Mission stations where two single ladies were robbed and beaten and their evangelist murdered by the brigands. What a terrible experience for the ladies.

It was most cheering to hear how the Hatherleigh folk have taken Changuping to their hearts and are giving so generously, and good of you, Mother, to take so much trouble on his behalf. He is still living on the compound until we know what the best thing is for him and meanwhile we are so pleased that, after at least eight months, his syphilitic sore is beginning to heal. It would be lovely if we could get him into a good Christian institution where he could learn a trade. It is hard to find a really conscientious Christian family who would take him for his sake and not for financial gain. Even our cook, when we were talking about selling one of our three dogs to save on expenses, said that it was more advantageous to feed the dogs as they were worth more than the blind boy because they protected us from thieves.

Thank you for forwarding Miss Davis' letter, but between you and me, Mother dear, if there has to be a choice, please send Mary's letters rather than any others. I've not heard from her for about a month, and even if the letter doesn't seem particularly "newsy" I just love to keep in touch and hear all the tiny details. Thank you for your lovely understanding letter, Mother, which was so cheering as I do so often feel I need my dear Ma, especially at this time. How I am longing to have a real talk with you again one day!

We have just heard the news that the King has abdicated which came as a great shock. I'm sure you must be awfully upset about the state of things in the Royal family.

December 20th

John seems to think things may be very serious for China as there are a lot of rumours that Kiang Kai-Shek has lost his power and the men who have deposed him want to make an alliance with Russia. I do shrink from any more evacuations especially with two infants to care for.

It has been a very busy time for us all as John and Meg have been running a ten day series of meetings for enquirers and leaders from all the outstations and I've been preparing the refreshments. Miss Sanderson is not coming until after Christmas after all.

With love
Ruth

Ruth
Chuhsien   December 26th

Dear Mother and Dad

It was good to welcome Amy Wilson just before Christmas. It was quite a quiet one which was lovely after such a busy period. On Christmas Eve we had open house for all the women and girls and about 70 came, including children. They had an uproarious time playing games etc, and John showed them his beautiful set of Christmas slides and explained the Christmas story.

The pastor gave us a goose which his servant brought round in a basket on his back, also a hen, a pound of sugar and about 40 oranges. We have had literally hundreds of oranges given to us, five chickens about 60 eggs and five packets of sugar. Of course, Mardi enjoyed the excitement and was spoiled by the number of presents she had.

I was amazed and overjoyed to hear that over £14 had been given for Changuping. Miss Wilson thinks it will be great if we can get him into the Blind School at *Hankow* and she is writing to ask a friend who knows the people who run it. For Christmas we gave him a lovely scarf, some nice woolly mittens and a mouth organ, the strains of which I can hear floating up to me at this very moment. Three of the women on the compound made him a nice pair of shoes out of the cloth of an old pair of shorts of John's, the first pair of his own he has had since he came to us, and he is very proud of them.

With love
Ruth

1937

Ruth
Chuhsien   January 2nd

Dear Mother and Dad

Dr Parke and Miss Sanderson, our new worker, have both arrived. She is very nice and I'm sure we will be very happy, though I shall miss Meg hugely.

January 8th

Everything is ready for the new arrival, and I'm anxious he/she will put in an appearance by the 17th as in Chinese eyes it would be a breach of etiquette to attend church for Meg's wedding in less than a full month after the birth. Meg's engagement ring and wedding dress material still haven't arrived from *Shanghai*. This morning three men came to make her a silk wadded quilt for her trousseau, a very posh garment which every bride should have. She has also had her sedan chair repaired and re-curtained so it is looking splendid and ready for the bridal journey.

Next weekend we are expecting quite a crowd on their way to the synod at *Shunking*. We have received the details of the school for blind children but it is only for blind *girls* and deaf *boys* which is so disappointing but we shall keep trying.

January 13th

Our son, Peter Ronald, was born.

January 14th

By now you will have received the cable telling of Peter's arrival. Thank you so much, mother, for your dear letter which John had ready to give me.

January 17th

Peter is a lovely healthy baby, much admired by his big sister. As I'm not too fit and can't get up until the tenth day Mardi is sleeping in Meg's room but is not well and Meg is being such a brick looking after her as well as entertaining the three synod guests. Miss Wilson is a wonderful nurse and even Dr Parke has been filling all the lamps every day.

January 24th

Unfortunately I have not been progressing as quickly as I should and there was the fearful thought that I might need the same treatment as I had following Mardi's birth. However, thanks to the expert care of Dr Parke and Miss Wilson I am much better and was allowed up for the first time yesterday, my birthday! In the afternoon John and Dr Parke carried me on my chair to the drawing room where there was a lovely fire and Meg had prepared a delicious tea including a birthday cake which John had iced most beautifully. Meg has had three of my precious pictures framed so the drawing room won't look so bare when she takes hers down.

The others have had a very busy week and I wish I could have been "up and doing" instead of watching them work so hard. Three visitors came and went and we had the whole Simmonds family and two other colleagues staying en route to the synod at *Shunking*. Three of our Chinese workers have also gone which meant that John, Dr Parke and Meg had to fill in for them on Sunday as well as all the extra work at home.

<u>January 31st</u>

This week has been delightfully quiet and restful after all the hustle and bustle of last week, but on Wednesday we expect another influx on their way back from the synod to their various stations. Dr Parke left on Wednesday. He has been wonderful and gone far beyond the call of duty. Miss Wilson is staying on until Meg's wedding expressly to make sure I don't overdo things! I shall miss her terribly. At present I'm not even allowed out of the house. The cook's wife is expecting her baby any day now and Miss Wilson is going to help her too.

Meg made her cake last week, and John decorated it magnificently with all the proper equipment which she got from *Shanghai*.

With love
Ruth

Ruth
Chuhsien   February 6th

Dear Mother and Dad

On Wednesday several people travelling back from the synod stopped here for the night. We were expecting them in the evening and had the meal all prepared, but just after dinner the Simmonds family and two other colleagues arrived with a whole bevy of coolies and you can imagine the hustle and clatter as they got themselves settled while we quickly rustled up a scratch meal for them.

Having ascertained the others would not be here until the evening, John, Mardi and I set out to meet them, me in a chair. It was a glorious day and I was thrilled to be getting out into the country for the first time for weeks, but we'd only gone round the corner when we met the party arriving! I could have wept.

Eventually 14 of us sat down to supper then retired to bed after we had juggled with the sleeping arrangements to accommodate everyone. Well, what a night! At 3.20 a.m. John came in for some matches. At 4.20 the cook and house-woman got up and started clattering about in the kitchen. Then I heard someone creeping about on the veranda and found the Simmonds' nurse with a colossal charcoal fire. Then their little girl started singing the first two bars of "Jesus loves me" over and over again. Three guests started getting up and talking in quite loud voices and Peter cried on and off all night. Then the first party left at 7 a.m. and the other at 8 a.m. and at last we could get some sleep!

Now we are just six, but not for long because over the next ten days, guests will be arriving for Meg's wedding so that by the end we will be a party of about 14 plus four children. I am slowly getting back into harness again but must say I shall be very glad when it's all over.

With love
Ruth

John
Chuhsien   February 10th

Dear Friends and Supporters
Bishop Houghton was consecrated at the sub-synod meetings last month and my position as young people's

worker continues although I have said I cannot do it full justice with all the local claims and family duties. One of my big tasks is to prepare and send out Sunday school course material which takes much time and thought but is well worth it as about 20 churches are now using it.

Also at the sub-synod I was elected as one of the delegates to attend the general synod of the Anglican Church in China in April. This is an annual event attended by delegates from all over China and is held in a different diocese each year. This year it is being held at *Foochow, Fulkien,* where I was born and spent the early years of my childhood when my parents were missionaries with the *CMS. It is being hosted by Bishop Jack Hind, who happens to be my Godfather and uncle by marriage to my late aunt. So it would be a great privilege and wonderful opportunity to visit my old home and see some old friends. After much deliberation, and with Ruth's blessing and my Godfather's encouragement, we have agreed that I should go, subject to funding becoming available. It won't be easy leaving Ruth and the children for nearly two months and it is so courageous of her not only to spare me but to encourage me to go for old times' sake.

Our colporteur, Mr Hsiao, wants to retire from his full-time paid work and devote his time to visiting any of the outstations we ask him to with just a little remuneration towards his travelling expenses. This is exactly what we need, as with so many outstations we cannot give them as much attention as we ought. He

---

*CMS   Church Missionary Society

would stay two or three weeks, seeking to attract new people, teach enquirers and build up the church members.

The new Sunday school has its ups and downs. Last Sunday it was market day and not one of the six teachers turned up because they were all looking after their shops. However, we rejoice that seven members were baptised at Christmas and another eighteen are ready for training.

You may remember that *Wu-chia-ch'an* was our "Forward Movement" objective for 1936 and I am pleased to report that the work there has been most encouraging. They have raised enough money to build their own church which is progressing well. The "objective" for 1937 is *Chin-Bien-Szu*, an old outstation which became defunct several years ago through lack of local leadership.

Yours sincerely

John Carpenter

Ruth
Chuhsien   February 15th

Dear Mother and Dad

Most of the wedding party have arrived and Meg and I have been busy preparing for the wedding feast and she is doing the finishing touches to Mardi's dress. I have taken over the housekeeping again so with the two infants to see to and all the other jobs, life is pretty hectic.

Sunday February 21st

Well, Wednesday was the big day! We had the wedding breakfast here and everyone was marvellously helpful making the dining room and drawing room look charming and laying the tables decorated with bowls of exquisite violets from the garden. Meg looked perfectly lovely in a cream dress and Ken in a smart new suit and they made a fine-looking couple and the whole scene was very pretty. Mardi looked so sweet and did her part beautifully. They went away in a cloud of confetti and rose petals and fireworks let off by the Chinese following the bridal chair.

The day before the wedding we had Peter's baptism, taken by Mr Hannah in the drawing room, with Ken as one of his Godfathers.

Peter's christening

Miss Wilson left straight after the wedding with the Bible-woman and her two children, also Changuping who is going to a proper school for blind children in *Chengtu*. He was thrilled and I do hope he will be able to learn something to enable him to be independent. He was such a cheery little fellow and really useful in looking after the gate and we will miss him.

It seems so quiet now that everyone has gone, the clearing up is done and we are just our four selves. We are so enjoying not having to bother thinking about posh food, interesting puddings, making cakes, using up left-overs and managing without stores we had ordered for the occasion but haven't yet arrived. There was extra to do because all the travellers had to have provisions for the road – cakes, biscuits, butter, jam, milk, tea, sugar etc. For the past few weeks I've hardly seen anything of John and I am so happy having him to myself and he has been so kind making sure I have a real rest. Mardi says quite long sentences now and it is priceless hearing her mixing up the two languages.

March 1st

The cook is going to leave the compound and rent rooms on the street for his wife and three children as he has adopted an orphan to be a sort of servant girl. I am not sorry because the children have unpleasant minds and the boy has a perfectly rotten temper and I don't like Mardi playing with them.

Parcels and letters are fairly pouring in for Meg. We're going to keep them until their stores arrive, i.e. those specially ordered for the wedding and honeymoon and then we'll send a coolie over to *Chowkow* with them. They spent a day with us after their honeymoon and it was lovely to see them though I felt awfully sad that the parting of the ways had come. It's been so pleasant having Meg with us and we miss her so much and it has been lovely having Ken blowing in from time to time. Miss Sanderson is back again, which is very nice.

March 6th

We are delighted that a good part of the money for John's travelling expenses to *Foochow* has come in, so he is definitely going and leaves in about a fortnight's time. It will be awful having him so far away for so long but I am completely fit now and both Mardi and Peter are in the best of health and Miss Sanderson is here so I won't be alone. I am so pleased for him to have this chance of a life-time.

March 14th

Bishop and Mrs Houghton arrived on Saturday and John arranged for a three bearer chair for us to meet them. After seeing practically nothing but the four walls of the compound for weeks it was a real treat to get out into the country. We met them after about 6 li and had a picnic tea by the side of the road.

With love
Ruth

John
Chuhsien   March 16th

Dear Everyone

I am thrilled at the prospect of this trip and so grateful to those who have made it financially possible and to Ruth for sparing me. How I wish she could come too because she needs the rest and change far more than I do; I'm the one who gets out and about while she has to stay mainly within the confines of the compound.

I have had a long talk with the Bishop about the work here and the possibility of another worker coming to relieve me of some of my responsibilities. He is considering making *Chuhsien* his headquarters because of its central location and road and river accessibility.

The evangelistic band's first visit to the old outstation of *Chin-pien-szu* was heartening and about 15 new enquirers were added. They are benefiting from the teaching of Mr Hsiao who is also seeing to the repairing of the old premises. One pleasing and unexpected result of the campaign was that another derelict outstation, not on our itinerary, was visited and found to have some real new life. The old leader had become very keen again after a lapse and had begun repairing the church which had suffered from the Communists' invasion a few years ago.

A week today I shall be setting off for *Foochow*. The synod itself lasts from April 17th – 26th, but there is a 3½ week journey either way by river and sea plus several days in *Shanghai*, a long time to be away from my family. How I will miss them.

With love
John

Ruth
Chuhsien   March 19th

Dear Mother and Dad
We have had an anxious time with Mardi because she is so poorly again with aches and pains and a temperature of 103°. I do hope she will be better soon as John won't be happy about going away if she is still unwell.

March 23rd

I can hardly believe it but John has gone! Mardi and I went down to the river to see him off. She is much better so he was able to leave with an easy heart. It seems so strange for him to be going so far away for so long – over two months.

<u>March 28th</u>

Easter Day! I do hope it is being a happy one for you. It's a glorious day here and spring is in the air, but my heart is sore as I think of John getting further and further away from me.

<u>Monday</u>

I have been pretty busy since John left but both the children being well has made it much easier. Mardi had a couple of days missing her Daddy terribly but has now got more used to the idea. This afternoon I took her for a walk and we passed a group of boys about 12 years old, one of whom poured out a mouthful of the filthiest things at her. She picks up everything so quickly and hears such indelicate subjects that I always have to be on my guard. Sometimes a great crowd of schoolgirls come specially to see her having her bath. They all stand round as close as they can, ask her to speak English for them and laugh at everything she says and in general admire her so that she absolutely plays to the gallery. If the nurse takes her up to the veranda to get her away from them they all crowd up the steps to stare at her. It is so difficult bringing up children here.

John and I exchange airmails twice a week and he sounds happy and is enjoying his experiences. He told me that at one point they reached a rapid which at present is impassable to anything but empty junks. They had to get out of the steamer and walk a few li with coolies carrying their luggage then continue downstream on a smaller steamer. In fact I gather that all our mail has to come that far up the river then be transferred to junks which take it as far as the rapid. Here the mail is removed and taken to the bank and carried up to the top while the boat is guided to the foot of the rapid by one man who then jumps out with the oar and goes to land. Then, with a tow-rope the empty boat is towed up this terrific rapid at the top of which it is reloaded with the mail. What a business and isn't the Chinese PO amazing in the way it deals with such a situation.

With love
Ruth

Ruth
Chuhsien   April 11th

Dear Mother and Dad

This week we had a houseful of visiting workers who came to lead a mission so it has been quite tiring with all the catering, secretarial work and babies to look after. I'm quite glad we are a quiet little household again, Miss Sanderson and the three of us.

I've had another cause to squirm at conditions out here. One night last week Margaret suddenly woke up screaming and screamed wildly in my arms for about ½ hour speaking incoherently, not able to tell me what was wrong. At last she dropped off to sleep but about an hour later she started again and a great terror got hold of me and I just sat on my bed and clung to her and cried, and prayed. That very evening a wire had come from some friends to say that their little boy was seriously ill with meningitis and was not expected to live and I immediately thought the worst. John was over a thousand miles away, but dear May Sanderson suggested it might be worms so we gave her some santonin, and she passed three huge worms. No wonder she has felt so unwell recently, but thankfully she is much better now.

It is such hot thirsty weather. The other day I found three dead fleas in my drinking water jug, proof that the rats had been drinking out of it – ugh!

I wonder what you are all doing at home. "Oh to be in England now that April's here". It must be looking lovely. We have got masses of beautiful pink and red roses out now. I wish you could see them and the multitude of grapes.

With love
Ruth

John
Shanghai   April 12th

Dear Everyone

I have completed the first leg of my journey and am now staying in *Shanghai* for a week and have done some shopping for the family, caught up with some dentistry, addressed two meetings and attended a cathedral service which was a great treat. I set sail for *Foochow* on Wednesday and am so thrilled to be going but am already quite homesick!
April 16th

There are about 20 *Foochow* delegates on board, mainly foreign bishops, priests and deaconesses.

We are now nearing *Foochow* slowly steaming round Sharp Peak with the Pagoda coming into sight and the port beyond it. The sea is quite calm and there are a number of junks fishing all round us and a few steamers. A small sampan has just come alongside and a man held out a boathook, hitched it on to the steamer and was swung right out of his sampan and clambered up his bamboo pole on board, simply hanging on by the hook! I'm glad I don't have to board like that. Wouldn't you love to be here? It would bring back so many memories.

<u>Saturday 17th April</u>

It took about an hour from the Pagoda Anchorage to the bund, passing familiar landmarks on the way and a new motor road. Another is being built to *Kuchang* which will reduce the 1½ days journey to four hours. The *Kuling* Hills were in the distance, and ahead the ancient Bridge of 10,000 Ages which has now been reinforced with concrete and a foot-walk added either side, leaving the middle for traffic but the stone buttresses are the same.

We drove through the city to Trinity College where we registered and were given about eight invitations to various feasts, concerts etc. and we were then taken to our hosts. I am staying in the house where we used to live, next door to the Theological College where you were principal, Father, but I don't remember much of it. A friend who is a synod steward gave me a conducted tour past many familiar sites.

Finally we reached the cemetery which was looking lovely with arum lilies everywhere, and I had no difficulty in recognizing "our" little grave. (*This refers to John's two elder brothers, both of whom died as new-born babes*.) It was looking so well cared for and I believe something flowers on it most of the year. I met the caretaker and gave him a small tip and asked him to do it up especially nicely and then I will try and get a snap. (Later John returned and found arum lilies had been put on it and the grave stone had been cleaned to show the writing.)

We also saw the graves of Miss Harrison and Miss Nettleton whose remains were discovered recently as the result of a series of almost miraculous coincidences and efforts on the part of friends. Although only bones remained and they were a mile apart, yet there were personal effects by them which identified them beyond doubt. They now lie at the end of the Kuchung Martyrs' plot. So far there is no grave stone because it is all very recent and the wishes of the relatives are awaited.

(Miss Harrison and Miss Nettleton were long-standing missionaries with the CMS and were evacuating to Foochow in July 1930 when they were captured by brigands on the river. They were held to ransom but were finally shot or beheaded at the beginning of October 1930 and their bodies remained undiscovered until the beginning of 1937. This case received extensive publicity at the time and appears in Hansard after it had been raised in the House of Commons)

Sunday 18th April

Today I went to four services including the main synod service at the Cathedral. It was good to meet at least a dozen of your old contemporaries and I had tea with my Godfather and four other bishops.

Sunday 25th April

It has been a very happy and stimulating week but I am not sorry to be going home tomorrow. The business meetings have not been particularly productive but it has been nice to meet so many people and hear different points of view. In our own house we were a very happy party of four and every evening we were invited out to dinner by different folk. One day we were invited to the CMS girls' school for tea followed by a drill display, chapel, feast and a sacred concert, a most enjoyable evening. Today the organist at the British Church was unwell, and I was asked to play for all the services!

With love

John

John

China Sea   April 26th

Dear Everyone

By the time we arrived at the Pagoda Anchorage to board our ship, it was nearly midnight and there was no accommodation ready for us. So we all crowded on to the first class top deck and laid ourselves about on the floor or the long chairs as best we could. After about two hours of fitful slumber I woke up cold and strolled round the ship to find a warmer spot. All the seats in the 1st class saloon were packed with ships' servants, and in the 3rd class (to which I was entitled) the public beds were occupied by about 70 Japanese wrestlers, huge brawny fellows, wearing either a kimono or pair of short pants with or without a vest. They were swarming over the beds, some asleep, others gambling or looking on, all with their hair brushed up to the top of their heads from back, front and around and tied in a little loop or top-knot.

I returned to the top deck and had another fitful sleep until about 6 a.m. when we were turned off our forbidden territory. We then found our apartments which had been vacated for us, and had a very good foreign breakfast prepared by deaconess Clark, one of our party. Our "apartments" are *part* of a bed. The whole bed is shared by a Chinese family of four, two Chinese delegates, three American delegates, a priest, deaconess Clark, all from the synod, and myself. The bed is a big platform about 11ft x 13ft covered with rush mats on which we live, sleep and have our food. The two Chinese delegates kindly laid out their *p'uk'ais side by side which just covers my patch too so at their invitation I am sleeping on their bed. I am writing this cross-legged on the common bed with others reading, typing or sleeping all around.

Deaconess Clark has provided two excellent meals today using two meths stoves. She travelled down this way but not with 70 Japanese wrestlers on board so they had more room.

<u>April 30th</u>

I'm in *Shanghai* again and by co-incidence met one of my old schoolmasters from Trent who is now Head of the Cathedral Choir School. He invited me to tea and we enjoyed reminiscing about the old days. One evening Mr Gibb, our General Director, invited me to his private flat for an informal interview. I felt very honoured and we chatted about all sorts of things and I took the opportunity of raising the question of Ruth's hair (*see her letter of May 10th*)

<u>May 3rd</u>   Somewhere on the Yangtze

I am travelling "Chinese First" which is much cheaper than the top deck and reasonably comfortable.

---

*p'ukai   Extra light very warm quilt made of silk "cotton wool" covered in bright patterned material

I am saving two berths for the new workers who will join us at *Hankow*. You will be glad to know that the $250 which I received from the kind donors will have covered all my expenses for the trip, and the additional gift has paid for expenses incurred in *Shanghai*.

Thank you all for your thoughts and prayers during these weeks. It has not been easy to be away from Ruth for so long, and I know it has been a lot harder for her with the little ones to look after. I am so longing to see them again.

Love from
John

Ruth
Chuhsien   May 2nd

Dear Mother and Dad

John should be on his way home now so we shall soon begin to count the days till his return. Margaret *will* be thrilled and so shall I.

These last two days we've had the rain which was desperately needed to fill the rice fields and the ground looks so refreshed. Three or four days ago the Rain Idol was paraded round the streets (a bamboo and paper creature borne aloft on poles) and gongs were beaten - and the next day it rained!

Margaret is supposed to be having her morning nap, but I found her standing up and addressing the large photo of you both which hangs at the top of her bed and saying in Chinese "are you laughing?" and "are you eating peanuts?" Then she spent some moments trying to put her hands into the same position as yours,

Dad! A most gorgeous and beautifully dressed doll has just come for her by post from friends of John's in Lewisham and she is quite enraptured by it.

<u>May 10th</u>

John is expected home on the 21st and we are beginning to get excited. He will have been away 9½ weeks.

I must tell you something rather important (to me). Some time ago we wrote to Mr Hannah, our superintendent, to ask if he would have any objection to my bobbing my hair, to which he replied that although he had no personal scruples he felt he must apply to the HQ in *Shanghai*. The reply came back that the matter would have to wait until the return of Mr Gibb, our General Director. So when John was in *Shanghai* he decided to take the bull by the horns and the perfect opportunity arose when Mr Gibb invited him for an evening at his flat. John brought up the subject explaining what a great trial my hair was to me in the hot weather and Mr Gibb willingly gave permission.

Well, I should like to have got your reaction before doing this but already it is quite unbearable, so heavy, hot and sticky, and as soon as John comes home I shall get him to do the deed. Please, dear Mother and Dad, don't think I'm rebelling and saying that I'm old enough to please myself, but I feel sure you wouldn't want me to go through any greater discomfort than necessary and I know John will prefer me to have bobbed hair because this bun is unbecoming. So please, dear parents mine, give me your blessing!

<u>May 16th</u>

It is very hot and if rain doesn't come in huge quantities soon, famine is very probable. Already food is very dear, especially rice, and the poor people are living on barley which has just been harvested. Lots of beggars have died. All fish and meat is banned from sale; fortunately we have our own chickens.

You will be very sorry to hear that Dr Parke is dangerously ill with typhus. It would be heart-breaking if he were taken. Dr Gray has gone to him but I expect Miss Wilson will put him in the hands of a Chinese doctor if she can get a good one because they are particularly good with typhus.

<u>May 22nd</u>

Now we have heard the tragic news of the death of Pringle Parke, our dear doctor. I can hardly believe it and wonder how it can be that one of the very best should be taken.

Dr Parke

The children and I were all set to go quite a long way out to meet John on Friday but, much to our delight he turned up unexpectedly on Thursday evening accompanied by our new worker, Mr Iliff. His return is a great joy to us all and Mardi follows him around everywhere. He brought back a huge pile of presents including a beautiful black silk kimono for me, embroidered all over in the richest shades of crimson and lined in pink silk.

Still no rain! Food prices are going up and up, all these big fertile valleys are gasping and the harvest is seriously threatened. Outside the houses there are sticks of incense burning and blue flags with characters beseeching the gods to send rain. I was saddened to see one outside the door of a woman who had professed faith and has now gone right back to idolatry.

May 30th

John has done the deed and removed my hair so I feel very nice and cool about the head but I had an awful shock to see how old I look!

It is really quite a problem getting enough food these days of dearth, especially with an extra mouth to feed.

With love
Ruth

Ruth
Chuhsien   Saturday June 6th

Dear Mother and Dad

This week has been a nightmare because we have had thieves five times in the middle of the night. The first night I was woken by the dogs barking so roused

John who went to the gatekeeper's lodge and roused the gatekeeper and her husband. They couldn't find anything so we went back to bed. About half an hour later they saw a man crawling along the wall and raised the alarm with the most bloodcurdling scream which woke the whole compound. The thieves made off leaving their booty all along the wall including Margaret's most precious doll and the next morning we found they had consumed half a steamed pudding!

Another night we found a wretched man dressed in the most awful rags hiding under the steps. He had a Chinese flag and old vest of mine ready to wrap up his booty. As the men were chastising him another man was seen making off over the back wall. We tied up the first man until morning and then let him off with a caution. Last night we took even more precautions and although we felt apprehensive we slept well through the night, only to find that they had been again but not taken anything. This time they had given the dogs opium! So far they have not actually got into the house but have taken things accessible from outside.

If you report these crimes to the officials you have to pay a lot for the man to be detained at your expense. The Chinese have all sorts of advice, e.g. "cut off one of his ears and he won't trouble you any more" given to me by the former head of the coolie office. Some thieves have the tendons of their arms and legs cut and others are beaten on the spot and let go. We probably made a great mistake keeping our man until the morning. It is all very worrying and will make us very anxious about leaving this place so inadequately protected when we go up to the hill. Actually, the most valuable thing we have lost is peace of mind and several hours sleep and it is very unsettling for everyone on the compound.

Sunday

Last night two armed police officers were stationed outside the north wall of our compound but even so we had a slight alarm. Apparently the police force has been halved this year due to the high cost of living, so the thieves are having a field day.

Our coolie has just got back from *Chungking* with a load of sugar. The road is terribly bandit infested so we do feel grateful that he has got through safely and the load intact. Sugar is a very expensive commodity nowadays.

June 21st

The other day I took pity on a woman whose baby was woefully thin and gave her half a dollar. She followed me home saying her little girl would be a Christian if I gave her some more money. I felt dreadful refusing but knew she'd always be asking if I gave in and others would follow. I continue to take my women's class and Miss Sanderson and I have started taking the older schoolgirls alternately and are encouraged by their interest and increasing numbers. John and I are also starting to do alternate market days.

We have been overrun with rats recently and have been using some poison we bought in *Chungking* which thankfully has got rid of a lot and we have acquired two new kittens which will help. The long-awaited rains have come and the rice is planted out but the prospects of a good harvest are slight.

With love

Ruth

Ruth
Chuhsien

June 28th

Dear Mother and Dad

Today I feel like a storm-tossed ship entering harbour. Last week Margaret suddenly became feverish and for four days ran a very high temperature and I was convinced she had malaria. Following Miss Sanderson's advice I gave her a small dose of quinine which brought the fever down but made her sub-normal and listless. Then yesterday, we had just taken her temperature and she was sitting on the bed trying to make the thermometer case whistle when suddenly she plunged into the pillow with it in her mouth and gave herself an awful jab at the back of her throat. She was in such pain and we were so alarmed that we thought of sending a telegram to a doctor asking for advice, but eventually she calmed down and went to sleep. It is lovely to see her smile again today although she is still not well and trails around after us and I hear her calling "Mummy, Mummy – I want to *look* at you"! We do thank the Lord for keeping her when she is so often unwell. Only recently two colleagues have lost little ones and our hearts grieve for them.

We're getting ready to go up to the hill. There is so much to take, including a lot of kitchen equipment, linen and stores etc. I wonder what sort of house we will have when we get back to England. It will be fun making do with soap-boxes and packing cases and any odds and ends we may pick up in sales. We have a lovely lot of crockery and linen to bring back and are going to buy a Chinese carpet as a great luxury, if we can afford it.

With love
Ruth

John
Chuhsien   July 1st

Dear Everyone

One day last week our various troubles were getting on top of us and we had a long talk about applying for early furlough as we really feel Ruth needs it. She is absolutely worn out and I am pretty tired too, and there was Mardi's illness which we couldn't account for with malaria-like symptoms, not to mention accidents, also a staff problem. Then we had second thoughts and decided not to write or try to pull any strings but pray that we would be given strength to carry on. Thank you, all three dear ones, for your prayers and love.

With love
John

Ruth
Chiu p'an shi   Sunday July 4th

Dear Mother and Dad

I'm writing to you from the cool heights of the hills, a tremendous drop of 30° from the city and the change of air is quite enervating. The clouds are all around and the mist is sailing in at the windows which are just unglazed wooden partitions, closed only by shutters which keep out the light.

We had a very wet journey up and a lot of our things, camp-beds, chairs etc., are still too wet to use. Bill and Lily have arrived with their children and Mardi and Joy are playing happily together. All Mardi's English is going to the wind because Joy and her parents speak

Chinese most of the time. We are still expecting about six more guests.

<u>Monday 5th</u>

John went down to the city again today for about a fortnight because he has a lot of work to do. Mardi isn't very well again and is very sad to see him go. She is a great worry as she seems to have so many accidents and illnesses.

We have masons here who are cementing the back veranda. They make the cement of clay or sandy soil, coal dust and lime and it is fascinating to see them put great lumps of lime into the trough with cold water and watch it boil and bubble and steam. The air around is quite hot and everywhere is covered with a thin film of lime. The carpenters are also busy making beds and cupboards and putting up a little shelter.

<u>July 11th</u>

We discover that our house-woman has been pilfering small things and I am quite upset as I thought she was completely honest. Yesterday Margaret fell down ten steps but fortunately wasn't hurt. Mrs Liu, the nurse, is very tolerant of the discomforts and is doing all she can to help but I am finding the children such a handful on my own in these conditions. We have had some very wet days but it is glorious now and I keep thinking of dear Dr Parke. He was so fond of this place and we miss him so much.

We have seen three motors going along the new road so at last we are getting linked up with the outside world.

With love
Ruth

Ruth
Chiu p'an shi   Sunday July 18th

Dear Mother and Dad

It was great to see John back yesterday, and now we are all here, a party of ten plus four children. We are having a big wardrobe built in our room, which will be the only real piece of furniture. Apart from that we live in boxes and have planks for shelves. Whenever it's wet everything that's hanging up gets damp and unwearable, so we will appreciate our cupboard.

<u>July 26th</u>

Last night we spent nearly two hours dealing with mosquitos in all four of our nets. Mardi's was the worst and as well as about six mosquitos we found three B flats (bed bugs) and this morning she had lots of little red spots where the little brutes must have been sucking her blood. I have had everything out and cleaned all the beds with Jeyes fluid and washed all the sheets.

John has built Mardi a dear little house in the shrubs. The walls are made of sticks woven with bamboo, and the roof is most marvellously thatched with straw bound down with string. It is covered with a network of branches and leaves so it is comparatively shady all day long. He has also made a swing for her dolls and she spends many happy hours in this little retreat.

I have been sitting in our thatched "hut" to be quiet for writing letters and it's pitch dark now. I can hear the murmur of John's and the Bishop's voices, a faint burr from the village below, the occasional shout from the hills behind where some woodcutters spend the night and all around crickets and other insects are buzzing and an occasional bird twitters.

August 2nd

It has been pouring solidly for three days, and yesterday the Bishop and Mr Iliff decided to go and explore and got lost! We set off in three search parties and John and I were the ones who eventually found them. We had a terrifically long walk right round the top of a range, climbing up all the way, beating our way through a thickly overgrown path. For about half an hour we were shouting to them across the valley until at long last we found them at the top of Leopard Hill. They had somehow been down into the valley and up the rock face. Just where we met, the "path" went over a lot of slippery rocks hidden by ferns etc. and within the space of a minute all four of us sat down in the mud one after the other. We just sat and roared! We found our way back by the light of a lantern and a torch, squelching at every step, and finally got home at 10 p.m. Neither of them had been here before so they could never have found their own way back.

On Sundays we are having regular Bible studies amongst ourselves and lots of hymn-singing accompanied by our organ, which is so nice.

The Bishop has bought a plot of land for another bungalow up here and John and the local pastor have been helping him draw up the plans.

With love
Ruth

John
Chiu p'an shi   August 17th

Dear Everyone

We have been thinking about you and wondering what you are making of this Japanese affair. We can get daily first-hand news on Desmond Guinness's wireless, theoretically at least. The last really clear news was from *Nanking* on Saturday some of which was corroborated by London relayed through *Hong Kong*. It was reported that 200 people had been killed in *Shanghai* as a result of bombing though reports are not always reliable, of course, especially now when the wireless is used for propaganda purposes.

We are wondering how we will get our letters through to each other as we understand that the mouth of the Yangtze has been blocked and believe the Siberian route is closed too. Also I am out of touch with my bank although fortunately there is quite a lot of station money at *Chungking* so I think we are all right for the present. Apart from that we are not affected in any way here, though it must be a difficult time for those in *Shanghai*.

We have heard that Mr Bevan, our colleague from *Tahsien*, may be sent to *Shanghai* to cover another man's absence which would be a great blow. He is one of the very few experienced senior workers in the Mission at present, the aftermath of the War when so few recruits came out, and there are very few younger men to replace them. Others are due to retire and about 18 workers are due for furlough during the next two years, including ourselves.

With love
John

Ruth
Chiu p'an shi   August 22nd

Dear Mother and Dad

The other evening John and I had a picnic supper at a beautiful spot by the side of the motor road. A little group of boys tending goats came and perched near us, silently watching, and we gave them each a sandwich. We watched the beautiful reflection of the sunset and a most exquisite pink sky and as we walked back we met the moon rising, a glorious huge ball, crossed by a cloud, a breath-taking sight.

We are now getting the London news relayed two out of three nights from *Hong Kong* and daily from *Nanking* and we were very shocked to hear of the desperate fighting and fearful loss of life in *Shanghai*. We are anxiously waiting for news of our missionaries. It may mean all foreigners will have to evacuate. Everything is quiet here but prices are going up noticeably.   Fortunately our store cupboard is well stocked in some things but we shall have to do without others, I expect.

August 28th

I thought I was going to have a nice quiet hour to write as John and Desmond have taken Mardi to see the workmen cutting stone for the Bishop's new house, but four small boys have arrived and are standing quietly watching me write!

We heard yesterday that the cables to Europe and America have been cut so *Shanghai* is cut off from communication with the outside world. If they succeed in bombing the wireless stations the isolation will be pretty complete. *Nanking* has been heavily bombed and evidently large numbers of Japs with ammunition have landed at *Shanghai* though we can't be sure of the facts. We missed the news from *Hong Kong* as the wireless is barely functioning.

September 6th   Chuhsien

We came down from the hill on Wednesday and it's quite nice to be home although I do miss the countryside, the fresh air and good places for Margaret to play. Here it is all stone which is scorching hot when the sun is beating down on it.   Today is our fourth wedding anniversary and it has been nice spending most of it on our own as a family.

With love
Ruth

John
Chuhsien   September 8th

Dear Friends and Supporters

We have been asked to go to *Tahsien* to stand in for Mr Bevan who has gone to the headquarters in *Shanghai* to cover a colleague's temporary absence. I am to be in charge of the pastorate which is a much larger parish than *Chuhsien* comprising several counties. There is no Chinese pastor as we have here, and the outstations are much further from the city. Our appointment has to go through the diocesan standing committee and will only be until the Bevans get back.

When I was in *Shanghai* earlier this year, I was able to make arrangements with the China Sunday School Union to print lesson notes of their course similar to those which I have been producing for use in *Szechwan*.

These will replace our local course as from next month, so that this will relieve me of a very heavy responsibility in connection with my young people's work. I was hoping to have more time to give to other branches of this work, but it doesn't seem likely now.

Yours sincerely
John Carpenter

Ruth
Chuhsien   September 13th

Dear Mother and Dad

We are getting ready for our departure to *Tahsien* in a fortnight's time, and also have four guests coming this week-end. I have been dealing with the ginger and it delights me to think I shall probably bring some home to you. We have scraped it and boiled the syrup for the second time today. We will do it again tomorrow and then, for the final time, together with the ginger. We started with 26 lbs ginger and 18 lbs sugar so it should make a nice lot.

We hear that all the CIM workers in *Shanghai* are safe and sticking at their posts, though the noise of cannon fire etc. can clearly be heard and one day a bomb was found on the roof of the home but no damage was done.

It is a very wet day and we're having an awful battle with mosquitos. They come in an absolute cloud and one can't sit anywhere in the house without feeling sharp pricks suddenly in unexpected places.

September 21st

The first repercussion of the war has been felt here today as the street crier went around early this morning announcing that all the local militia must leave today for *Wanhsien* and probably they will have to go on to the war zone. Our house-woman's second son and our younger church-warden have to go, so it really does bring it near to home.

<u>September 26th</u>

We leave for *Tahsien* on Tuesday and have about 33 boxes packed with clothing, books, stores etc, and are also taking quite a lot of furniture, high-chairs, baths etc. which can't be packed into boxes. We will send it all by boat while we go by land and will require eleven men. We are delighted that Mrs Liu, our nurse, is coming with us.

With love
Ruth

Ruth

Tahsien   October 3rd

Dear Mother and Dad

Here we are at *Tahsien* after three days journeying on the most ghastly roads. We spent the first night at *Tachu* Mission house and the second at an inn. We were off by 5 a.m. arriving at *Tahsien* at about 7 p.m. after travelling for 14 hours in the mud! The last 30 li was appalling and we had to grope our way and were so glad when the cowboy turned up with a lantern to meet us! We *were* tired! John not only walked about 80 – 90 English miles in the three days but also carried the children for long stretches. He is marvellously strong and it doesn't seem to affect him and happily both the children stood the journey very well.

This place is *immense*! There is a long wide corridor down the middle of the house with nine bedrooms leading off, dining room, drawing room, kitchens and servants' rooms. All the rooms have fireplaces and are beautifully large and light. There is a big garden, somewhat overgrown but still full of glorious flowers and numerous fruit trees and there is a lovely big space for the children to play in.

We have three male co-workers, Donald Temple and Paddy Crockett who spend most of their time at *Kiachang*, an outstation 1½ days' journey away, and Desmond Guinness who lives here. Our two lady workers, Miss Dix and Miss Elliott, live at the other side of the city and have been so kind and welcoming. There are also three Chinese ladies, the finest honorary workers I have met. We have a cook, table-boy, cowboy, old gardener, house-woman and gatekeeper, most of whom have, I believe, been taken on to give them a job. The church is larger in size and membership than at *Chuhsien*.

<u>October 10th</u>

It was such a joy when, on Mardi's very birthday, your two lovely parcels arrived with presents for her and so many other wonderful things. What thrilled me most, Mother, was the lovely pot of homemade jam! It is delicious and just like you always used to make and reminds me so much of home.

This has been a hectic week, unpacking, altering curtains and getting the house straight, seeing to food, making Mardi's birthday cake, preparing rooms for three guests and entertaining them, and taking my first women's class. Also Mr Temple and Mr Crockett arrived on Tuesday.

<u>October 17th</u>

Our gardeners have sown about 14 different types of vegetable which are already showing signs of growth and we are still harvesting other crops. There are at least 11 pomelo trees, and something called a "soap bean" tree which is huge and has pods which we are selling. Two men climb the tree and knock them down to the ground then pick them up with the help of a small boy. They will probably pick over 200 catties for which we will be paid a copper per catty, so we will get over $2! It's called "dzow-goh" and the people use it for washing their clothes.

We are much enjoying the company of our fellow missionaries and they are so good with the children. They have all gone off in different directions now so it is just us four rattling around in this enormous place.

With love
Ruth

Ruth
Tahsien   October 24th

Dear Mother and Dad

We have had a visit from two men who told us that the thieves who stole some things from here just before we came had been caught. They advised us to try and get our things back so John went to various prisons and offices, wrote statements etc., and now the two men, who are probably members of the same gang, keep demanding money.

Yesterday in the middle of dinner John was called urgently to the ladies' house where a whole crowd of soldiers were trying to install themselves. Fortunately he seems to have succeeded in getting them to leave.

Wireless notes have come from *Chungking* giving details of terrible atrocities. There is constant bad news about the war and it is becoming apparent that ways of retreating from the country are all rather precarious if we do have to evacuate. It's not an easy time, but the peace of God *does* keep our hearts and minds. It is rather amazing how letters and parcels keep coming through. We are getting wireless notes now but they take five to eight days and it's strange to think that you know the news much sooner although you are 5,000 miles away.

Sadly Mardi broke the lovely plate Meg gave her last Christmas and her grief was great, but yesterday she spent an enthralling half hour watching the riveter mending it. With 11 pairs of brass rivets he has made a very neat job of it.

<u>November 4th</u>

Desmond's wireless is working again so we can keep in touch with the outside world.

We have been working out the October accounts and it has been the most expensive month for our board since we came to China. This place is too big for such a few of us and the cook seems to have got into very extravagant ways. We have two quite superfluous servants, one of whom has been stealing but we have no means of dismissing her. I'm doing all I can to keep costs down but everything is so much more expensive than it was at *Chuhsien*.

Last week I took Mardi to see Teh p'u, the six year old adopted son of our deaconess. He calls her "Diehdieh" (Daddy) as an unmarried Chinese woman who adopts a child is always called "Father". It would be a great insult to call her "Mother". To get to their house we had to walk through the grave-hills which was strewn with coffins half out of the earth. In one place the coffin had been broken open by dogs and there was a little pair of blue cotton trousers to show that there had been a child's body there, but devoured by the scavengers. The wealthier people have their dead buried much more deeply.

I am gradually getting to know more of the women church members who are a friendly crowd and I do wish I had more opportunities of getting amongst them. But there are plenty of dedicated workers here so I feel it's up to me to do my own job of looking after the home and family as well as I can. Truly it is a huge place to look after and Mardi and Peter both need such a lot of attention.

With love
Ruth

Ruth
Tahsien   November 12th

Dear Mother and Dad

This is my Christmas letter and it brings lots of love and good wishes from all of us. This will be our seventh Christmas in China and quite likely our last and next year we will, God willing, be spending it in one of our family homes. Won't that be simply wonderful!

I have made each of the children a silk-wadded quilt and had silk covers made for them. I bought the raw material by the catty sold in pieces about a foot square.

Then two men came and made them up. Using a Chinese quilt mattress to work on they laid down about six squares and put a bench upside down across them. Then, standing at opposite sides they both put a foot on the bench to hold it down and pulled the silk out from the hard lumpy state it was in to the utmost soft silkiness finally rubbing it down with a flattening instrument.

November 15th

Last night Mardi had awful fits of screaming and was writhing about in agony just like that time before when she had worms. We gave her some santonin which produced one worm. I wish I could keep her clear of it – it's so horrid and gives her *such* pain. I felt overwhelmed with misery and had an overpowering desire to bring her home to sanitary England. One of the girls has started helping a bit with Peter, but yesterday I learned that her head is full of lice, so I've forbidden her to nurse him. Today I found a louse on my pyjamas.

John is studying as much as possible and intends to take his 5th exam before Christmas whether he is ready or not. He must get it over with as he will not be allowed to take the sixth and last for six months after that and we don't want anything to hold up our furlough.

November 21st

I don't know which way your letters are coming but it has been a tremendous comfort to continue receiving them regularly all these weeks when we feared there would be hold-ups or they might not come at all. I'm afraid mine to you may not have got through with such regularity.

It is trying living in such uncertain times and we wonder very much what the future holds. Sooner or later we may have to evacuate. A journey at this time of year with two little ones would be pretty grim if we hadn't the normal methods of travelling from *Chungking* to *Shanghai* and the idea of "getting out by the back door" makes me shudder. We hear that the capital of China has been moved to *Chungking* and that the Japs are pushing up the river and are only 85 miles away from it.

November 28th

The other day we met a very long procession of schoolchildren, alternate squads of boys and girls, all members of the Jong tsi chuin (like the Boy Scouts) with their triangular knotted ties and caps. Each batch had its own uniform and their teachers marched alongside. One was immaculately dressed in plus-fours and a smart western overcoat, correct shoes and stockings and a trilby hat! Children from the city famine relief centre brought up the rear, all neatly dressed in black wadded coats and trousers, their heads shaved bare, and behind them the soldiers. It was a most impressive sight and was in honour of a high-ranking official who has just taken up residence in *Chungking*.

The girl who has been causing us such problems is leaving to get married which is a great relief.

With love
Ruth

John

Tahsien   December 2nd

Dear Friends and Supporters

We have been here two months now and are very conscious of weakness in the men's work. There is no Chinese pastor and the workers are few and inexperienced. There is one cheerful young man aged about 20 who is a good preacher and hopes to be ordained but he is too young to take any responsibility. We have opportunities to preach in the two local prisons for men and women, but it is difficult to follow up those who have shown interest. However, as well as our two lady workers, we have three very fine Chinese ladies who run a daily dispensary and have started classes for women and children in their area.

Desmond visited some of the country churches last month. His impression was that there are a few real, if uninformed, believers but the majority, even some of the leaders, are simply nominal Christians whose life-styles are far from Christian.

Yours sincerely
John Carpenter

Ruth
Tahsien   December 5th

Dear Mother and Dad

We have suspicions that the cook is misappropriating provisions. Although we are living more simply and economically than we did at *Chuhsien* I still haven't been able to keep the cost down and have to be on the look-out all the time which is wearying in the extreme.

<u>December 19th</u>

For Christmas I have bought a Chinese fiddle for Desmond who is rather partial to weird musical instruments. The jolly young shop apprentice showed me a selection of strange instruments demonstrating each one. While I argued the price the surrounding mob got thicker and pressed closer. The apprentice was very amused and finally I chose the cheapest which he wrapped up in a Chinese newspaper so that we didn't look like street musicians.

Last week, with his exams behind him, John kindly looked after the children for a day while I went with Ada Elliot on a trip to the hills to collect greenery for Christmas. We took our cowboy with his *pei-teo and walked up to the *Tahsien* summer bungalow about 15 li away and found lots of lovely red berries, flowers and leaves and some tall graceful silver-grey grasses. We also saw an old man carrying a magnificent golden pheasant which he sold us for 40 cents which, plus a chicken, will do for our Christmas dinner. It was a lovely day and a real treat.

We enjoyed having Paddy Crockett with us for a few days and he took back a Christmas cake and pudding I'd made for him and Donald Temple. They will be back for the New Year. On Christmas Eve there is to be a social for the church members followed by a service, then another service on Christmas morning and a lantern service in the evening. We are busy getting presents for the servants and families who live on the compound – quite a job!

December 27th

We had such a happy Christmas with Desmond, Miss Dix and Miss Elliott and the four of us. The house was brightly decorated with the berries etc. which Ada and I had collected. We also bought eight huge Chinese lanterns from a man on the street who very skilfully

---

*pei teo   Back basket

painted a design on them copied from some jolly Christmas paper John gave him. We hung one in the dining room, one in the drawing room and the other six on the beams right down the long whitewashed passage which runs the whole length of the house. We put candles in the lanterns with festoons of evergreens in between and it looks so pretty. I cooked the chicken and pheasant for dinner and I don't think we lacked any of the delights that make up Christmas.

We had been looking forward so much to hearing the King's speech on Desmond's wireless, but by the time he had got it working it was all over. It *was* disappointing.

Thank you, my dear ones, for your very generous present with which we are proposing to buy a COW! We had already decided we must get one for our personal use rather than sharing with the household and we shall use about three-quarters of your gift for that. When we leave we will sell it again and probably get nearly as much as we paid for it.

With love
Ruth

Ruth

Tahsien   January 3rd

We had a houseful over the New Year with lots of fun and relaxation, and now everyone has gone their separate ways, including John on his visitations.

John

San Ch'ing Miao   January 4th
(small market about 35 miles from Tahsien)

Dear Everyone

Fred Skinner, Donald Temple, the evangelist and I arrived here yesterday and it is the first of about ten places we hope to visit briefly in this coming fortnight. It was originally a "mass movement" run entirely by voluntary Chinese leaders as a result of which thousands from the country came to faith at opium-breaking campaigns. However, the work was interrupted by the Communist invasion just when it was at its height and is now a shadow of its former self although some of the little village congregations are still quite large. Opium is grown in this county (*Suanhan*) which is one of only two in *Szechwan* where it is still authorized. The pastorate, of which I am in charge, consists of five counties two of which stretch right up to the border of

Shensi province but apart from this mass movement area there aren't many outstations. There are three main leaders who are still active, living lives of faith and taking opium-breaking campaigns wherever they are invited.

San Ch'ing Miao (Three Streams Temple) is a typical little market, just one street with about 15 houses each side, a temple (no idols) and school. The local Christians have rented two houses at one end of the street and knocked out some walls to make a church. They have the most elaborate pulpit which looks strangely out of place but apparently is quite common in these little country churches. We held three meetings here today.

January 5th

This morning we set off at 7 a.m., walked 15 li and stopped for breakfast in a farmhouse where I took short prayers. We continued for another 15 li to a little "gospel hall" in a farmhouse. However, everyone had gone to market two miles further on, so we went on and saw several of the Christians including one of the leaders, a boy of about 16. On we walked for a final 30 li to *Shuang ho Ching* after what would have been an interminable journey had it not been a beautiful day.

The usual meeting place here is in a country house, but last time Desmond came he had a difficult time and advised us not to visit again unless we were invited. So we are only staying in the village tonight because we couldn't avoid it and just had evening prayers in one of the houses.

It is quite a long time since I last had to be away from Ruth and the children, and it doesn't get any easier. I don't want to neglect my heavy and happy family responsibilities, but I'm afraid I may have to be away a good deal during the next few months.

With love

John

(No further details of this trip)

Ruth

Tahsien

January 13th

Dear Mother and Dad

John returned yesterday after two weeks and the children went nearly wild with excitement. He leaves again tomorrow to go to *Kaichiang* for the weekend. Peter has enjoyed his first birthday today and among other things was given 106 oranges by Uncle Paddy!

January 22nd   Kaichiang

John and Paddy had the idea that I should take Mardi to *Kaichiang* for ten days, plus four days travelling, to help Paddy and Donald with the women's work and teach the cook how to make some foreign dishes. John and Mrs Liu are looking after Peter.

Mardi and I have a nice room, with plenty of fresh air as, on one side, the wall only comes half way up to the roof and there are just beams and tiles between us and the elements. Paddy has arranged for a nice young woman to help look after Mardi and last night he took me to the house of a Christian family to join in their evening prayers. He and Donald are living very much *amongst* the Chinese here, rather than being shut off in a great park as we are at *Tahsien*.

<u>January 23rd</u>

The men were very bucked today when their cook produced a pukka "foreign" dinner with roast beef, vegetables and gravy followed by steamed pudding with custard, their first foreign dinner since they came here. The cook is a delightful man and looks after the two bachelors very well. He does everything for them except for the washing and mending which his wife does. In the afternoon I took singing with the Sunday school then taught five women for an hour while the "uncles" looked after Mardi.

<u>January 29th</u>

Mardi and I are still at *Kaichiang* and I'm really enjoying the change and rest. It is very much a bachelor establishment but homely and both Paddy and Don lead very methodical routine lives, get a lot of work done and have a good relationship with the Chinese. There is a lovely big drill ground at the back where Mardi and I can walk. I have taught the cook to make several things and given him a few tips about using up scraps which pleased Don's economical mind. Every afternoon I teach a little group of keen Christian women and in the evenings we go to various homes for family prayers which is a joy. The stocking industry seems to be the chief one here and they all work away, old and young, with their spinning wheels and stocking machines.

John has been writing daily to reassure me all is well at home. We are leaving on Tuesday escorted by Paddy and a Chinese friend.

<u>February 5th</u>

There was a very festive atmosphere all the way home as people were celebrating the Chinese New Year and we were treated to all sorts of special delicacies, very different from the normal travelling. It's nice to be home again feeling very rested and John and Mrs Liu have looked after Peter very well. By the evening about 30 men had arrived for a week of leaders' meetings and we had them all to supper. There was a lovely surprise waiting - Margaret's birthday parcel from Chislehurst which, after four months, we had given up hope of ever arriving.

Dad, you ask why the Mission has such a place as this. Well, it was built privately in the early days by a wealthy missionary who was one of the original Cambridge Seven. His idea was that it should be a sort of retreat for missionaries needing rest and refreshment, but more recently it was used for new workers to come and be acclimatized to Chinese conditions and study without too many distractions.

Last night we heard on the wireless that the Japs had asked the British officials to evacuate all nationals north of the Yangtze and bombing has started in *Szechwan*.

February 14th

The leaders' meetings are over, a busy but happy week. Every evening we had four to supper and had to show them how to handle a knife because hardly any of them had ever used one before! Desmond was due to go to an outstation for five days for some meetings but he isn't well so it's John to the rescue.

John has written to Mr Gibb, the General Director, to ask if he will consider us for furlough in the autumn. It isn't a foregone conclusion because no-one has been able to get back after furlough and a lot of folk are due so it may not be possible to spare us. The plan was for Mr Bevan to have eight months in *Shanghai* and then return here so we very much hope that will be soon. We will probably not have a definite reply until after the council meets in April. Our letter was sent via the Bishop whose endorsement is necessary.

February 23rd

Desmond has gone to relieve John who won't be back until tomorrow so apart from my two chicks I'm having three days quite alone. I don't feel nervous at night because the house-woman and her little girl are sleeping in the house.

The boys' and girls' schools are having a month's military training. I can see hundreds of girls having a PT session in the big drill ground, all in neat uniforms, also three big groups of boys marching around very smartly.

With love

Ruth

John

As from Tahsien   February 23rd

Dear Everyone

I am sitting in a little Chinese bedroom in a large country farm-house which, with one other room, comprises the church premises in this village. I have had the unenviable task of conducting my first ex-communication which involved the old leader who had fallen deeply into sin. It has been a most uncomfortable experience as I was named as the accuser yet I have never seen the man or had a chance to speak to him. But the whole church is united in wanting him removed, even those who indulge in some of the sins themselves.

February 24th

I am back in *San Ching Miao* leading some follow-up meetings after our visit here last month and Desmond has now come to relieve me.

Yesterday was market day and we had 150 people packed into a small room so you can imagine the hubbub. The two main speakers were outstanding opium-breaking workers, and were as different as chalk from cheese! One was very thoughtful and balanced, whilst the other one ranted and screamed at the top of his voice and said some outrageous things, such as "all Christians should be poor and the poorer the keener". He himself has given up much and suffered much for the Lord, but unfortunately doesn't realize that God calls different Christians in different ways.

At the close of one meeting he got up and announced: "I oppose Mr Carpenter; he has interpreted that parable wrongly"! I thanked him for his interpretation and said that mine wasn't actually opposed to his and both were true, but he insisted otherwise. This morning he escorted me further than anyone else, holding my hand, as is the custom when saying good-bye to a friend. As we parted I told him how touching it had been when he preached on the love of Christ and urged him to preach more of that love and of what He has done and suffered for us and less of what we must do and suffer for Him. He just held my hand and didn't say anything.

While staying there I had every evening meal with the Chinese folk which consisted of very plain "dry rice" and vegetables boiled in the rice water. I was away for my birthday and in my load Ruth had put a cake and a box of fudge from Mardi and Peter which were much appreciated. This morning I walked 6½ hours on a rough mountain road with nowhere to rest, and have an early rise tomorrow with another 40 mile walk home.

Regarding furlough, the Bishop has replied saying he is only able to give us a conditional endorsement, *if* Mr Bevan is sent back to T*ahsien*. It is lovely to think our application is actually on its way to *Shanghai*.

February 25th

I got home in good time yesterday, thanks to a lovely day and a good coolie. About a mile outside the city, walking along the path at the top of the river bank I suddenly heard a very excited little voice from down below calling "Daddy, Daddy – I come to meet you; you come home again". There was little Mardi waving her arms like windmills and Ruth, Peter and the nurse. It was so nice to have such a lovely welcome, and now we have four days of happy family life all to ourselves in this huge house.

Thank you for two letters one of which was marked "by safest route" and took 4½ months to get here. It was written just after you had received mine sent just after the war really started. God has graciously supplied all our needs and we have no difficulty getting money and all food is available locally, *Szechwan* being a very self-contained province.

Meanwhile we hear of dreadful atrocities in *Nanking*, even of some American lady missionaries being murdered, yet things go on as usual in *Szechwan* and people seem oblivious as to what is happening elsewhere. We understand there is also very serious news from Europe.

With love
John

Ruth
Tahsien   February 28th

Dear Mother and Dad

Great news! Meg has had a baby girl.

How lovely England will be looking when you get this – April! Do the foxgloves still flourish in Hatherleigh and what about the wild daffies and primroses? And have you had many violets and snowdrops in the garden?

<u>March 7th</u>

More good news! Paddy is engaged to a Canadian lady doctor called Lila Jackson who is stationed at *Paoning*, five days' journey away.

You ask me to tell you a bit about *Tahsien*. It is a big city, more up-to-date than *Chuhsien* with bigger schools and better shops, a big drill ground with a playground, a park and a library. Several places have wireless and electric lights are about to be installed but would probably be too expensive for us unless we could have a meter. Usually a monthly lump sum is charged per light which is switched on and off from the station at set hours so that individual households have no control. Desmond would be able to get his wireless batteries charged if we had electricity.

The city has walls and gates at which there are always soldiers with bayonets on guard. Huge lurid pictures of the horrors of war are posted on the gates and when it is wet they are brought down to the big gate archway under the city wall as the paint is not waterproof. The chief feature of these pictures is blood and explosions. Yesterday as I passed I had a good look but didn't like to stare too much for fear of doing anything which might be misconstrued. The central figure was a practically naked woman who had fallen backwards, clutching a baby to her breast and blood spurting out from her body, and all the other figures were equally gruesome. Oh the horror of modern warfare. How dreadfully poor China is suffering and what is the end going to be?

The mission station was opened in 1899 by one of the Cambridge Seven. There are about 15 country churches with no "mission premises" but generally with their own church and meeting room. The most distant is at a wild and lonely spot on the border of the province, nine or ten days' journey away. I am told that in the early days a missionary couple spent several months up there with their two small daughters, taking servants and cows and living out of sugar boxes. What a life with young children. Missionaries in the old days really were pioneers!

The city church is a big building in our compound and at the end of some long paths is the "foreigners' house", set in solitary glory, so we see few Chinese people unless they call or we go out. From the point of view of the children it is very nice to be so far from the street, but from the point of view of accessibility to those we are trying to reach, it is far from ideal.

With love
Ruth

Ruth
Tahsien   March 15th

Dear Mother and Dad
Everyone, including John, has gone to the sub-synod in *Chuhsien* for ten days and the children and I are

alone with the servants in this big place. So it has been especially nice to have had five letters from you to cheer me up in my loneliness!

I have just had to go and "anoint" with iodine a coolie who was bitten by one of our three foul dogs. We really must get rid of the ringleader, not a nice specimen. There is a man here drawing a pattern on black silk to be embroidered by a lady in the church, as Paddy's birthday gift to Lila. It is a kimono but is going to cost much more than the ready-made one John bought me in *Shanghai* which was done by "sweated labour".

Meg writes happily about her baby. She and Ken hope to move to *Chuhsien* soon and I plan to take Mardi for a visit in April. John thinks I should have another break as he is aware of how confined and sometimes lonely I feel whereas he is out and about a lot of the time.

March 20th

This morning we received a missive from the Provincial Government Centre instructing us to have all our outside walls and any whitewashed parts of the roofs etc. painted grey. They commented on how very clean and white our walls are in the compound. This is to be done within the next five days! It so happens that we are in the throes of whitewashing so the timing couldn't have been better and the workmen were able to start straight away. Two days later the government decided to have a mock air-raid and all the men were commandeered to build a "house" which was set fire to and then had to be put out. All morning the city was cordoned off and various shots and even machine-gun fire were to be heard.

Today the schools marked the end of their month's military training by having a big show on the drill ground. A crude "theatre" was built and acting and music went on all afternoon. We had a good view from our garden, standing on stools, and the cowman sat up in a tree with Mardi on his lap with other children perched around them; even the nurse climbed a tree to look! The costumes were gorgeous - vivid colours and great flowing sleeves, old-fashioned Chinese style. Some of the actors were masked and had headdresses and there was weird languid flapping about and posturing. The music consisted of drums, cymbals and tuneless squeaky pipes and plenty of noise. There must have been well over a thousand people watching mostly on tables which the school servants carried out.

John should be back tomorrow but may have to stay on for some extra meetings. It is hard having all these separations and I worked out that of the first 55 days of this year, we have been apart for 35 and it looks as though John will have to go out again soon on a tour with the Bishop. After this I'm hoping to take Mardi to *Chuhsien* to see Meg and Ken and the baby, though this will, of course, mean leaving John and Peter to take care of each other once again.

I had a lovely big crowd at the women's meeting this week and they were most responsive and wanting to discuss the message.

Furlough is still a thing shrouded in the mists of uncertainty and therefore not to be longed for too much, but I *do* long to see you all and for you to meet the family.

March 29th

John got back from *Chuhsien* on Thursday, having done 90 miles in two days and we were all thrilled to see him. Miss Dix has been asked to go to *Wanhsien* for five months to work among the refugees and dear May Sanderson from *Chuhsien* is coming here.

    With love

    Ruth

Ruth

Tahsien   April 5th

Dear Mother and Dad

    The Bishop has written giving permission for my visit to Meg at *Chuhsien*. We have also had a very nice letter from Mr Gibb saying he has received John's application for furlough and will let us know the council's decision as soon as possible after the meetings are over. Well, the meetings *are* over as both Desmond and the Simmonds have had telegrams to say they can go and they are leaving in less than a fortnight.

April 11th

    We're living in hopes that the order for stores which we sent to *Shanghai* six months ago will soon arrive. Tea and cocoa were becoming a problem, but Desmond produced a 2 lb tin of tea and a 1 lb tin of cocoa which he won't need. Mainly we live on native produce, cooked in foreign fashion. We have our own cows so milk and butter are not a problem, and I sometimes make cheese. Beef, pork, chicken and fish can all be bought locally as can eggs, flour, sugar, oil, rice, cereals and bountiful successions of fruit and vegetables in their season, so we are very well provided for.

    On Friday we gave a feast for the members of the Church council. We were a party of 28 and we hired a professional cook. It was a really posh feast, probably too posh because we are not experienced in these things and didn't know much about the delicacies so were a bit shocked at the price. Altogether we bought 29 different items including two pigs' brains and one pig's stomach. It is a great relief to have this over with and I hope we never have to give another feast!

After rather a quiet period, this week promises to be hectic with a lot of comings and goings. Then I will have a week alone before John returns, and once he is settled I hope to take Margaret on our long-planned trip see Meg and Ken and baby in *Chuhsien.*

Group with Mardi and Peter

April 19th

Desmond left yesterday for furlough and Donald, Mardi and I and some Chinese men went down to the bank to see him off. The Bishop came last Thursday and left on Saturday for a tour of the outstations and he will meet up with John who has already gone. Paddy got back last Tuesday, feeling elated after his time with

Lila, and returned to *Kaitiang* on Wednesday. Donald arrived on Tuesday and leaves tomorrow to join the Bishop and last but not least Miss Sanderson (alias Auntie May) arrived from *Chuhsien* on Saturday to replace Miss Dix who left last week. She is such a dear and it is so nice to have her with us again.

With love
Ruth

John

As from Tahsien   April 28th

Dear Everyone

This month The Bishop has been travelling through the *Tahsien* pastorate while I have preceded him preparing candidates for confirmation. We met up for the Easter weekend, and on Easter Day at the first village he confirmed 27 people and at the next he confirmed our youngest leader, a brilliant 15 year old who can preach and take services like a pastor. To reach our next village we had to cross into *Suanhan* county where the growing of opium is still permitted. It is probably going to be banned completely next year so everyone seems to be making the most of it while they can. We found this, and all the other churches in the area, deeply involved in opium, smoking, planting and trading, not least the once keen church members and even some of the leaders. Some Christians pray fervently for the Lord's blessing on their harvest or praise Him devoutly if it is an especially good one!

The poppies come out in April and are at their most beautiful now, acres and acres of fields full of lovely white, dark purple, pink and red flowers. When the petals fall off they leave a head much larger than ordinary poppies. With an instrument made of four or five sharp knife-points, the men scratch or cut the poppy head from top to bottom. Immediately a white fluid oozes out in thick drops which in a few seconds turns a yellowy-pink, gradually getting darker until it looks like Bovril. The next day the men scrape off the fluid, which by this time is pretty stiff, and put it in a jar made of hollow wood or bamboo. The poppy heads are cut again on the other side and scraped again the next day, and so on. Then it is dried in the sun and sold for 50 cents an ounce of which the Government claims, perhaps, 20 cents. Large poppy heads will go on giving out opium for seven or eight days. You see everyone at it, young and old, men and women and children, though planting and growing does not necessarily mean they smoke it.

<u>Wednesday</u>   The Bishop and I separated and I went on to *Huang-Chin-k'eo* (HCK) to prepare candidates for confirmation in advance of his visit. I had written to the candidates from two other villages asking them to come to meet me at *HCK* for instruction, but on arrival I found no-one there and the church premises were just a heap of rubble in process of being renovated. It transpired that the leader had written to the candidates from the other villages telling them *not* to go to *HCK* because there were no candidates there and that he would ask me to go straight to them, but the message never reached me! Immediately I wrote to the candidates asking them all to meet me the next day in one of the other villages and sent it off with the runner.

<u>Thursday</u>   It was raining hard when the coolie and I set off. Twice we lost our way on the hill tracks and

then came to a river which we were unable to cross. Nearby was a small cottage where a woman was sorting beans on her lap, and she informed us that *if* the rain stopped the river might be passable the next morning. So there we were, stuck in the wilds of the hills, dripping wet and hungry! The old lady gave us some dinner, and when it became clear that there was no hope of our continuing she said we could stay the night. It was a filthy little cottage but we were so grateful to her for coming to our rescue. I was given the only bed, the previous occupant having evidently used opium and left part of his paraphernalia behind.

<u>Friday</u>   We were up at dawn and just able to clamber over the river and continue on our journey through very wet and narrow paths until we reached *Hsiapak'eo* in time for breakfast. It had taken 22 hours to do 40 li! But there were no candidates, presumably because my letter hadn't reached them or it was too bad to travel. I had intended having classes and interviews here all day and going on to *Ch'ing-Ch'i-Ch'ang* on Saturday and so catch up with my programme. Reluctantly I decided to stay at *Hsiapak'eo* for the week-end, and sent another letter to the candidates urging them to come as I was staying for their benefit. I also sent a special messenger to two other places ahead to tell them of the delay, and one to Ruth which I was especially sorry about, as she was going to be alone with the children in that huge house and compound.

At the evening meeting, one of the older Christians, Mr Wang, was challenged by the talk and confessed to growing opium and promised to root it up the next day.

<u>Saturday</u>   It rained all night and all day so not only were we unable to go to Mr Wang's fields, but the river

was impassable again so there was no sign of the candidates, of course.

Sunday   The rain stopped but the candidates still didn't turn up and we had to hold the morning service without them. In the late afternoon, having put it off as long as I could, we had the baptism service for three local candidates and I had just pronounced the blessing when in walked all the others!   One wanted to be baptized which I duly agreed to, having tested his Scripture knowledge and been given a good report of him.

Monday   We left early to witness the destruction of Mr Wang's opium fields.   It was further than I'd expected, a two hour walk including wading through a swollen stream. What a surprise I had at Mr Wang's house.   The central room was clean, tidy and white-washed, with a "Ten Commandments" scroll at the top and texts pasted down the wooden side pillars and 12 brand-new very well-made benches arranged for a service. He explained that there were more than ten believing families in the district so they had services there nearly every week attended by 20 or more, as it was too far for them to go to the nearest church every Sunday and impossible in wet weather.   All this alongside growing opium!

Mr Wang called his friends and neighbours and we had a service followed by breakfast then walked to his fields.   About 25 people gathered on the bank singing hymns and praying while the farm-hands set to work with hoes and hands demolishing the eight fields of opium. They had been growing it since September and it would have been ready to harvest in a few weeks' time so he had missed out on using the valuable land for growing anything else. Furthermore there were the government complications, so it was a real sacrifice and a real victory, as testified by the joy in his face.

We then set off for *Ching-Ch'i-Ch'ang*, 90 li away. Mr Wang sent one of his farm boys to show us the road to the first village, which was just as well because it wound in and out of paddy-fields and along the narrowest of tracks through the woods and over the hills, with frequent places to go wrong and no-one to ask. The next stage was easier to follow but was long and very slow-going. We came down one of the grandest gorges I have seen in China, so narrow and steep that it was quite overpowering. Thick woods covered both sides, while the road, mostly steep steps, followed the edge of a river still swollen after the rains. There was not a house to be seen for miles, nor even a field. It was very lonely but I thoroughly enjoyed the walk. The azaleas were almost over, but still showed on the hillsides in masses of bright red colour – the Chinese call them "thick mountain red" flowers. We finally reached *Ching-Ch'i-Ch'ang* just as it was getting dark.

<u>Tuesday</u>   I had a meeting arranged for the morning but the church leader told me that everyone was involved in the opium harvest and not many would be able to attend. Nor could he recommend any for baptism or confirmation except one old man of 87 who lived on the other side of the river. We safely negotiated the hazardous crossing to see him and I promised to recommend him for confirmation and send a mountain chair to get him over the river. Back at the church a number of people did turn up but they said the opium-planting was too far advanced to give it up this year.

In the afternoon I went on to another town where again all but the leader and one other family were involved in opium, so again there were none to prepare for confirmation apart from the leader's wife.

<u>Wednesday</u> I visited the last place on my itinerary, the most discouraging of all. I knew none were ready for baptism and confirmation but had to see a man about some money Mr Bevan had lent him and a cow which should have been returned long ago when it calved and was in milk. Also there was rent owing on Mission premises for 1936 and 1937. Not surprisingly, all was unprocurable. The Christians came in from the fields to talk to me with opium scrapers in hand and the wooden container tied round their waist. I then headed straight for home and it was so good to see Ruth and the children again.

With love
John

Ruth
Tahsien   April 26th

Dear Mother and Dad

Margaret's first words when she woke up this morning were "Daddy's coming today" and she was so excited. So it was a big disappointment when a letter arrived saying he had been held up and would not be back until Thursday at the earliest. I feel so horrid inside. All my plans for today have completely gone by the board.

Yesterday one of Margaret's eyes was a little inflamed. A nasty eye trouble has been going round, so

I wanted to get her to the ladies' compound urgently to ask Miss Sanderson to treat it before it got any worse. I couldn't take her myself because I had a meeting, but Donald very kindly went with the gatekeeper carrying her in a basket on his back. Miss Sanderson duly treated her with Golden Eye ointment which seems to be helping. Oh dear .... she's weeping .... "I want Daddy to come home *today*". Poor little girl, she is so disappointed, and what with her eye, a hoarse throat and cough into the bargain she is feeling very miserable.

Having given permission for me to visit Meg, the Bishop is now saying that except for work, people ought not to leave their stations! It is perfectly acceptable for people to go away to be bridesmaids or best men etc. so why, I ask, is it disapproved of when one wants to visit a friend? I'm longing to be home where clergy wives don't have to ask permission to venture from their husband's parish for a few days.

I wish our letter telling us definitely about furlough would come. Life seems to have been quite wearing lately and I long to go in the autumn and will be very disappointed if we have to wait till next year. Do pray that I may have grace if this has to be.

<u>May 1st</u>

John got back on Wednesday, a day earlier than he said, so it was a lovely surprise.

<u>May 9th</u>

Today we all went up to the summer retreat belonging to this station as John had to see about some repairs. He and I walked the five miles, Peter went in his bamboo bed carried by two men and Margaret travelled in a hua-kan. We took a pre-cooked dinner which we heated up there and an apple pie like the ones you used to make when we went on picnics, Mother, but not nearly as nice. When we come home and have a picnic, please make one just as you used, but it must be in an *oblong* tin. We did so enjoy the day, the first time we'd all been out for a picnic as a family.

The house on the hill seems very light and airy and two big soap-bean trees and a hill at the back provide shade most of the day. I think it will be a very pleasant refuge from the heat of the summer and though not as cool as *Chiu p'an shi*, it is much nearer.

We were so pleased to hear news of Changuping from the missionary in *Chengtu*, He has settled happily, is well liked and learning to read. He has been kitted out with clothes and there is enough money for the next two years. I wonder what will happen to him then.

The garden is looking so pretty with many lovely flowers, the vegetables are coming on and there is a big crop of soy beans for the cows. The oil seed is nearly all harvested and we shall probably be able to raise a dollar or two on that. I have been rather intrigued with two striking birds that have started frequenting the garden. They have sandy-red coloured breasts with black and white cheeks and striped wings and black tail and are about the size of a pigeon. When they get excited they spread their wings and open out their crown like a fan. (*Later identified as hoopoes*)

With love
Ruth

Ruth

Tahsien   May 17th

Dear Mother and Dad

Two home letters came last week and I'm glad to hear that in spite of being mixed and muddled mine are getting through to you. We heard from Desmond today from *Hankow*. He witnessed a big air battle which he said was a gruesome sight.

All is quiet here except the strains of the boys singing at the big Government school quarter of a mile away. They sing popular patriotic war songs for about an hour every night, e.g. "arise, arise, arise, youth of China". I'm trying to get hold of the words of the Chinese National Anthem which I hear sung twice nearly every day as the flag is raised in the morning and lowered at night. I'm quite tired of it but would nevertheless like to know the words so that we can sing it to you when we get home.

May 22nd

We have just heard that two of our colleagues have had their furlough delayed again because of shortage of funds, so we are wondering if the same will happen to us. I got very down-hearted the other day as it is rather a strain not knowing definitely about furlough but fortunately such moods don't last long. We are enjoying being our own little family here, but it will lovely to see Paddy and Don when they come for a few days next week. We go up to the hill at the beginning of July but John will probably have to come down every other Sunday to take the services and he has to study hard for his exam so it won't be much of a holiday for him.

May 30th

It's the end of May, and already we're "rejoicing" in August weather. Margaret and Peter are a mass of prickly heat and we are constantly fanning and mopping ourselves and drinking buckets of water.

On Friday Paddy, Don and I took our lunch up to the hill to inspect the workmen's progress. Mardi came too and it did her a lot of good because she's had two nasty attacks of malaria. On Saturday I took her to watch John and Paddy bathe and we both wanted to go in too. It was stifling and airless in church yesterday but the Chinese don't seem to mind and we had a good attendance. I am finding my afternoon meetings very encouraging with a nucleus of lively, spiritual women and quite a few new members.

June 2nd

Now we're wrapped up in our winter clothes as the rain has come and the temperature has dropped about 20°. The prickly heat has disappeared as if by magic. This is not a healthy climate, but it is nice to feel cool and not sticky all the time. Today we sold a crop of oil seed and 25 catties of scarlet runners (approx. 31 lbs) for about $5 (approx. 6/3d).

June 6th

John has had a new light bamboo bed made for Mardi. Peter's bed can fit into it when they're not sleeping so it can easily be carried up the hill and will take up less space when travelling. It only cost 60 cents, including a mosquito net.

Still no news from the coast!

With love

Ruth

Ruth *Airletter*
Tahsien   June 9th

Dear Mother and Dad
   Wonderful news! Furlough has been granted, funds permitting and we shall probably leave here at the end of August if the Bishop has no objections. So far there is no-one to take our place. We hope to sail from *Hong Kong* at about the end of September. The nurse is very sorry we're going – she does love Mardi and Peter so. I shall be glad to get away from this heat and dread Mardi having another malaria attack. Last night we found a B flat and several mosquitos in her bed.
June 11th
   We have heard from Mr Bevan and to our delight he hopes to come back to *Tahsien* in July which means that, all being well, everything is clear for us to leave and I do hope nothing will prevent his coming. I do hope too that the *Hankow/Hong Kong* route will remain open for us to leave the country that way.
   With love
   Ruth

Ruth
Tahsien   Monday June 20th

Dear Mother and Dad
   I can hardly believe that we are coming home and feel as though I shan't be able to let myself go in complete joyful anticipation until we are past the danger zones of *Hankow* and the railway journey. One step in the right direction is that Mr and Mrs Bevan leave

Shanghai tomorrow and should be in the province in about three weeks' time. John is very tired and in great need of furlough, and I am longing for him to be able to relax and cease from his many responsibilities.

We've had a gloriously cool June though the farmers are complaining there's too much rain and the crops are likely to rot; the rice is already breeding worms. So for the people's sake we hope the sun will soon shine but for our sakes we much appreciate this long cool spell when normally the heat would be pretty unbearable.

June 28th

Oh dear! There's many a slip 'twixt cup and lip". Mr Bevan has been called to relieve a sick colleague at *Hankow*. Also we know that funds are low and we may not be able to sail in September. So we may not know for some time if we can go when planned. Moreover there is the great question of *how* we are going to travel. If we have to go out some back way it will be awfully trying for the children and will mean we can hardly take any luggage. So we daren't get too excited, but we are thankful for present mercies, Mardi and Peter both well and happy, the weather not too bad and all our needs supplied.

Wednesday

Last Saturday we were expecting Lily Thow on her way through to *Chuhsien* for her wedding this Friday but she didn't arrive, so we thought she'd probably gone another way. However, on Sunday morning, she and a young Chinese Bible-woman turned up in the middle of the service. They had met brigands who stopped them, threatened them with pistols and took them into a filthy house. They proceeded to search them, making them remove their outer garments and feeling them all over and tossed all their belongings on to the filthy floor including Lily's wedding dress.

Then the leader said: "you're Gospel Hall people, aren't you? We treat Gospel Hall people well. We don't want your things". Hurriedly they started packing them up but were then shut into a tiny room and commanded to sit on a bed which was alive with B flats and told that if they spoke or moved they would be shot. There they sat for two hours, not daring to move until at last they were released, coolies and all. The whole episode lasted about three hours. What an ordeal for them, but Miss Thow seemed very calm and said they had found comfort in a verse of scripture. She set off yesterday in a small private boat, and should have reached *Chuhsien* this morning. Donald, who is best man, left very early today.

Mary's new house sounds lovely. I am longing to live in a civilized house with civilized furniture and a kitchen that has "lino" and not just a beaten mud floor, curtains at the windows instead of just thin dusty paper in the winter and empty frames in the summer – it seems like something too good to be true"! The stove here is a dilapidated old "foreign" range built into a mud stove with a big pit in the floor at the side into which the daily ration of coal is tipped. I found some dead cockroaches in the flour the other day and one in the lard tin. The bread is kept in an old tin with a board top. The pantry is a hanging wire mosquito-netting cupboard in the kitchen courtyard and has to be reached by a little step-ladder.

I wonder what you will think of our little ones. They really are treasures but Margaret is decidedly a hoyden! Hopefully she'll not shout Chinese slogans such as

"Down with Japanese Imperialism" at the top of her voice after a month or two of not having any Chinese playmates!

With love
Ruth

John, Ruth, Mardi and Peter

Ruth
Tahsien   July 6th

Dear Mother and Dad

Mr Griffin at HQ has provisionally booked us on the steamer which sails from *Hong Kong* on September 29th and will let us know as soon as sufficient funds are available.

<u>July 10th</u>

We have had a letter from the Bishop re our furlough which he apparently thought was granted on condition that Mr Bevan got back to *Tahsien* first, as per his proviso. However, there has evidently been some lack of communication between him and HQ who have quite clearly stated that furlough has been granted subject to funding, and have provisionally booked our passages, despite Mr Bevan's return being delayed. The Bishop still feels that we should wait, but to be kept back indefinitely for Mr Bevan to leave *Hankow* would be most gruelling, especially as he had actually set out to return here when he was waylaid. The Bishop is, of course, in rather a difficult position with this big diocese to staff and so few ordained men, either Chinese or foreign.

So perhaps we won't be able to come on the steamer that leaves on September 29th after all, but I do hope nothing will prevent us from getting the next which is only about three weeks later.

With love

Ruth

Ruth

Tahsien Hill Bungalow   July 18th

Dear Mother and Dad

We are up on the hill now and already I feel much better for the change. Yesterday I took the morning service. The congregation was mainly made up of the tenants, the Way family which comprises an old woman and her son and his wife, five girls, two adopted sons and a baby boy who is extra special because their other son was drowned in a cess pool. Mrs Way Junior works from dawn to dusk out in the fields and organizes the children in their jobs looking after the three big water buffalos, turning the hand mill and cooking. She is now making shoes for the family. The old woman minds the baby and sometimes sits on a low stool with her blue cotton trousers rolled up to her knees making the tough hempen string which is used to sew together the many layers of old cloth that form the shoe soles. Mr Way is a carpenter and goes marketing.

Old granny with baby

At meal times the whole household sprawls all over the place eating bowls of rice with a few beans or pickled turnips. Mrs Way is such a cheery soul and thinks nothing of walking five miles to church in the city in fine weather. They have all heard the Gospel, of course, but whether they have received it I don't know.

<u>July 25th</u>

We have just heard from the Bishop saying we definitely *can't* go on furlough until Mr Bevan returns. Who knows how long that might be? John has written to Mr Gibb, our General Director, telling him various reasons why we feel we *should* go as planned. As you know our plans were well ahead so to have them shattered like this is an enormous blow and we are trying hard to be patient.

With love
Ruth

John

Tahsien Hill Bungalow   July 24th

Dear Everyone

Well, what a week! I have never known rain like it! On Wednesday the gardener came up to tell us that the compound wall had collapsed in several places so I went to investigate and found five breaches between 5' and 25' wide and subsequently another 40' collapsed. We had to make temporary arrangements to block it up as the walls are made of earth and can't be rebuilt in wet weather.

The flood was horrifying. On the way down to the city we have to cross a little bridge over a stream about a foot wide. Not only was the bridge submerged but it took us about five minutes rowing among the house roofs and tree tops to get across to the road the other side. We hear that several low-lying villages have been completely washed off the map and can well believe it. From time to time I went down in the morning until quite late in the afternoon and there was a continuous stream of wreckage of houses, beds, tables, poles, rafters, water-tubs etc. swirling past as far as one could see. People were clinging on to anything they could and being carried bodily down the rushing torrent, crying out to be saved, but nobody dared venture in, and beggars were wading nearly thigh deep in mud scavenging,

The river was at its highest when I started back in the afternoon. The street was quite unwadeable and the water was half-way up the doors and right up to the South Gate which faces the river. People with ladders and boats were rescuing furniture etc. from upstairs windows and taking it to higher places. There is a row of houses built on tall poles at the back, and at the front of one of them, folk were calmly carrying on with their business making mien, shoes etc. while you could see the river right through the house swirling within a foot of the floor with the poles submerged. As I climbed the hill I could see another stretch of houses where the brown water was almost up to the roofs. It was a scene of utter devastation and has been an enormous calamity for the people.

With love
John

Ruth

Tahsien Hill Bungalow   August 7th

Dear Mother and Dad

We are having trouble with our cows and they are only yielding ½ - ¾ pint per day. So Miss Sanderson's cowman and ours are scouring the countryside for a new one. We have had two on trial, both unsatisfactory, and now the cowman tells me he has heard of two more which we can test.

Both Mardi and Peter have had upset insides but seem better now. This hot weather is extraordinarily tricky and I do hope they will not succumb on the journey.

<u>Tuesday 16th</u>

At long last we have heard from Mr Gibb. He doesn't insist that we wait for Mr Bevan's return but says we must stay until arrangements can be made for our station to be manned and is writing to the Bishop with some suggestions. At least we won't have to wait indefinitely but I'm almost sure we won't catch the September 29th boat but will have to get the next one on October 21st. I have reached a stage where I feel almost numb about the whole thing. We've been living in a state of mental upheaval since February and I'm longing to be safely home, though in some ways I shall be glad of a bit of extra time and it will be cooler for travelling. So if we can leave in the autumn I shall be happy.

Yesterday we had a tea-party for ten Chinese girls who are staying nearby. Afterwards we played games on the top "lawn" where the cows were tied. Suddenly one of them took fright and broke loose. It careered madly all over the place, down the valley to a dangerous cliff edge, and right out of sight! The cowboys, house-woman and tenant's wife between them managed to round it up and get it safely back.

<u>August 22nd</u>

This week I have got the cowboys to take the cows out for a walk every afternoon and this has already resulted in slightly more milk. One day I took one out myself! The custom in the city is to keep cows tied up in their stalls or to a tree all day, and they don't get nearly enough exercise. So when I go down I'm going to put them in the little paddock and get the old gardener to take them out every day which I think should increase the yield.

<u>August 25th</u>

The Bishop is waiting to hear whether the Williamsons would be willing to come here temporarily and if so we may be able to leave soon. We still don't know which route we will be taking out of China because there are going to be dangers whichever way, but please don't be anxious because we are confident that the Lord will look after us.

<u>September 1st</u>

Wonderful news! The Williamsons are coming to relieve us!

With love
Ruth

Ruth

Tahsien   Wednesday September 7th

Dear Mother and Dad

We are hoping the Williamsons will be able to come on Saturday and meanwhile we are very busy packing and making arrangements for our big move.

I have had the brainwave that we should come home via India *(where Mary and Ronald, John's sister and brother were both missionaries)*. We would take a ship from *Hong Kong* to Calcutta, go by train to Kachwa, spend a week or so with Ron and Molly, visit Mary at Mirzapur and then travel by rail to Bombay where we would embark again. We haven't seen them for seven years and are not likely to do so for some time yet and it seems too good an opportunity to miss. We have sold John's lantern and slides to our hill guests, the organ to the Bishop, some medicines to Miss Dix and will be selling the sewing machine and various other items, including the cow(!), so altogether we reckon we can make about £20 which should cover the extra cost of the travelling. We have written to Mr Griffin, HQ, asking him to book us that way.

The route by which we will travel to *Hong Kong* is a big question which occupies a great deal of our thoughts and, alternately, worries and thrills us. Mrs Liu, the children's nurse, is coming with us as far as *Chungking* which will be a great help.

September 8th

The Williamsons don't think they'll be able to get here until next Wednesday which would mean handing over to them on Thursday and leaving on Friday and hopefully getting to *Chuhsien* for the weekend. It's cutting it rather fine and the weather has broken into torrential rain so I'm afraid it may delay them. Oh my dear ones it will be wonderful to see you, and how thrilling if there were a peal of bells to welcome us.

Wednesday 14th

No sign of the Williamsons yet and it is now unlikely that they'll get in tonight so probably we shall not be able to start this week – uncertainty right to the last! When we know just when they are arriving we will be able to calculate when we start from here and reach *Chungking*. Beyond that we can't plan though we hope to be catching the steamer leaving *Hong Kong* on October 21st. Mr Bevan has written and advised us not to attempt the *Hankow* route. He says the last 80 miles of the railway is impossible, though it seems it can be done by launch so we shall have to see.

We have had a very nice send-off from the folks here, and many leaving gifts, including a rooster and 40 eggs!

Thursday Night – the Williamsons arrived!

September 18th

I'm overjoyed to say that we have, at last, started on our long journey which leads to "Home Sweet Home".

With love
Ruth

HOMEWARD JOURNEY   *Combined account by John and Ruth*

Sunday September 18th   On the River

Finally we said good-bye to *Tahsien* yesterday and have at last really started on our journey to England! It is hard to believe it! The Williamsons arrived on Thursday night having started out on Monday. They had awful weather and had to come across country where the recent floods had completely washed the road away in places and vast tracks of land were buried under deep mud. All the way they heard rumours of brigands but they finally arrived safely, for which we thank the Lord, and we were up till 10 p.m. discussing the hand-over.

First thing on Friday John went to book a boat and we were finally all on board at about 11 p.m. intending to start early the next morning and reach *Chuhsien* in one day. However, the water was too high and we had not gone far when the boatman drew into the bank at the foot of a small market and announced that we must stay there until the next day as we couldn't get over the rapid a few miles further on.

It was almost impossible to go ashore as the bank was so steep and muddy and the people stood in big groups watching us nearly all day. In the evening the boatman found a quiet inlet where we could stop for the night. Today we didn't leave until noon, by which time the water had receded by 10' and we had a most thrilling few minutes crossing the dangerous rapid! Now we're heading for *T'uch'i* for the night (where Ruth worked for three months at the end of 1932).

We stayed Tuesday night at *Chuhsien* and had a really lovely time with Ken and Meg and the baby. Meg has made their house so pretty and the baby is perfect. We also visited the Bishop and Mrs Houghton, who are now living in our old house which has been completely transformed.

The last 10 li before reaching *Kwangan* (where Ruth was evacuated for two months in 1933) is one continuous rapid called the "Four Seasons Rapid" as it is dangerous all the year round whatever the water level. Because the water was high there was not much trouble from rocks which were all submerged but the waves and currents were bad. We had to have a special pilot on board who took the helm. At one very rough point he turned the boat to meet a wave head on, and my, didn't we meet it with a vengeance! It came all over the front deck where the men were rowing and about two-thirds of the way along our "cabin" till it finally spent itself by pouring through the cracks between the boards on to our luggage below! At *Kwangan* we had a very brief time with the Denhams who gave us very serious news of Europe.

Friday September 23rd

Yesterday we were held up for a day at *Hochow* (where Mardi was born) and stayed the night with the German ladies who gave us a lovely welcome. Imagine our surprise when in walked Donald Temple on his way to *Chungking* for emergency dentistry! So we are all travelling together by steam launch for the last bit of the journey. Donald was a God-send as we had to start at 4.30 this morning when it was dark and there were no rickshaws, and he and John each carried a child all the way down to the launch.

Apart from the restricted space and having to sleep on the floor it has been quite comfortable travelling in our little wooden boat and we ate ordinary food which we cooked on our charcoal fire. Mardi and Peter have stood the journey well so far though they are a handful in this tiny boat with all the stuff round and not much room to move.

Sunday September 25th

We arrived in *Chungking* yesterday but have not had any clear guidance as to how to proceed from here to *Hong Kong*. Mr Bevan has advised us not to take the *Hankow* route, though comparing that with what we are hearing about the *Kweichow* route, it may be the lesser of the two evils. But we would need to go soon because the Japs are reported to be 50 or 60 miles from *Hankow*, and the way won't be open much longer.

We still haven't heard about our proposal to return via India but a letter will probably be waiting for us at *Hong Kong*. We would also like to visit Jack in Egypt if he is back.

<u>Sunday October 9th</u>

In the end we decided to go via *Hankow* being the least dangerous and less complicated route. At last a steamer came in and on Wednesday (5th) we were all packed up and ready to go when there was an air-raid alarm! We all rushed down to the cellars and hardly got down when we heard aeroplanes overhead and the noise of anti-aircraft guns. It was all over in about ten minutes but we stayed down until the "all clear". A bomb was dropped a few miles out, but nothing actually hit the city.

We had just got all our luggage down and were calling coolies when a telephone message came from the shipping office saying the steamer had engine trouble and we must wait for the next which was due out on Saturday – board Friday night (7th). We immediately sent an airmail to Mr Bevan asking if the delay would affect our going via *Hankow* as the situation was changing almost daily. The next day there was another air-raid warning but the planes apparently turned off in another direction. On Friday we once again did our final packing and having had no word from Mr Bevan, we set off on the ferry which took us to our steamer which was moored right over the other side of the Yangtze.

Yesterday morning, two weeks after we arrived in *Chungking*, we started on the second stage of our journey. Eventually we entered the Gorges which were as majestic as ever and we anchored for the night up a little creek right in the middle of them. We were off early this morning (Sun 9th) and passed through some more lovely gorges and quite exciting rapids and got in to *Ichang* at 1 pm.

Tuesday October 11th

Peter is cutting teeth and both he and Mardi have been very much off colour with bad coughs and colds. The cabins were terribly hot and meal times were simply awful as neither of them would eat. At *Ichang* we had to trans-ship so we took the children ashore to let them have a bit of a run while John was negotiating the tickets. At the shipping company offices Ruth met a young man who turned out to be a doctor with the Scottish Mission. She told him about the children's ailments and he directed us to his wife who was a paediatrician. We walked a short way along the bund to the Mission Hospital where they both work and live and found his wife who was such a kind, charming young lady. She examined Peter and said he had quite a bad touch of bronchitis which was quite a shock as we'd thought it was just a heavy cough and cold. Mardi only had a bad head cold and a touch of stomatitis in her mouth. The doctor gave us some medication and they both seem better today.

The river is very wide now and this ship is much bigger than the last. We have two most luxurious state rooms, a big dining saloon, better food and very nice stewards. The head steward asks what the "babies" will eat and prepares it all very nicely. You can imagine the thrill for Mardi and Peter having a bath in the big bath and turning on the electric lights and fan. We are due in *Hankow* the day after tomorrow.

On our previous ship the Captain, First Officer and Engineer were most friendly, particularly the First Officer. When we trans-shipped at *Ichang* he arranged for some of the ship's hands to put our boxes across for $1, far less than getting coolies. Then he himself carried Peter over while John took Mardi. As we pulled out of *Ichang* this morning he and the Captain shouted "Goodbye – have a good journey"!

Wednesday October 12th

Today the scenery has been flat and marshy in places with very few houses, mainly little brown thatched mud huts. Most of the few people we have seen were fishing with big nets from the bank. We have passed a few steamers packed with people fleeing for their lives from *Hankow*. All the time the conversation on the steamer is about the situation. Some say we'd best sit tight in *Hankow* until the Japs have entered and taken it, then just go by British boat down to *Shanghai* with all the other British boats, gunboats etc. It would be very gruelling to be there during the fall though we are told that it ought to be perfectly safe for foreigners in the Embassy. It would probably be the best thing to do but would probably mean missing our boat at *Hong Kong*.

We should reach *Hankow* tomorrow and then we shall see what arrangements Mr Bevan has made or is making for us. We do hope it won't mean a long separation if Ruth and the children have to go by plane. We don't know what the situation is with the railway but today's wireless news says the Japs have entered *Bias Bay*, north of *Hong Kong*. This may make it harder than ever to get there. Still, we are quite at peace about our journey as we are in the Lord's hands.

What awaits us at *Hankow* we do not know but we are informed by a fellow passenger that the Chinese have just had a big success in that area, which should mean an easier and safer journey from there onwards. He is a Times Correspondent, a most friendly and well-informed man who was a passenger on the river gun-boat, USS Panay, when she was sunk by the Japanese on the Yangtze last December. *(This incident is well documented on the internet and mentions "Colin MacDonald, Times Correspondent" as being one of the passengers, presumably the person John and Ruth met.)*

We are getting so excited – only ten days till our boat is due to sail from *Hong Kong*. We hope we can make it in time!

Saturday October 15th   Hankow

Here we are in the city which is probably being talked about all over the world! We arrived on Thursday evening and were met by Mr Ebeling, the CIM business manager, whose first words were "What a pity - I've just had to give up your bookings on tonight's train"! However he has booked us on the train which is scheduled to leave tomorrow night and it is touch and go whether we will catch our steamer at *Hong Kong* on the 23rd. If we miss it we will have to stay there for three weeks which would cost a small fortune. We have really been glad of the three days' break here because Peter had diarrhoea badly and we've just been able to get him over it and we were able to get some washing done. Also, we have been vaccinated for smallpox so we won't be prevented from entering *HK* on that score.

The missionaries in charge here are Mr and Mrs Lewis-Jones. Ironically, Mr Bevan left yesterday to return to *Szechwan*! The Consul has issued an order for foreigners to leave and the place is being gradually evacuated. Shops are closing one by one, though some are still selling up their stocks and what *is* left is very expensive. John took Mardi shopping this morning and bought some basic provisions as we may be seven or eight days on the journey. If so we will miss our steamer but if we can get through in four or five days we might just do it as long as our passages have been kept open right up to the last.

This is a lovely city compared with *Chungking*. The CIM is very near the bund, situated on the corner of two wide tarmacked streets along which motor cars, lorries, bicycles, horse carts, rickshaws, coolies with hand-carts or carrying-poles, cyclists and pedestrian all pass. The children love standing on the verandas of our two rooms watching everything down below. The house itself used to be the British Concession and is very nice with such luxuries as sprung beds, easy chairs, electric light, water in private bathrooms, full length wardrobe mirrors etc. There is a lovely big tennis lawn opposite and masses of flowers and big buildings all around. But all the streets along the border of the foreign Concessions are bristling with barbed wire and the dike along the side of the river is honeycombed with dugouts. There are huge gates at intervals across the roads to stem the tide of refugees and looters.

This afternoon we heard a siren but nobody seemed to take any notice. We took the children out to play on the lawn where there was a huge Union Jack spread out. A man explained that the siren was the first warning and the second would go when the planes were near. When the second one went we took the children in and were just deciding what to do when we heard the "All

Clear". Mrs Lewis-Jones told us that the people simply carry on with what they are doing when they hear the siren because there are so many false alarms.

<u>Wednesday October 19th</u>

On Sunday morning Mr Ebeling went to get our tickets and came back and announced "no trains going". Our hearts sank because we realized instantly we'd missed our steamer. Immediately John went to enquire about the Eurasia aeroplanes, but they said there was no guarantee of a flight, and anyway there were already a hundred people on the waiting list. Then Mr Lewis-Jones had the idea that we might go to *Changsha* then by train to *Nanchang* and *Kinhwa* and thence by bus to *Wenchow* on the coast, and up to *Shanghai* by steamer. This route is said to be open at present, and we have sent an urgent telegram to *Nanchang* asking their advice and are awaiting a reply.

The first step was to find a way to *Changsha*. The steamship companies told us that the last ship of the season had just left (water too shallow during winter months) and the bus company informed us that the last bus had been commandeered for military purposes. Then we were told there were no trains today but to go back tomorrow. Mr Ebeling went this morning and was told to go back this afternoon. He has been again this afternoon and was told to ring up at 5 p.m. and if there is a train we must leave straight away! We will only get third class seats and will have to sit up all night. Of course we will be lucky if we get away at all. John tried the boat office again today and was told there was a slim chance there might be boat in five or six days' time.

We have never been in such a predicament! But if we hadn't just lost the booking for the train the night we arrived, we might well have landed up in *Canton* when the terrible bombing took place. It is now completely cut off from the coast and there is no CIM there and we know nobody. It may be that we just have to sit tight until this city falls, and then there is every probability we could get to *Shanghai* by British boat under escort. Still, we wouldn't want to be here during the fall – it would be such a bad experience for the children. We are having a big testing time but know that our Heavenly Father is with us and has us in His hand.

Today all the rickshaw coolies have disappeared. We heard they all fled in the night for fear of being commandeered as soldiers. Since we came we have had air-raid warnings nearly every day and one day there were lots of planes flying overhead but there has been very little anti air-craft shooting.

It is, of course, a crushing blow to have lost our steamer but we have been so preoccupied with how we are going to get out of this doomed city that we haven't felt it quite so keenly. What *is* worrying us is not being able to let you know. There is no airmail from here, and the ordinary mail may well not be able to get through via *Canton*.

So this has been our taste of *Hankow* which we will probably be interested to read one day when it has all faded into the dim and hazy past! *(Six days later Hankow fell to the Japs)*

Thursday October 20th

Excuse the pencil but you'd hardly expect me to have pen and ink in a ditch in *Hupeh* province! We're on a train going to *Changsha* and had just finished breakfast when the steward came along and said "air-raid warning – everybody out". So the train stopped and everyone scrambled down and made for cover. We have found a beautiful deep ditch not too far from the train, covered with long grasses and an ideal place to hide should the need arise.

12.30 p.m.

We are back on the train after about an hour, having thankfully seen no planes.

We had such a shemozzle getting away from *Hankow* yesterday. We only had about half an hour after hearing there was a train before we had to leave the house! We tried to pack up and let the children amuse themselves but first Peter got hold of the inkpot and took the cork out and put it in his mouth! He *was* an inky mess. Then he pinched his thumb in the Venetian doors and was in such pain that the only thing that would comfort him was to carry him around. It was also his normal bed-time and he was very tired. While John was seeing to the luggage I (Ruth) set off, carrying Peter and leading Mardi, escorted by one of the servants, and John was to catch us up.

We had gone two blocks when the table-boy came rushing after us and told us we were going the wrong way. We turned back and soon Mardi started to drag. It was a long way and such a relief when Mr Ebeling caught up with us and promptly took Peter and I carried Mardi. Meanwhile John had run all the way to the launch where we had to cross the river and finding we weren't there had come running back to find us. I was so glad to see him. It was a quick crossing and while Mr Ebeling dealt with our luggage John and I walked about a quarter of a mile to the station carrying the children. Mr Lewis-Jones was waiting for us with the good news that he'd been able to book a compartment for us - a luxurious first class sleeper, the last on the train!

Saturday October 22nd

The travelling time from *Hankow* to *Changsha* is normally 12 hours; it took us four times as long! We arrived late last night and hired two rickshaw coolies at the station who assured us they knew the way to the Mission station. Clearly they didn't as they took us to the north of the city and we landed up at the Yale University Mission! A kind man gave us directions to the CIM station and sent a "boy" to accompany John walking, while Mardi had to sit alone in one rickshaw and Ruth sat in the other with the nearly asleep Peter. Imagine the little procession making its way through the streets of *Changsha* so late at night! There were not many people about but quite a lot of cars and we passed a lot of wrecked houses and many other signs of the war. There were also some badly wounded soldiers waiting at the station.

It was nearly midnight by the time we arrived at the Mission. We were greeted by Mr and Mrs Ettling, such a kind young German couple, who were amazed to see us because the telegraphic news, which overtook us, said that *Hankow* was now a closed city except the road to *Szechwan*. This means that our train was probably the last one to *Changsha*. Our hosts quickly got two rooms ready for us and by 2 a.m. we were all in bed! We weren't up until after 9 a.m. and had just finished breakfast when there was an air-raid warning - another false alarm.

Sunday October 23rd

We left at 7.30 a.m. this morning and these dear people not only prepared all our food for the journey but they also came down to the station and helped carry the children.

We sat in *Changsha* station for two hours and then set off, but after an hour the train stopped and we were told there was an air-raid and we all had to get off! This time we were in a large expanse of sugar cane fields where we found a delightfully shady, completely hidden spot. We hadn't been there long before we heard the drone of planes and systematic "thud, thud, thud" away in the distance, over *Changsha*. We did thank God that we had got away in time, and as far as we knew, the Ettlings would have been back in their compound before it started. After two or three hours we were able to get going again but we had many long stops while the track ahead of us was repaired after being bombed. By 10 p.m. we'd only actually been moving for about 3½ hours the whole day.

Monday October 24th

We've been able to make good speed today with no further delays or air-raid alarms and should be in *Nanchang* in about half an hour.

These air-raid warnings are the order of the day and we have had three altogether. The train is fitted with wireless and when the steward is alerted that aeroplanes are around, he walks calmly down the corridor looking into each compartment to tell the occupants there is an air-raid warning. There is no panic and there always seems to be plenty of cover within ¼ mile of the train. We believe that no train has yet been hit by a bomb, though sometimes the planes come low and machine-gun the whole length of it, so it is no use sitting still. We had a bullet hole in one compartment and a smashed window in another which we vacated.

<u>Tuesday October 25th</u>

We got to *Nanchang* yesterday afternoon, a journey which took 30 hours instead of the normal 16 hours. There was no-one there to meet us, but one of our fellow-passengers kindly helped us hire three rickshaws. On arrival at the CIM mission house we were given tea, met a bewildering number of people and two hours later were back at the station to continue our journey. We were able to get a double berth carriage again and should be arriving at *Kinhwa* in about four hours. Then we will go by bus to *Wenchow*.

The reasons the journeys are so slow are:- 1) air-raid alarms 2) military trains taking precedence as it is only a single line track and trains can only pass at stations and 3) repairing the line in front from the last bombing, which happens nearly every day. It is amazing how the Chinese can get it repaired so well in three or four hours! Fortunately for us it has been just over the new moon period so we had no danger of night raids either in cities or on the train so we slept in peace, but when the moon is full, night raids are quite common.

<u>Wednesday October 26th</u>

Our colleagues at *Kinhwa* had heard we might be coming and were wondering where to put us all as they were expecting seven people from *Shanghai* en route to *East Szechwan*! However three ladies were accommodated elsewhere and we were able to stay in the house. The party didn't arrive till late last night and imagine our pleasure to find it included Mrs Bevan and her 4½ year old daughter and Elsie Fearn who used to work with us at *Chuhsien*. They were on their way back to *East Szechwan* from *Chefoo* School.

We had to leave at 7 a.m. this morning and today's conveyance was an open truck, a lovely powerful, well-sprung lorry! The children and Ruth were fortunate enough to ride in comfort by the driver while John scrambled into the back with the luggage and the crowd.

We had a very good 3½ hour journey to *Lishui* and were welcomed by the three charming German workers. We leave early tomorrow morning and hope to reach *Wenchow* in the evening.

Friday October 28th

Yesterday was a really tiring day. We got up at 5 a.m. and our hosts and another colleague came down to the bus station and helped us. One bought the tickets and two scrambled on to the bus as soon as it arrived to bag our seats while we looked after the children. Ruth handed Mardi through the window to one of the helpers and then climbed on to the wheel and followed her. John then handed Peter to Ruth and after all the luggage was safely packed on to another truck he got on! We drove for about four hours along an excellent road, mostly by the riverside and through magnificent scenery, and finally reached the bus park where we were to pick up the launch. Here we found a quiet spot by the river where we were soon joined by a crowd of children come to see the strange foreigners. We enjoyed a picnic lunch which our dear German friends had got up at 4 a.m. to prepare for us and Mardi and Peter were able to have some exercise. Both were awfully tired.

Boarding the launch was bedlam but eventually we found a space under an awning on the roof of the main passenger room and managed to keep the children happy for about 4½ hours until we reached *Wenchow* – the *coast*! Then it was a long way by rickshaw, over cobbled streets, to the CIM house where again we received a warm welcome from the two workers and will stay a couple of nights until we leave for *Shanghai* on Sunday. We have just been listening to the news on the wireless and it was nice to hear Big Ben again!

Another party is here on their way through from *Shanghai* and they told us HQ are rather anxious about our whereabouts and fear we are caught in *Canton*! The airmail John sent from *Hankow* evidently hadn't reached them. He sent another as soon as we had bought our tickets to *Shanghai* telling them when to expect us. *(A few days later we heard that Wenchow harbour was to be closed any day, so we got out just in time)*

<u>Monday October 31st</u>

We left *Wenchow* yesterday and are now steaming towards *Shanghai*, due to arrive tomorrow. There are no direct boats to *Hong Kong* so we have to go this way. We don't know how long we will have to stay in *Shanghai* before proceeding to *Hong Kong* or what our plans will be thereafter but will send you a cable so that you know we have arrived safely at the coast but have missed the steamer on October 23rd. Meanwhile, we are having a very enjoyable trip and thankfully Peter is much better. We are thinking of you and hoping you aren't worried about us.

<u>November 1st</u>   Shanghai

We have certainly had many adventures since leaving *Tahsien* 6½ weeks ago and are full of thanks to the Lord for keeping us safe and at peace during this testing time. Not only has He protected us from so many dangers but we have received the most wonderful hospitality at mission stations all the way and not had to spend a single night in an inn.

Seven long years are nearly over and we can hardly believe that now, God willing, it is only six or seven weeks before we will see you. We won't know until we reach *Hong Kong* whether or not we will be able to go via India, but we shall send a letter at the earliest opportunity to tell you exactly what our plans are.

<u>Sunday November 13th</u>

We left *Shanghai* on Friday and are now on the briny heading towards *Hong Kong* where we are due to arrive on the 15th.

We had a wonderful ten days in *Shanghai*. There were about 70 people staying in the home including two big parties from England and America, a fine set of young men who filled the place with their freshness and jollity. We renewed acquaintances with several people and had invitations to tea with a couple we met when we first came out and with the headmaster of the *Shanghai* Cathedral School who was a master at Trent College when John was there.

Among the party of new workers were three who were going to *East Szechwan* and we took them down town for a Chinese meal at a restaurant which served typical *Szechwan* food. Three others came to make up the eight, the correct number for a Chinese feast, and we had a most delicious meal and a thoroughly enjoyable time. We went by tram and it was fascinating to see *Shanghai* at night.

We can definitely come home via India and if all goes to plan, our itinerary will be as follows:- November 19th depart Hong Kong; December 6th arrive Calcutta; December 17th leave Bombay; (Christmas Day meet Jock at Port Said?); January 5th arrive Plymouth!

I (Ruth) do so hope you will come and meet us. In fact I can't imagine a home-coming without you, as whenever I've allowed my thoughts to run to that glorious day I've always pictured you waiting at the quayside! It is thrilling to think that we are at last really on the way home and there's such a song of joy in my heart!

John and Ruth left Hong Kong on November 19th, and on their homeward journey spent ten days in India with John's sister and brother and Christmas Day with Ruth's brother in Egypt where they had a picnic lunch beside the pyramids.

They finally reached England on 5th January 1939. What a homecoming it must have been!

**Hatherleigh Vicarage garden with Ruth's parents.
Home, Sweet Home!**

1939

To Friends and Supporters   March 1939

We have been advised to take a curacy for a year for the sake of my wife and the children who have had such a very unsettled time, and I have been offered a post at St Paul's Braintree.   John Carpenter

Braintree Parish Church Magazine   June 1939

Dear Friends

On behalf of my wife and myself I want to thank you all for the welcome you have given us as we have come to live and work among you. You can hardly realize what it means to us to enjoy the peace and rest of a home of our own in this quiet little Essex town after our experiences in war-torn China.

Our last memory is of a 6½ week journey to the coast with two children and 14 pieces of luggage, a journey when we came within 25 miles of the fighting line, passed through constant air-raid alarms for three of which we had to evacuate from the train and hide in fields nearby, and had many other adventures which helped to break the monotony. But the Lord kept us through it all and though we saw the havoc wrought by bombs, heard the bombing at a distance and once even had enemy planes flying right over us, yet He spared us from anything near enough to alarm the little ones.

On our travels we were blessed by the kindness of missionaries, some of whom we had never met before, but who welcomed us into their homes and helped us on our way, so that our difficult journey was made just as easy and happy as it could have been in the circumstances.

And now we are looking forward to a time of fellowship with you all at St Paul's and sharing in the work with the vicar. He has appointed my wife as CIM Secretary for the parish and we both hope that our coming among you may inspire a new interest in the land which needs your prayers and help as never before, and the Mission which has meant so much to us in these difficult times.

Yours sincerely
John Carpenter

Epilogue

Ruth was still in her late twenties and John in his early thirties when they returned from China, and after all the turmoil of the previous seven years, enjoyed only a few months' peace before WW2 broke out. The family was increased by another son and daughter, and they settled down happily to life in England.

After nine months in Braintree John served as rector of St Ebbe's, Oxford during the war years and continued his ministry at Uphill, Weston-Super-Mare for nine years, Christ Church, Surbiton for 17 years and Peldon, Nr Colchester for three years. In 1974 he and Ruth moved to West Sussex where initially he assisted the vicar of four country parishes. They ended their days very happily in Lindfield. John died in 1985 and Ruth ten years later after a lifetime of dedicated service to their Lord.

Postscript

From time to time during the course of typing this journal, I have digressed and randomly searched the internet for more information about life in China in the 1930s. On one occasion, completely unbidden, an Ebay page appeared on my screen featuring an American collectables company advertising hundreds of Chinese stamps, postcards etc. Suddenly amongst it all, I spotted a tiny envelope in my mother's handwriting addressed to her parents in Hatherleigh, dated January 1937! How it turned up in America 80 years later I cannot imagine but could not resist buying it and reuniting it with its original contents! JWG

Lightning Source UK Ltd.
Milton Keynes UK
UKHW011056011121
393195UK00002B/156